GROW LIKE TECH

Dave Morrissey

Copyright © 2024 by Dave Morrissey

All rights reserved.

No part of this book may be reproduced in any form or by any electronic or mechanical means, including information storage and retrieval systems, without written permission from the author, except for the use of brief quotations in a book review.

CONTENTS

Introduction	i–x
1. Change Is Constant	1
2. The Why of Tech	19
3. Culture Is Religion	36
4. Growth Is God	78
5. Data Is the New Gold	103
6. Be Open	124
7. Fail Fast	138
8. Leadership	150
9. Managing People	196
10. Customer-First Building	242
11. Meetings, Meetings, Meetings	274
12. Storytelling & Marketing	290
13. Community at Large	307
14. Tech Yourself	321
Conclusion	337
Acknowledgments	339
Bibliography	341
Endnotes	351

INTRODUCTION

What worked last week won't work this week. Beware.

Tech is coming for your breakfast, lunch and dinner. TLDR: If you can't beat them, join them.

Tech is made up of the companies you want your company to be, you want to work for, or you want your child to work for. Look at the impact of a handful of these tech companies; who doesn't love a winner?

Meta (formerly known as Facebook, Inc.) is the most successful thing in the history of humankind according to business thought leader of the moment, Scott Galloway. There are 7.5 billion people in the world, and 3 billion have a daily relationship with Meta.[i] Facebook (#1), Facebook Messenger (#2), and Instagram (#8) are among the most popular mobile apps in the United States. The social network and its properties register fifty minutes of a user's typical day. One in every six minutes online on a desktop is spent on Facebook, and one in five minutes spent on a mobile is on Facebook. No matter how you skin it, Facebook's newly christened holding company, Meta, is the largest nation, or religion, on Planet Earth.

Introduction

But wait. Only very recently, ChatGPT saw one million new users within five days versus Instagram that took two and a half months, Facebook ten months, Twitter twenty-four months and Netflix forty-one months. All of a sudden there is a new horse in the race for global dominance.

Google, unlike most products, ages in reverse, becoming more valuable with use. It harnesses the power of two billion people, twenty-four hours a day, connected by their intentions (what you want) and decisions (what you choose), yielding a whole that is infinitely greater than the sum of its parts.

Tech companies, in a quest for market dominance, want to become the Swiss army knife to your everyday needs. WeChat in China has become the first 'super app'. To begin with, 60 per cent of the total population of China is on the app,[ii] with its original use being that of a messaging app akin to WhatsApp or Messenger. Users of WeChat can now pay bills, transfer money, book tickets, create company accounts, and so on – all in the convenience of a single platform. It's social media, entertainment, e-commerce and fintech all rolled into one. Get a loan on a car while you take a selfie.

Thirty per cent of US households have a gun, and 64 per cent have Amazon Prime. Wealthy households are more likely to have Amazon Prime than a landline phone. Half of all online growth and 21 per cent of retail growth in the United States in 2016 could be attributed to Amazon. When in a brick-and-mortar store, one in four consumers check user reviews on Amazon before purchasing.[iii]

Amazon is the most referenced tech company in this book, as they are the best executioners on the planet, in my opinion. When they set their eyes on a target, they operate with ruthless efficiency and begin to take over.

It started with retail, on their quest to become the 'Everything Store', dominating the online retail category with 350 million products to avail customers of. Amazon Web Services (AWS) is the leading provider of

Introduction

cloud infrastructure services in the US, and is used by more than three million active customers (that's three million businesses) around the world. AWS offers more than ninety fully featured services for computing, storage, networking, database, analytics, application services, deployment, management, developer tools, mobile, Internet of Things (IoT), artificial intelligence (AI), security, hybrid and enterprise applications. AWS is the undercurrent of the cloud-based internet.

Amazon is also coming for the health industry, with the launch of Amazon Pharmacy. The tech company may even become your newest sports broadcaster: Amazon is now in the NFL broadcasting game, with Premier League football on the horizon.

According to a BBC report,[iv] there are 350 million products available on Amazon – and they're not just books. They're everything from diapers to cars and everything in between. The report also states that Amazon has become a major competitor in nine of the top ten GDP industries – including healthcare and financial services – and that it's only getting bigger as Amazon continues to expand into new markets.

Apple is also up there in terms of focused execution and dominance; however, their secret sauce doesn't make up much of the tech curry available for public consumption. Apple operates as a secretive anomaly in the modern tech era where openness to open source is a virtue of profound growth. There can be no denying that Apple's secretive approach has paid off, with it being the most valuable company on the planet. Indeed, Apple became the first ever company to reach $3 trillion in market cap valuation at the turn of 2022.[v]

What do the US, China, Germany and Japan have in common? They are the only four countries in the world with a higher GDP than Apple's market capitalisation. Staggering.

Size is one thing. Speed is a whole other ballgame. ChatGPT, the popular chatbot from OpenAI, is estimated to have reached 100 million monthly active users in, wait for it, just two months after launch, making it the fastest-growing consumer application in history.

Introduction

'Software is eating the world' as they say in tech land. But it's not, really. How people think and act in their work is what's creating a ravenous Cookie Monster in the business world. Companies with distinct cultures are devouring business segments with a level of disruption and impact never seen in history. Why these companies exist, and how they execute that why, is the reason why tech companies are eating every business, outside of tech's lunches.

The era of big tech is the talk of modern business media and any current affairs discussion, as if it is the second coming of the Industrial Revolution. Indeed, the internet and smartphones have ushered us into the Information Age where 'data is the new oil'. Unlike other shifts in technological progress, there aren't seemingly abstract forces at play with unknown players wallowing in the B2B space. There are companies that are more omnipresent in our daily lives than any other brand or business institution in history.

We can check our Facebook and Instagram up to one hundred times a day. We can speak in our kitchen, and batteries arrive the next day from Amazon.

Netflix claims its real competition is 'sleep'. Google isn't just an internet search company with maps, shopping and more. It's a verb.

These companies have changed how we work. Resumes are hurtling towards irrelevance thanks to the social vetting system that is professional social media network LinkedIn. You can set up a business from your living room that ships products, that you don't have to handle, across the globe thanks to Shopify. A Starbucks store manager can now engage with the CEO on Workplace by Meta.

These companies have changed how we earn. E-sports now pay more than winning Wimbledon. An eight-year-old is now the highest-paid YouTuber globally. Fortnite has become the biggest live music venue in history.

These companies have changed how entire industries look and operate today. Communications, retail, travel and entertainment have all been

Introduction

disrupted beyond comparison to what they were before tech companies got their mitts on them. And it's not stopping there. Logistics, health and education are now ripe for tech annihilation. Amazon just unveiled a next-gen 100 per cent electric delivery vehicle. They aim to have ten thousand on the road by 2022 ... and one hundred thousand by 2030. That's more than FedEx Express's entire global fleet. You see that 'Heart app' on your iPhone that you keep looking at to check your step count? That app could well be your GP in years to come.

Medicine is getting the tech treatment. 'Silicon Valley now owns Hollywood' according to actor-turned-techie Joseph Gordon-Levitt.

These companies have changed the look of the world economy. In the past ten years the market cap of these companies has grown to insane new heights.

The 2010s saw the rise of the first reasonably valued trillion-dollar companies – all of them tech stocks. Apple, Microsoft and Amazon are the three that have hit the mark. Alphabet (Google), valued at nearly $900 billion, is likely next.[vi] And many tech companies have grown to dizzy new heights without making a significant profit, such is the value investors price their impact and potential.

The iPhone is the most successful consumer product in history. All the iPhones ever sold stacked end to end would reach the moon.[vii] Staggering. No wonder Apple became the first company to be valued at one trillion dollars in 2018 – and then hit three trillion dollars at the turn of 2022.

But many look on at these companies with an air of jealousy or even outright bewilderment. The antidote to this is to ask why and how these companies became, well, these companies. This brings us to the purpose of this book.

I am not here to go into what they are doing with the power they have amassed, but rather how they amassed that power through business and people practices. I will say that I believe big tech is on the whole net positive; I am a techno-optimist if you will. It's humans behind the

Introduction

scenes who are riddled with biases, capable of poor decision-making that can affect society.

With great size comes greater responsibility to counteract these biases to protect against teen bullying and depression, political polarisation and data misuse. But that's another book in itself. For the duration of this book, let's just go with believing Google's value of 'Don't Be Evil' is a lived truth by them all.

The vision and drive of these companies are rightly put on pedestals for bringing product development and business acumen to untold levels of ingenuity and proficiency. One of the singular attributes of tech is its unabashed drive for value creation. It celebrates innovation, and failure, and recognizes the necessity and vitality of market competition in a hyper-Darwinian environment, in ways not seen in any other industry in humankind.

I hear a lot from people working in industries outside of tech about 'agile' this and 'lean' that or 'scrum' there – supposedly new techniques to move projects along with greater speed and alignment. Great. But it's usually hot air. Those 'new' practices are merely the mindset of tech put on paper.

This book serves to look into why and how these companies became the way they are. More importantly, it examines how you can apply the behaviours and practices to your work, to your industry. And even to yourself. As a means to emulate these tech companies, their virtues and successes. Whatever industry or market you are in, there should be plenty of lessons from big tech companies in this book that you can 'steal with pride' (techies' term, not mine).

Why the hell should you listen to me? Well, I've lived in tech for well over a decade. On both sides of the tech spectrum, from start-up to tech giant. I was working in an e-commerce start-up back in 2012, then I joined Facebook, growing partner businesses for the likes of LEGO, Alibaba, Very, Gymshark, Web Summit and many more. I then went back to start-up land to the cutting edge of AI-powered creative execu-

Introduction

tion, leading partnerships with Meta, Google, YouTube, Snap, TikTok, Pinterest, LinkedIn, Amazon and more in EMEA. More recently I have been leading an e-commerce growth team at arguably the platform of the next decade, TikTok.

Not only the companies I have worked in, but also the companies I have worked with, gifted me with a range of learnings and perspectives.

Throughout, I spent time working with traditional companies across sectors, and also with hyper-growth, 'automate-the-hell-out-of-everything' digital natives. Every company I worked with wanted to do things faster and more impactfully. Oftentimes I was sharing learnings about how Facebook and other tech companies were doing it. Understanding how tech companies tick, from how they hire to how they motivate and feed their workforce, and sharing the learnings has been a brewing passion of mine. From Fortune 500 companies to scrappy fifty-person start-ups, it's the 'digital natives' amongst those who I have gleaned a ton of insight and learning from.

I am also a corporate culture nerd. I've grown to be obsessed with how people work together. The norms that form and transform. The power of collaboration and collective belief. Added to that, I have dived into over eighty books on management, culture and the tech companies themselves. Not to mention countless web articles and many, many hours extracting nuggets from podcasts.

Tech was, is, not my first love. Music is.

Electronic music in particular has been my guiding cultural force from twelve or so years of age. Not only was I in love with the records, I was also obsessed with the business element. I dreamed of putting on my own music festival. I studied festival line-ups religiously, intrigued by the hierarchy and make-up of acts on a festival poster.

The music industry beckoned, working with promotion companies and nightclubs. A chaos, a thrilling chaos. But a lack of structure – what I

Introduction

learned after moving industries – scalability and accountability were totally absent from the industry's culture.

Tech drew me in. But tech subtly coexisted with music as a honey trap for me. The punk ethos is alive and kicking in hacker culture after all. Both boast freedom and rebellion through creation.

The opening credits of *Hackers*, the 1995 film about a group of teenage hackers in New York City who take on a bastardly corporation, was the perfect collision of the two worlds. Orbital's 'Halcyon On and On's' lush melancholic timbre that leads into utterly delectable beats informs the opening scenes where the protagonist, Dade Murphy aka 'Zero Cool', crashed 1,507 computer systems (including Wall Street's) with a hack at the age of eleven. My favourite record of all time, soundtracking people taking on the man with their computers. Hook, line and sinker for an impressionable me.

Tech had me. Creative. Innovative. Disruptive. Global reach. With structures and accountability.

And it was also becoming part of the culture.

In 2012 when I was first properly entering tech, it was nascent in culture. Since then tech has proliferated in culture. Gone is the niche demesne in which tech played, the nerd culture if you will. Films like *The Internship* and the two flicks portraying Steve Jobs, to TV shows like *Silicon Valley*, have opened up tech to the mainstream. Tech *is* culture today.

In the today's society, culture starts on tech platforms. Creators are the modern punks, albeit usually more toned and washed. The music industry infrastructure is being upended, as artists are building careers from their bedrooms. Human creativity is exploding on individuals smartphones, not in Hollywood studios. Funny how things come around.

This book could be viewed as a start-up playbook. Start-ups and tech are intertwined. Every tech start-up wants to work and feel like a start-

Introduction

up forever, even when they get to ten thousand-plus employees across the world. If anything, tech is the embodiment of start-up DIY culture. Where anyone can build anything anywhere.

The best thing this book can do is help reframe your mindset. Tech is at its soul, a mindset. People thinking, and most importantly doing, in bigger and bolder ways. Cynics will complain about them, but to that I say shut the fuck up, a wee bit. Don't hate them, learn from them.

We're living in a golden age of innovation, where technology is reshaping our lives. *Grow Like Tech* will help you understand how to be part of this new generation of entrepreneurs and innovators, becoming an innovator yourself. The best-in-class companies and their cultures featured in this book cover a wide range of industries, from commerce to hospitality to media and more, supercharged by the tech way: Airbnb, Apple, Uber, Amazon, Meta, Google, Netflix, Alibaba, WeChat, Pixar, OpenAI, Tesla, Asana, Stripe, Wayflyer, Web Summit and Spotify, to name but a few.

These companies are encroaching on every area of your life. From your job to your home. So keep going on about the 'evil of big tech' or, maybe just maybe, you could look closely at how they think and work. There is a lot to learn from them. From smartphones to smart homes, tech is doing the smarts for us, so we can become more human together (that's the hope at least).

Ideas are cheap and plentiful. Ideas brought to life, at enormous scale and impact, that's what this book opens the black box on. This book is about how tech brings ideas to life. How their means of execution, primarily through the lens of culture, have dominated society's leaps in modern times and changed the way of work as we know it.

In the chapters ahead, you will learn about the cultures and processes behind the world's most revered tech companies. How Amazon makes decisions. How Netflix pays employees. How Facebook/Meta likes to fail. How Google hires people. From visions to meeting structures, from testing to partnering. The nuts and bolts of all the world's leading tech companies get a look-in up ahead.

This is a book looking at how others are doing it, but ultimately you should take the lessons and look inwards. What can you and your company start doing differently?

This is the mindset behind world-changing innovation. This book reveals how these tech companies create and execute world-changing ideas.

Chapter 1
CHANGE IS CONSTANT

IT IS NOT THE STRONGEST SPECIES THAT SURVIVE, NOR THE MOST INTELLIGENT, BUT THE ONES MOST RESPONSIVE TO CHANGE.

— Charles Darwin

Change is the only true constant in life, whether you like it or not. How many times have you heard the term 'unprecedented change' since the beginning of 2020? Covid-19 brought a level of change so disruptive to health, economics and society at large, that it will take us years to unravel what happened and how it truly affected us. The only thing it turned out that we could control was our individual selves, our mindset and actions, throughout.

In business, change happens in real time, particularly in the modern era. It should be seared into the psyche of anyone in any business, any department, that *what worked last week won't necessarily work this week*. And in tech, change is even more pronounced. In large part, this is due to its lifeblood – software.

Software will eat the world, the tool of change in tech

One of tech's most celebrated figures, the entrepreneur behind Netscape and later turned investor, Marc Andreessen, opined that 'software is eating the world' back in 2011. He claimed that 'we are in the middle of a dramatic and broad technological and economic shift in which software companies are poised to take over large swathes of the economy.' Think about how you now check the weather (ask Alexa), how you buy stuff (one-click buy from Amazon), how you travel (getting an Uber to your Airbnb), how you navigate new places (Google Maps) and so on. Software has seeped into our everyday lives.

Eventually most productivity tools will become software-mediated. Software could be the final industrial revolution. It might subsume all the revolutions to come.[i]

To be an accelerant you must have the raw materials. Just as the electricity plant used to be built near the coal mine, the raw materials today are top engineering, business and liberal arts graduates. This is because tech – software – is eating the world. You need its builders, people who can program software, and who have a sense for the intersection of tech and something that adds value to the enterprise and/or the consumer.[ii] That's not to say you yourself need to become a software developer, but you sure need to understand their value to you and your business. Think like them. Follow them.

Mass systems of public education were developed primarily to meet the needs of the Industrial Revolution and, in many ways, they mirror the principles of industrial production. They emphasise linearity, conformity and standardisation. One of the reasons they are not working now is that real life is organic, adaptable and diverse.[iii]

Software is the weapon of change as it is so malleable; software can be bastardised beyond belief. It can be changed and iterated upon to have new forms and functions, allowing the creator to keep up with consumer use. If it's not working, it can be changed to work in a few hours. The speed of adaption that software gifts the business world has unlocked a whole new world of serving customers. It has led to a whole new pace to business development.

And if you don't believe digital and its vehicle of software is taking over, you are on the wrong side of history. An article in *The New York Times* in 1939 concluded that 'Television will never be a serious competitor for radio.' If you're listening to the radio, you can get on and do other things. To experience television, the NYT argued, 'People must sit and keep their eyes glued on a screen.'

Everything is going digital. Digital-first product development and service deployment are becoming the norm. The digital revolution is fundamentally rewriting the rules of general management. Software simultaneously lowers transaction costs, demolishes barriers to entry and accelerates the pace of change.

The Covid-19 pandemic accelerated the adoption of lots of digitisation. If you look at all the companies that did really well, they're digital companies that are digitising the physical world. The mall became Amazon, money is becoming crypto, hotels are becoming Airbnbs. Digital is benefiting.[iv]

STONE AGE. BRONZE AGE. IRON AGE. WE DEFINE ENTIRE EPICS OF HUMANITY BY THE TECHNOLOGY THEY USE.

— Reed Hastings, co-founder, chairman, and CEO of Netflix

Change and competition accelerating

Change is constant.

Convention hobbles innovation.

And whether you like it or not, change is accelerating at quite a clip. The diffusion and adoption rates for new technologies have risen over the years. It took approximately four years for the internet to reach fifty million users, but it took Facebook only three and a half years to reach that same milestone. It took about thirteen years for mobile phones to reach a global adoption rate of 25 per cent, while smartphones took only five years to reach the same level of adoption. It took Facebook only two years to reach fifty million users, while it took television thirteen years and radio thirty-eight years to reach that same milestone. Global electric vehicle sales have risen from just seventeen thousand units in 2010 to over two million in 2019, with China being the largest market.

The term *disruption* is rife in the tech world. To be crude, it means your business is getting fucked. Someone has come to the table and is scoffing down your lunch while you are still arranging the cutlery. Tech is brimming with stories of so-called innovative tech players being disrupted by new kids on the block …

Just as the search engine Alta Vista preceded Google, and Myspace dominated before Facebook, Taxi Magic would become the highest-profile precursor to Uber; the company was the first to seize, and squander, the opportunity to revolutionise the taxi industry.xiii

Again looking at Google, no one would have ever dreamed of a search engine becoming a threat to Microsoft. This too is a lesson for strategic innovation: your next major rival can come from anywhere.[v]

But there is gold in those hills of change. Leaning into this software-come- digital-come-tech way of doing business is a proven winner. According to the pioneering work of Nobel Prize winner Robert Solow, technological innovation is the ultimate source of productivity and growth. It's the only proven way for economies to consistently get ahead – especially innovation born by start-up companies. Recent Census Bureau data shows that most of the net employment gains in the United States between 1980 and 2005 came from firms younger than five years old.[vi]

And when the world zigged like crazy thanks to Covid, the leading innovators in tech zagged to the beat of the drum with aplomb. A Twilio study of 2,569 companies published this summer found that, on average, the pandemic accelerated digital communication strategies by six years.1 Data from a McKinsey article showed that in three months of 2020, US e-commerce penetration grew as much as it had in the past ten years.2

In Microsoft's Q3 2020 earnings call, CEO Satya Nadella said, 'We have seen two years' worth of digital transformation in two months.'3
vii

Research from Accenture has found leading companies that scaled their technology innovation during Covid are growing revenue five times faster than lagging adopters. 'Leaders' are now growing revenue at five times the rate of 'laggards', exceptionally higher than the doubled growth rate leaders reported just a few years ago. In sharp contrast, many laggard companies just recently invested in newer technologies for the first time, largely to maintain business and technology operations during the pandemic. This put laggards even further behind and in the position of playing catch-up.

The report shows that evolving technology strategies deliver greater success when companies master these three imperatives:

- Re-platform to the cloud to build systems strength, reducing redundant technologies and disconnected data across the IT stack, while gaining computing power and flexibility. For instance, 80 per cent of leapfroggers (those companies who blast past everyone else) had adopted some form of cloud technology by 2017, but that figure rose to 98 per cent by 2020.
- Reframe to an innovation-first technology strategy. Leapfroggers excel at shifting their mindset and viewing potential downturns as opportunities to innovate with new technology. Scaling new innovations became the top priority

for leapfroggers during the pandemic, and 67 per cent seek to aggressively increase revenue from non-core business lines.
- Reach by expanding access to technology across internal business functions and embrace a broader value agenda by addressing personalised employee upskilling, well-being and mental health. Nearly two-thirds (65%) of leaders prioritise employee happiness by providing digital-based flexible work arrangements, compared to just 43 per cent of laggards.[viii]

Tech is changing your social behaviours; look if you will at the rampant rabbit warrens that are dating apps. If you haven't noticed, the dating game has changed.

In times past, if you wanted a date, you had to go out and find one. You'd go to school or work, then maybe hit up a bar or a club with friends and hope the right person would cross your path. And then there was online dating – a way of narrowing down your search and finding someone who was looking for what you were looking for.

But now? The app handles all of that work for you! Swipe right, swipe left … swipe left, swipe left, swipe left …

And then there's Thursday: a counterpoint to the melee of swiping all day every day. It's a dating app that only allows users to talk on Thursdays – so no more Tindering your way through life. It creates a sense of urgency by unlocking the option to match at midnight every Thursday and giving users just twenty-four hours to connect with and message other users. Thursday also focuses on getting people to meet in person instead of just messaging other users, and it encourages users to forge deeper relationships. And they pride themselves on users deleting the app, because that is success for the user, they found their partner. Imagine telling an investor, 'Yeah so we really want to get them off the app as quick as possible, give me money, thanks.'

Decentralisation and democratisation

THE FUTURE IS HERE, IT'S JUST NOT EVENLY DISTRIBUTED YET.

— David Bowie

As we have seen, the democratisation of technology has led to a decentralised system. The tools and platforms that were once only available to the elite have now become accessible to everyone with an internet connection.

The internet has created a new paradigm for communication, collaboration and sharing. For example, it is possible for someone in one country to collaborate with someone in another country without ever having met them or even spoken to them on the phone.

The tech tsunami of change has rewritten the rules of the game. In a sense, it's all to play for. With a new culture of working and capitalism, decentralisation has taken hold.

There has never been a more exciting or unpredictable time to be in business. The internet has enabled the democratisation of opportunity by allowing us to find and connect with potential customers anywhere in the world, and increasingly it provides new ways to succeed by helping entrepreneurs and innovators to create value for the people they want to serve.[ix]

A stark example of this is in the hyped-up world of Bitcoin, but more so its underlying technology, blockchain. Decentralisation is an idea whose time has come. The internet is large enough and liquid enough to accommodate decentralised models in new and more pervasive ways than has been possible previously. Centralised models were a good idea at the time, an innovation and revolution in human coordination hundreds of years ago, but now we have a new cultural technology – the internet – and techniques such as distributed public blockchain ledgers that could facilitate activity to not only include all seven billion people for the first time, but also allow larger-scale, more complicated coordination, and speed our progress towards becoming a truly advanced society. If not the blockchain industry, there would probably be something else, and in fact there probably will be other complements to the blockchain industry anyway. It is just that the blockchain industry is one of the first identifiable large-scale implementations of decentralisation models, conceived and executed at a new and more complex level of human activity.[x]

Remix and recycle culture

Fresh, original ideas are few and far between nowadays. Yet existing ideas combined are everywhere, and seemingly accelerating. It's the era of remix culture, where older ideas are meshed with new updates (just look at the slew of remakes and franchises spewing out of Hollywood, how many Spiderman movies can there be?) Thanks to software and the internet, that glorious highway of information, ideas can spread with more ease and dexterity.

For the entrepreneurial class, the doers, this spells out opportunity. Matt Mason, in his astounding book *The Pirates Dilemma: How Youth Culture Is Reinventing Capitalism*, coined the term *punk capitalism*. He used the term punk capitalism to describe the new set of market conditions governing society. It's a society where piracy, as the co-chair at Disney recently put it, is 'just another business model.' A society where the remix is changing the way production and consumption are structured, rendering the nineteenth-century copyright laws we use obsolete. A world where advertising no longer works quite the way it did. It's a place where open-source ways of working are generating a wealth of new public goods, niche markets, knowledge and resources – free tools for the rest of us to build both commercial and non-commercial ventures. It's a place where creativity is our most valuable resource. It's a marketplace where things we used to pay for are free, and things that used to be free have to be paid for. It's a world where altruism is as powerful as competition, inhabited by a new breed of social entrepreneurs, a creative resistance who make money by putting as much emphasis on truly making a difference as they do on turning a profit.[xi]

In tech, they have a cleaner, more digestible term for their Patagonia and chinos-wearing minds. We are entering what lead Google economist Hal Varian calls a new period of 'combinatorial innovation':

This occurs when there is a great availability of different component parts that can be combined or recombined to create new inventions. For example, in the 1800s, the standardisation of the design of mechanical devices such as gears, pulleys, chains and cams led to a manufacturing boom. In the 1900s, the gasoline engine led to innovations in automobiles, motorcycles and airplanes. By the 1950s, it was the integrated circuit proliferating in numerous applications. In each of these cases, the development of complementary components led to a wave of inventions. Today the components are all about information, connectivity and computing. Would-be inventors have all the world's information, global reach and practically infinite computing power.

They have open-source software and abundant APIs (Application Programming Interfaces) that allow them to build easily on each other's work. They can use standard protocols and languages. They can access information platforms with data about things ranging from traffic to weather to economic transactions to human genetics.[xii]

As a result of this new world, product development has become a faster, more flexible process, where radically better products don't stand on the shoulders of giants, but on the shoulders of lots of iterations. The basis for success then, and for continual product excellence, is speed.[xiii]

Paul Romer, an economist at New York University who specialises in the theory of economic growth, says real sustainable economic growth does not stem from new resources but from existing resources that are rearranged to make them more valuable. Growth comes from remixing.[xiv]

Dave Morrissey

THERE ARE NO NEW BEGINNINGS

UNTIL EVERYBODY SEES THAT THE OLD WAYS NEED TO END.

— Kae Tempest

It's coming for your industry

But the tech industry is the tech industry, I hear some of you say. That is what, in tech terms, is known as 'siloed thinking' – having a narrow opinion not open to data and perspective. You need to get that out of you sharpish. Tech is in every industry now. Every industry is tech.

Let's call tech, quite simply, 'innovation' for a moment. It's been the narrative du jour of the business world for some time now.

According to the *Wall Street Journal*, some form of that word appeared in the annual and quarterly reports of US companies over thirty-three thousand times in 2011 alone.[xv]

The success of single tech companies like Apple can hollow out entire markets, even regions. The iPhone debuted in 2007 and devastated Motorola and Nokia. Together they have shed one hundred thousand jobs. Nokia, at its peak, represented 30 per cent of Finland's GDP and paid almost a quarter of all of that country's corporate taxes. Russia may have rolled tanks into Finland in 1939, but Apple's 2007 commercial invasion also levied substantial economic damage. Nokia's fall pummelled the entire economy of Finland. The firm's share of the stock market shrank from 70 per cent to 13 per cent.[xvi]

This tech method is repeating in every industry. Take razors: start-up Harry's has started to challenge the incumbent Gillette. In investing, start-up Robinhood is challenging Fidelity, T. Rowe Price and other century-old institutions for your brokerage account. Opendoor is shaking up the real estate business by changing the way houses are bought and sold. In industry after industry, digital native companies are using technology to bring a new kind of product to market, faster, cheaper and with a better customer experience than the incumbents. Another way to think of this: software has moved from being a cost centre to the profit centre.[xvii]

Even your everyday pizza is impacted. Domino's CEO Patrick Doyle admitted ten years ago that their cardboard pizza was the 'worst'. But what they did was improve the quality of the pizza, somewhat, and leaned mightily into tech.

Getting hot pizzas to customers like Amazon gets you books is Domino's schtick. They are admittedly not a pizza company, but a tech company. Its share price has performed better than Alphabet's/Google's in the past decade as a result. The reason tech continues to eat more of the world's GDP is a gestalt that says we need to make a much better product and lower price.[xviii]

The business playbook has been rewritten; in fact there is no playbook, every element of business is up for grabs, ripe for disruption. Even financing. Tech has slapped Wall Street silly in recent times, telling them, 'No, we aren't into profits, we are into adding value to customers for the sake of growth.'

If you, your company and your industry don't buck up and look to innovate like tech, you are likely to lose. In *Corporate Innovation in the Fifth Era: Lessons from Alphabet/Google, Amazon, Apple, Facebook, and Microsoft*, the authors analysed the biggest losers of economic value over a ten-year period from 2002 to 2012. The study showed that for the 103 biggest losers of economic value out of all public companies analysed over the time frame, over 80 per cent of the time the reason for the significant value destruction was a strategic and/or innovation blunder, for example, being caught by surprise by a disruptive innovation launched by a competitor or new player, or by a strategic inability for a company to keep up with innovations in its industry.[xix]

The losers appear to be those that can't keep up with the new strategies of their industries and competitors: they are laggards in innovation in one way or another.[xx]

And this is before we even lean into the elephant in the room murmurs, from AI's big swinging dick. *Artificial intelligence automation may impact 66 per cent of ALL jobs.* Goldman Sachs research gave these sobering insights:

- Seven per cent of workers will lose their jobs completely in the ten years if generative AI reaches half of employers.
- Eighteen per cent of the global workforce could be automated by AI but this is more of a DM rather than EM theme.
- Forty-six per cent of administrative jobs and 44 per cent of legal jobs can be substituted by AI.
- Twenty-five per cent of all current work tasks could be automated by the US and Europe.[xxi]

Your industry, and job, as you know it, will be very different in ten years. Darwinian times, and then some, ahead.

It's where your employees are going

Your customers going to competitors is one thing, but what about your staff? Why would a twenty-something bright-eyed buck want to work for a miserly laggard company when over the road there is a glistening aura of fun and progressiveness emanating from the doors of another company?

Tech companies, and those companies trying to emulate them (I see you Ryanair, putting a slide in your office like Google has, chancers) are the star prize for young people today. Everyone wants to work for them. And the data points to a mass migration to these companies. WPP is the world's largest advertising group. Some two thousand of its former employees have migrated to Facebook or Google. By comparison, only 124 former Facebook or Google peeps left to go work at WPP.[xxii]

Change starts with truth

YOU CAN'T STOP THE WAVES, BUT YOU CAN LEARN TO SURF.

— Jon Kabat-Zinn

For change to happen, realness has to take hold. An acknowledgement, hell, an almighty bear hug of the truth is vital. You and your business have to look at hard data and/or anecdotal evidence about where you are, what your strengths are and where you need to go from there. Bias, be gone. What worked last week won't work this week. (Repeat that 100 times.)

Getting to the truth is what the best companies do. Take the animation studio at Pixar for instance, a tech company essentially, brought to life in a big way by Steve Jobs. Its CEO, Ed Catmull, had this to say:

What makes Pixar special is that we acknowledge we will always have problems, many of them hidden from our view; that we work hard to uncover these problems, even if doing so means making ourselves uncomfortable; and that, when we come across a problem, we marshal all of our energies to solve it.[xxiii]

Change starts with mindset and urgency

MANY LEADERS OF ORGANIZATIONS, I THINK, DON'T BELIEVE THAT CHANGE IS POSSIBLE. BUT IF YOU LOOK AT HISTORY, THINGS DO CHANGE, AND IF YOUR BUSINESS IS STATIC, YOU'RE LIKELY TO HAVE ISSUES.[xxiv]

— Larry Page

Covid and change – my apologies, that's the last time I mention them in the same sentence again. It's important to note this breakdown of thinking and action from Airbnb's CEO Brian Chesky who outlined how they adapted to Covid when it hit. This is an exceptional restructuring of a huge company, truly telling of the mindset of tech people:

Airbnb started like all companies start. They start as functional organizations. You have a marketing leader and a design leader and a product leader, engineer leader, finance, HR. Then the Andy Grove law of large organizations is that all organizations eventually become matrixes. Very few companies, when they grow, stay functional. The only large functional organization in the world is Apple, and even Apple is only quasi-functional because they have a whole services group now, which is a little bit quasi-divisional. But Apple is a functional organ; they're an anomaly.

If you take the Fortune 500, every other company is a conglomerate or a divisional. Before the pandemic, we were divisional and we had subdivisions. We had actually 10 divisions: a homes division which had core host, pro host, business travel, luxe, plus. Then we had experiences, transportation, content, and a few other things – about 10 or 11 divisions. We were really scattered.

In hindsight, we were not so focused. Of course, you don't know until after. It's kind of like those movies where you think your life is great, and then the plot happens. The whole point of the movie is you realize that your life wasn't as great as you thought and you grew from the experience.

That's kind of what it was for us. We lost 80 percent of our business. I had to stare into the abyss. I never thought the company wouldn't exist, but a lot of other people did. I had to stare into making some hard decisions. We had to lay off 25 percent of our employees. It was the hardest professional decision I've ever had to make.

We also lost about 10 percent of people that were contractors. A whole bunch of people tend to resign after a layoff because they're like, 'Okay, well, there's not a lot of opportunities.'

So we lost almost half of our company. We had to shutter most of those divisions. We only kept the core. We kept homes and experiences. We put those under one group that we called Host.

The radical thing is we went back to a functional organization. I studied a number of other companies that were in crisis, and the most dramatic crisis I had encountered was Apple. In 1997, Apple was 90 days from bankruptcy. They were a divisional structure. Steve [Jobs] comes back. He shutters most of the divisions. The other thing Steve did is he went back to a functional org. I went to a functional org, as well, primarily out of necessity to cut costs and integrate, but something remarkable happened. When I got to a functional org, suddenly I took the very best people and I put them on one problem. Not only did we save money, we started growing faster.

One of Alibaba CEO Jack Ma's favourite sayings proved to be true when they were in fierce competition with Yahoo in the 2000s:

'Today is tough, tomorrow is tougher, and the day after tomorrow is beautiful. But most companies die tomorrow evening and can't see the sunshine on the day after tomorrow.'[xxv]

The tech mindset is one which is only now being spoken about in everyday life. Twilio's Jeff Lawson observed that over the past decade, he met so many people who exhibit this mindset, in every function – from finance to customer support, from marketing to operations, from sales to product – who are building the future of their respective companies as digital businesses. All of those people are builders. There's a misconception sometimes that digital disruption is all about developers. It's not. Yes, companies need developers to build software. But really it's about the successful collaboration between all the functions and the software developers who actually write the code. It takes a village.[xxvi]

Curiosity and urgency, or persistence, are the cornerstones of this mindset. Curiosity is crucial to success. What worked yesterday is out of date today and forgotten tomorrow – replaced by a new tool or technique we haven't yet heard of. Consider that the telephone took seventy-five years to reach fifty million users, whereas television was in fifty million households within thirteen years, the internet in four ... and Angry Birds in thirty-five days. In the tech era, the pace is accelerating further: it took Microsoft Office twenty-two years to reach a billion users, but Gmail only twelve and Facebook nine. Trying to resist this tide of change will drown you. Successful people in the digital age are those who go to work every day, not dreading the next change, but asking, 'What if we did it this way?' Adherence to process, or how we've always done it, is the Achilles' heel of big firms and sepsis for careers.

And the urgency in which tech bestows to change is something else. Amazon's Jeff Bezos's mantra is every working day at Amazon is Day 1 for the company. Day 1 means that Amazon will always act as a start-up – every day has to be as intense and fevered as the first day of running a new business.[xxvii]

Management consultant Will Hogg believes that effective organisational change requires four key stages. The absence of any one factor will inhibit culture change and often make it impossible:

- A case for change
- A compelling picture of the future
- A sustained capability to change
- A credible plan to execute[xxviii]

Ryan Holmes, founder of Hootsuite, called out five phrases that need to be eradicated from everyday work chatter, in order to be a more innovative environment capable of surfing the waves of change:

1. *'That's not my job'**: Great, but should it be? If not, who's the best person to reach out to?
2. *'That's not how we do things'*: Well, why not? Traditions are meant to be broken.
3. *'That will never work'*: Maybe it won't ... but maybe it will.

The best ideas – from antibiotics to the iPhone – started out as long shots.
4. *'That's too complicated': Complex problems often yield the biggest returns ... if you keep at 'em.*
5. *'We already tried this': So what? Companies evolve; circumstances change. Sometimes, it's worth revisiting a challenge with fresh eyes.*

*At Meta, posters famously adorn the walls with the saying 'Nothing is someone else's problem.'

ONE OF THE MOST VALUABLE THINGS YOU CAN DO AS A FOUNDER IS TO CULTIVATE A BEGINNER'S MINDSET AND BE WILLING TO CONSTANTLY LEARN AND ADAPT.

— Sam Altman

A shortcut to ride that wave of change

Remember, software is changing the world, and it itself changing every instant. Daunting perhaps, but it's still humans pulling the strings. The humans hold the key.

There is a simple solution to this wave of change for you and your work, from that old adage, "If you can't beat them, join them." Jeff Lawson again spells it out:

To truly thrive in the digital era – either as a disruptor or those fending off the disruptors – you need to think like a Software Person. Now, a Software Person is not necessarily a developer – it's anybody who, when faced with a problem, asks the question: 'How can software solve this problem?' That's because being a Software Person is a mindset, not a skill set.

Every kind of company can become a software company (read, a tech mindsetted company) – all you have to do is internalize the value of rapid iteration. You don't need to be Elon Musk or Jack Dorsey; you just need to believe in the power of iteration, and Darwin will be on your side. But of course, to iterate, you first need to build. You can't iterate on something you've bought off the shelf. That's why it's Build vs. Die.[xxix]

As Mark Zuckerberg, founder of Facebook, remarked, 'The biggest risk is not taking any risk … In a world that is changing really quickly, the only strategy that is guaranteed to fail is not taking risks.'

And if you want to stay on top of where tech will go next, follow the porn. Porn was first to make use of the internet for distribution at scale, much to Pamela Anderson and Tommy Lee's horror. Video and streaming, porn blew first. With VR and AR, you will know they are mainstay technologies for your business and endeavours when they hit critical mass in the world of porn.

Chapter 2
THE WHY OF TECH

WE ARE HERE TO MAKE THE WORLD A BETTER PLACE.

— **Every tech leader, ever**

'Make the world a better place' is a well-worn saying in meeting rooms across the land of the tech giants and wannabes (i.e. start-ups). It's the idealistic vernacular that drives their impact on society. Given the backlash against big tech, that mantra feels terribly contrived. And from experience in tech it does work as a valuable heuristic, but can also be a bastardised statement, to rationalise one person or a team out of an immoral shithole. Let's look at the positives for this chapter.

Each company has a distinct WHY. The power of that one word, *why*, is understated in society. It helps people find purpose. It helps people remove a point of friction. It helps people pave a path forward. It helps people frame their place in the company. It helps people call out bullshit. For a company and its people, having a crisp, well-defined, almost holier-than-thou *why* brings purpose and untold levels of employee engagement. This dominoes into employee ingenuity and performance which brings innovation, market share and industry impact. And money, lots of money.

The *why* is an idealistic driving force that propels ambition, long-term thinking and heightened levels of engagement. In Maslow's hierarchy of needs, the top of the pyramid, self-actualisation, is where the *why* comes alive. To Maslow, self-actualisation is the ability to become the best version of oneself. Maslow stated: 'This tendency might be phrased as the desire to become more and more what one is, to become everything that one is capable of becoming.'[i]

Seeing and working towards a big-ass purpose, something bigger than yourself, that will make a dent in the world, may seem like an idealistic viewpoint, but that belief system works. We are overly hardwired for purpose as humans, so get with the program, your brain's program.

History is layered with stories where a heightened belief in a *why* brings unprecedented results. The story of three bricklayers is a multifaceted parable with many different variations, but is rooted in an authentic story. After the Great Fire of 1666 that levelled London, the world's most famous architect, Christopher Wren, was commissioned to rebuild St Paul's Cathedral.

One day in 1671, Christopher Wren observed three bricklayers on a scaffold, one crouched, one half-standing and one standing tall, working very hard and fast. To the first bricklayer, Christopher Wren asked the question, 'What are you doing?' to which the bricklayer replied, 'I'm a bricklayer. I'm working hard laying bricks to feed my family.' The second bricklayer responded, 'I'm a builder. I'm building a wall.' But the third bricklayer, the most productive of the three and the future leader of the group, when asked the question, 'What are you doing?' replied with a gleam in his eye, 'I'm a cathedral builder. I'm building a great cathedral to the Almighty.'[ii]

In the modern day, a clear vision of the *why* fuels the world's most impactful and valuable tech companies. It is vital to tech. Modern management guru Eric Ries explains in his must-read book *The Startup Way* how it brings necessary focus, and then some.

The vision makes plain what the start-up hopes to accomplish. It is the primary coordination device as the team acts in a decentralised fashion. As General Stanley McChrystal wrote, 'The key reason for the success of empowered execution lay in what had come before it: the foundation of shared consciousness.' Vision provides a profound sense of motivation and energy and an unparalleled recruiting advantage.[iii]

Before we get carried away with ourselves, here is a wee sobering note from Google's Sergey Brin to not let tech get ahead of itself …

Silicon Valley has outgrown the time of being wide-eyed and idealistic about tech and needs to show responsibility, care and humility. Advances in artificial intelligence represent the most significant development in computing in my lifetime. There are very legitimate and pertinent issues being raised, across the globe, about the implications and impacts of these advances. How will they affect employment across different sectors? What about measures of fairness? How might they manipulate people? Are they safe?[iv]

It's always good to have a reality check from time to time. And then kick back into idealistic inspiration.

IF YOU WANT TO BUILD A SHIP, DON'T DRUM UP THE MEN TO GATHER WOOD, DIVIDE THE WORK, AND GIVE ORDERS. INSTEAD, TEACH THEM TO YEARN FOR THE VAST AND ENDLESS SEA.[v]

— Antoine de Saint-Exupéry

Missions and visions in tech

WORK TAKES ON NEW MEANING WHEN YOU FEEL YOU ARE POINTED IN THE RIGHT DIRECTION. OTHERWISE, IT'S JUST A JOB, AND LIFE IS TOO SHORT FOR THAT.

— Tim Cook, CEO of Apple

The *why* is comprised of the mission and vision of the company. Which comes first can vary. Some companies nail down both early on, some cobble them together over years, or as new people join the company to give it better direction. A company that doesn't know what it is doing and why it is doing it is a rudderless beast, tame it or it will sail off into the Bermuda Triangle of business.

But ideally the mission comes first as that's the larger piece of the *why* pie. The mission describes the organisation's visible, tangible work in the world: what the company does, who it does it for, and how this helps the client. It explains the tangible activities and overall approach that the company takes as it translates the big-picture vision into everyday action. Some companies are solely mission-driven, while other companies have a mission fused with a vision.[vi]

In tech, the loftier and more ambitious the mission, the better. Facebook's is famously around connection, to give people the power to build community and bring the world closer together. People use Facebook to stay connected with friends and family, to discover what's going on in the world. Fintech poster child Stripe has a cracker, with a mission to increase the GDP of the internet. Both really make you pause and reflect, and spark the imagination into what could be possible.

Some go beyond one-liners. E-commerce darling Etsy has the following:

At Etsy, our mission is to enable people to make a living making things. The engineers who make Etsy make our living making something we love; software. We think of our code as craft.

Patreon is the membership platform for content creators. You know the one, where every podcaster under the sun tries to direct you to give the equivalent of the price of a pint for access to more of their ramblings. Patreon has two missions:

1. Fund the emerging creative class
2. Create a company where teammates build fulfilling lives

This is smart, as it puts focus on the people most important to the business, the staff and customers, not the bloody shareholders and investors.

A company's vision on the other hand articulates the business's medium- to long-term goals and aspirations. Looking years into the future, and if everything goes according to plan, the vision describes how the company will change the world. To be powerful and inspiring, a vision statement should be compelling, meaningful, and boldly ambitious, capturing the essence of why the company exists and what it would make happen if anything were possible.

LinkedIn's vision is the following:

Create economic opportunity for every member of the global workforce.

Coinbase is similar but has a crucial distinction, with 'freedom':

Create economic freedom for people around the world.

Check out the compelling use of language used by the web-hosting mainstay GoDaddy:

We will radically shift the global economy toward small business by empowering people to easily start, confidently grow and successfully run their own ventures.

Through the word 'radically' you instantly get the sense of urgency and desire in the company's *why* from one word.

And the company with arguably the best mission of them all is Calm, the meditation app, which aims 'to solve the world's mental health crisis.'

VISION WITHOUT ACTION IS A DREAM. ACTION WITHOUT VISION IS A NIGHTMARE.

— Japanese proverb

Many will think that the *why* is all a bit of hot-air fluff. Fluff sells in the corporate world, people. Let's look at the impact of these missions and visions on businesses.

A mission is exciting. It will give energy to both you and everyone around you. It's also what gets customers behind you. Simon Sinek claims that people don't buy WHAT you do, they buy WHY you do it.[vii]

In his popular TED talk and book, Sinek argues that if we want to inspire people, we should start with *why*. If we communicate the vision behind our ideas, the purpose guiding our products, people will flock to us. This is excellent advice – unless you're doing something original that challenges the status quo. When people championing moral change explain their *why*, it runs the risk of clashing with deep-seated convictions. When creative non- conformists explain their *why*, it may violate common notions of what's possible.[viii]

The world's most valuable company, Apple, was the perfect example for him to point to ...

Apple's *why*? Everything we do, we believe in challenging the status quo and thinking differently.

Apple's *how*? Our products are beautifully designed and simple to use. Apple's *what*? We just happen to sell computers.

Everything we do, we believe in challenging the status quo and thinking differently.

In money terms, that's $2 trillion in value, and counting.

The people impact

I WANT SOMETHING GOOD TO DIE FOR, TO MAKE IT BEAUTIFUL TO LIVE.

— Joshua Homme, Queens of the Stone Age

Undoubtedly, a good *why* brings talent in and keeps them engaged and loyal to the company. It's a 360-marketing tool in itself. It's a key component of a Zappos founder, the late Tony Hsieh, in his landmark book *Delivering Happiness* saw it this way. He explained:

Happiness is really just about four things: perceived control, perceived progress, connectedness (number and depth of your relationships), and vision/meaning (being part of something bigger than yourself)[ix]

Beyond the theory, the data points to the *why* being a catalyst for a buzzed-up workforce. Research suggests that an employee who is satisfied with his or her work is 40 per cent more productive than an unsatisfied one. But an engaged employee is 44 per cent more productive than a satisfied worker, and an employee who feels inspired at work is nearly 125 per cent more productive than a satisfied one.[x]

And they sell more product. Employees who are inspired by their leadership and work at Dell are 30 per cent more likely to recommend Dell's products to a family member or friend compared to employees who are merely satisfied.[xi]

Look at the customer and within

The *why* of tech companies – well, the successful ones – begins with the people they are serving, the users or customers. Not shareholders. Not their partners or parents. Especially not themselves.

Apple didn't become the most beloved brand in the world by making beautiful stuff; they got there by making sense of what the future would look like and by making meaning for the people who would live in that future. Steve Jobs and Jony Ive didn't start with an idea for a product; they began by thinking about who it was for and what mattered to them. Apple design to serve, serve to design.[xii]

Apple's current CEO Tim Cook recently revised Apple's vision and mission statement to further emphasise the central position of customer-focused innovation, opening their black box of purpose even further. He wrote:

We believe that we are on the face of the earth to make great products and that's not changing. We are constantly focusing on innovating. We believe in the simple, not the complex. We believe that we need to own and control the primary technologies behind the products that we make and participate only in markets where we can make a significant contribution. We believe in saying no to thousands of projects so that we can really focus on the few that are truly important and meaningful to us. We believe in deep collaboration and cross-pollination of our groups, which allow us to innovate in a way that others cannot. And frankly, we don't settle for anything less than excellence in every group in the company, and we have the self-honesty to admit when we're wrong and the courage to change. And I think regardless of who is in what job those values are so embedded in this company that Apple will do extremely well.[xiii]

Missions within teams in companies that are geared towards the customer win. Twilio's Jeff Lawson learnt this:

Teams do their best work when each member of the team feels accountable to the customer, and a deep sense of purpose to serve the customer. Small teams enable that kind of connection and purpose, with a mission that comes from inside the team, driven by a primary interaction with the customer and their problems, not from executives.[xiv]

Add value

TRY NOT TO BECOME A PERSON OF SUCCESS, BUT RATHER TRY TO BECOME A PERSON OF VALUE.

— Albert Einstein

This focus on the customer reframes what good output looks like, and in tech lore, it means adding value to the customer. Adding value can be construed as make more money from people. This is a shallow and somewhat cynical take.

Tech companies look to add value by providing more access (Facebook to your friends' lives), making products cheaper (WhatsApp for calls across countries), increasing self-service with more control (Uber for moving from A to B), increasing in convenience (Amazon, one-click buying and getting the product the next/same day), allowing information access (Google) and saving time with automation (Squarespace when setting up a website).

We have more to come on tech adding value to customers and users in the 'Customer-First Building' chapter.

'Dream big – really big'

Another term bandied around micro-kitchens (imagine your local corner shop, on every floor of the building, brimming with snacks and drinks, free of course) at every tech company for a mission is its North

Star, the big audacious pie in the sky. It evokes an epic challenge in the mind, which fires the brain into thinking bigger and bolder. In tech, the bigger and bolder, the better.

Google's founder and CEO, Larry Page, often pushed employees, saying, 'You aren't thinking big enough' – which was later replaced by the Larry Page directive to 'Think 10x.' It encompasses the art of the possible … and the impossible.[xv] 10x-ing everything and anything to do with revenue generation or efficiency scaling is a common trope amongst the meeting rooms of tech companies, God forbid they have to get out of bed for 9x growth.

Start by asking what could be true in five years. Larry Page often says that the job of a CEO is not only to think about the core business, but also the future; most companies fail because they get too comfortable doing what they have always done, making only incremental changes. And that is especially fatal today, when technology-driven change is rampant. So the question to ask isn't what will be true, but what could be true. Asking what will be true entails making a prediction, which is folly in a fast-moving world. Asking what could be true requires imagination: What thing that is unimaginable when abiding by conventional wisdom is in fact imaginable?[xvi]

Don't be a goldfish. Tech expands attention span, and then some. It's a mental framework that leads to bigger, bolder decision-making. Jeff Bezos points out:

Just by lengthening the time horizon, you can engage in endeavours that you could never otherwise pursue. At Amazon we like things to work in five to seven years. We're willing to plant seeds, let them grow – and we're very stubborn.

We say we're stubborn on vision and flexible on details.[xvii]

Go big and bold, but not too far. Elon Musk, the CEO of SpaceX and Tesla, who some are calling the Leonardo da Vinci of our time, harks caution:

Certainly don't try to set impossible goals. I think impossible goals are demotivating. You don't want to tell people to go through a wall by banging their head against it. I don't ever set intentionally impossible goals. But I've certainly always been optimistic on time frames. I'm trying to recalibrate to be a little more realistic.[xviii]

It's not just the US-based big tech dreamers who subscribe to a big and bold *why*. In the past decade Chinese companies like Tencent, Baidu and Alibaba have been seen to mimic their US counterparts. Over to you, Jack Ma, founder of Alibaba:

From the first day we started Alibaba, we had three main goals. We want Alibaba to be one of the top ten websites in the world. We want Alibaba to be a partner to all businesspeople. And we want to build a company that lasts 80 years![xix]

'Dream big – really big,' he always says. Whenever Jack asked his managers to set goals for the company, they would provide their most optimistic projections. Jack would usually come back and triple or quadruple our goal.

Despite initial resistance from managers, Jack dared them to dream: 'If you don't imagine it will happen, it will never happen,' Jack told them all. At the end of the year they nearly always found that they had not only met but exceeded those lofty goals.

Be different

Dare to not copy these guys. Dare to be different. All too often you hear of companies wanting to be the next Facebook or Alibaba, and they copy their make-up. 'To be the Uber of ...' is a common utterance among any aspiring entrepreneur. This distracts from that company being true to its customers, and itself. So when setting out the *why*, make it unique to who and what is being served.

Outside of tech, albeit they are now becoming a digital-focused company, LEGO espouse a pitch-perfect *why*, 'To inspire and develop the builders of tomorrow.' This is a collective desire – to spark kids to pursue ideas through 'hands-on, minds-on.'[xx] What a space to own, the 'builders of tomorrow'.

Paul Graham, founder of Y-Combinator, arguably the most exciting and impactful tech start-up incubator on the planet, tells it like it is, or should be. One of his questions for founders who apply to Y Combinator: 'What are you doing that the world doesn't realize is a really big fucking deal?'[xxi]

Write it down, share it

Research shows that writing something down means you are more likely to achieve it, 42 per cent more likely in fact.[xxii] Put it on paper. And repeatedly do so. Take a tour of any tech firm and you will be guaranteed to see the *why*, be it the mission or vision, or some combination of them, adorning the walls in poster format, or graffiti. And you better believe it's on many a PowerPoint slide.

Later on we shall see the virtue of writing the *why* (and *how*) down in tech land, where the mission adorns posters on walls, coffee mugs and general chit-chat.

Go forth, and with your group of colleagues, sit down to brainstorm your mission, and don't leave until you have it concisely and meaningfully figured out. Put it on a poster. And let the better times roll (well not really, you have to execute on that mission like your life depended on it).

Process of discovery, not invention

'It's all about the journey'. One of the most thrown-about, bastardised lines said in the tech world. A journey implies you are going from A to B, from Dublin to San Francisco. No company has such a linear path, it's an adventure, not a fucking journey.

Mr Sinek saw the lack of linearity in finding a company's way with its *why* as its guidepost:

Finding WHY is a process of discovery, not invention. Just as Apple's WHY developed during the rebellious 1960s and '70s, the WHY for every other individual or organization comes from the past. It is born out of the upbringing and life experience of an individual.[xxiii]

In *The Four*, Scott Galloway's seminal book that looks at the dominance of Facebook, Google, Amazon and Apple, he gave the benefit of hindsight to these behemoths with regard to their adventures:

Tech giants, of course, don't start out as globally dominant megalodons. They begin as ideas, as someone's garage or dorm-room project. Their path looks obvious and even inevitable in hindsight, but it's almost always an improvisational series of actions and reactions.[xxiv]

Every *why* will be a product of its environment. No environment is the same. Journeys can be pretty much the same. Adventures not so. Prepare to go on an adventure.

Missions are malleable

The beauty of tech's grand missions is that there is no true end in sight. There is always more to do. There is always hunger to achieve. Hunger to serve. Hunger to innovate.

Crucially, we can never achieve our mission, as there will always be more information to organise and more ways to make it useful. This creates motivation to constantly innovate and push into new areas. A mission that is about being 'the market leader,' once accomplished, offers little more inspiration. 'The broad scope of their mission allows Google to move forward by steering with a compass rather than a speedometer',[xxv] explained Laszlo Bock, former SVP of People Operations at Google.

This level of foresight is crucial to the mindset of tech. It's a fine line between bold ambition and bloody stubbornness. Pushing forward but with check-ins to reality is key. Netflix CEO, Reed Hastings, saw this on reflection of Netflix's history:

It's impossible to know where a business like ours will be five years from now. Trying to guess and plan around those guesses is sure to tie the company down and keep us from adapting quickly.[xxvi]

In 2017, then Facebook, took its mission down another path. Previously, the mission had been 'To give people the power to share and make the world more open and connected.'

We used to have a sense that if we could just do those things, then that would make a lot of the things in the world better by themselves,' Zuckerberg told CNN Tech. 'But now we realize that we need to do more too. It's important to give people a voice, to get a diversity of opinions out there, but on top of that, you also need to do this work of building common ground so that way we can all move forward together.'

Lo and behold, a refreshed mission was born: 'To give people the power to build community and bring the world closer together.'

The *why* informs all strategy

Tech's ability to cast its bright eye into the long distant future doesn't just light the self-actualisation fireworks and spark unprecedented engagement in business practices, it gives tech the ability to lay out strategy like other industries can't, or won't bother their arse to.

At Meta, for example, Mark Zuckerberg and his team have defined an innovation strategy that focuses on three future innovation domains that they believe are fundamental to achieving their mission to 'Give people the power to share and make the world more open and connected.'

These three innovation domains are:

- Connectivity – including terrestrial solutions, telco infrastructure, free basics, satellites, drones and lasers
- Artificial intelligence – including vision, language, reasoning and planning
- VR/AR – including social VR, mobile VR, Oculus Rift, touch and AR technologies

This list of innovation domains is well understood by the entire Meta management team and board who are actively exploring and communicating about these exciting topics.[xxvii]

Tech, when it comes to its *why*, tends to think in five, ten, twenty-year leaps. The ten-plus years being the 'moonshots', those audacious leaps forward such as enabling a person to see photos from a friend's weekend via electrical charges in human skin (hello, Meta, something they are working on). You and your business may not be there yet, so start with the first five years and work backwards, as Eric Schmidt put forward in *How Google Works*:

The right strategy has a beauty to it, a sense of many people and ideas working in concert to succeed. Start by asking what will be true in five years and work backward. Examine carefully the things you can assert will change quickly, especially factors of production where technology is exponentially driving down cost curves, or platforms that could emerge.[xxviii]

Going deeper, Schmidt outlines what good strategic planning should look like.

A good strategy statement articulates a company's purpose, its means of competition, and its unique advantages by answering the most basic questions about what a company does and how it does it:

- *Who we serve*
- *With what sort of products or services*
- *What we do that's different or better*
- *What enables us to do that*

And it has these qualities:

- *It is reasonably short and parsimonious.*
- *It is specific.*
- *It states what the company does and why it matters in a way that anyone can summarize without having to quote it literally.*
- *It avoids jargon, such as 'best of breed,' 'best in class,' or vague words such as superior, expert, and empowered.*
- *It is affirming, but not grandiose or self-important.*
- *People easily recognize that it's you.*

Actually, hold on, we might be getting ahead of ourselves again. All too often, strategy is another convoluted term bandied about in business at large. Let's clarify what strategy is specifically, as spelt out in Cynthia Montgomery's *The Strategist: Be the Leader Your Business Needs*.

Strategy – the system of value creation that underlies a company's competitive position and uniqueness – has to be embraced as something open, not something closed. It is a system that evolves, moves and changes. Strategy is about serving an unmet need, doing something unique or uniquely well for some set of stakeholders. Beating the competition is critical, to be sure, but it's the result of finding and filling that need, not the goal.[xxix]

The pivot

Now that we know how tech thinks its way forward, and what strategy actually means, prepare to change. This is where a constantly-relevant tech verb comes into play, the pivot, which is a change in strategy without a change in vision.

Tech start-up history is filled with legendary pivot stories. Among them are PayPal, which went from a money transfer mechanism for only Palm Pilots (handheld devices way back when) to the web-based version we now have, and Netflix, which moved from mailing DVDs to its customers to streaming.[xxx]

You remember that last chapter? Always be wanting and willing to change.

Chapter 3
CULTURE IS RELIGION

'CULTURE EATS STRATEGY FOR BREAKFAST.'

— Peter Drucker

I opened this book by pointing out that it isn't the software or inherent technology really driving this industry, but rather the people behind it all, collaborating and making decisions. How people work together; the unique and nuanced way people in different groupings operate in tandem; how they think, talk and act – that is the culture of a company. And in no other time in the history of business has a company's culture been looked at as a means of competitive advantage until the prevalence of tech in the past two decades.

Culture in every other sector meanders along as a nice-to-have in the minds of management, or maroons itself as an afterthought. Worse, it sinks before the ship sets sail, never even considered at any stage.

Not so in tech. Tech sees culture as another system to optimise. Another way to differentiate and extract as much value from a resource as possible. Tech has changed the game so much on the culture front, I'd argue that tech's approach to company culture could be its greatest gift to the world of business. On the whole, employees are shinier, happier people working at these companies thanks to that big C word.

Culture may seem airy-fairy but it works, incredibly, especially when it is considered and optimised. Drinking the Kool-Aid has a psychological effect, it's the self-actualisation boost that catalyses the workforce. It steps people's mindset up a level. Employees go bigger and better every day. And you know what that means, more business growth and money.

Ninety-four per cent of executives and 88 per cent of employees believe a distinct workplace culture is important to business success according to a Deloitte 'Culture in the Workplace' study. Heidrick Consulting just completed a six-month study of five hundred top CEOs and found that companies led by CEOs who value culture and focus on people first have financial performance (assessed by a three-year revenue CAGR – compound annual growth rate) that's more than double that of other companies surveyed.

There is a startling disconnect between the elements of culture CEOs think are most important to improving financial performance and what elements actually are most prevalent in their companies today ... most aren't practising what they preach.

Culture can take on a dark side when not cared for. The Netflix documentary on airline manufacturer Boeing, *Downfall: The Case Against Boeing*, highlighted the ugly side of culture, resulting in lost lives.

The film details how Boeing's quest to save money and time led to deadly corners being cut in the development of its new 737 Max aircraft. As a result, two crashes occurred, killing a total of 346 people. The film makes it clear that Boeing's priorities were misplaced, and that its employees were under immense pressure to deliver a safe product. However, the culture of the company made it impossible for them to speak up about the problems they were seeing. As a result, two planes full of innocent people lost their lives.

Truth-telling and safety were far from practised.

A *Harvard Business Review* study found proof that positive work cultures are more productive.[i]

Companies with disengaged cultures have:

- 37% higher absenteeism
- 49% more accidents
- 60% more errors

Companies with low employee engagement scores experienced:

- 18% lower productivity
- 16% lower profitability
- 37% lower job growth
- 65% lower share price over time

On the flip side, companies with highly engaged employees enjoyed 100 per cent more job applications.

Group culture is one of the most powerful forces on the planet. We sense its presence inside successful businesses, championship teams and thriving families, and we sense when it's absent or toxic. We can measure its impact on the bottom line. A strong culture increases net income by 765 per cent over ten years, according to a Harvard study of more than two hundred companies.[ii]

While successful culture can look and feel like magic, the truth is that it's not. Culture is a set of living relationships working towards a shared goal. It's not something you are. It's something you do.

'Culture eats strategy for breakfast'

Management guru Peter Drucker came out with the famous saying, 'Culture eats strategy for breakfast' about work culture back in 2006, and it still rings loud and clear today, especially in tech and innovative industries at large.

Pixar's Ed Catmull puts it simply:

Getting the right people and the right chemistry is more important than getting the right idea.[iii]

Look at ants. An ant colony is an emergent system. The whole is greater than the sum of its parts. A similar irony applies to human groups. Pretty much all the most challenging work today is undertaken in groups for a simple reason: problems are too complex for any one person to tackle alone. The number of papers written by individual authors has declined year on year in almost all areas of academia. In science and engineering, 90 per cent of papers are written by teams. In medical research, collaborations outnumber individual papers.[iv]

The most innovative companies say that the cultural attributes that drive innovation are:

1. A strong identification with the customer and an overall orientation towards the customer experience (and constantly making sure it is competitive and getting better).
2. A passion for and pride in the products and services being offered by the company (including ensuring that they are leading edge and fully competitive with those of other players in the industry).

At Apple, innovation for the customer is a strategy woven deeply into their culture. In an Apple store the focus is entirely on the customer and identifying their needs, making sure they understand the options that Apple can provide, and then helping them to make their own choices regarding which Apple products to take home. An Apple store swarms with Apple employees who are trying their very best to serve each customer. And there is enormous pride among the Apple people in their company and its products and services. In fact, getting an internship or job at an Apple store is a substantial undertaking itself with many more people being turned away than accepted. Apple people like to say that it is easier to get into Stanford than to get a job at Apple.

This may or may not be true, but there is a feeling of privilege to work there and to have the opportunity to serve customers and fulfil the Apple mission.[v]

What culture is

Work culture – what is it? It is the visible, and invisible, behaviours and actions within a workplace. The nuanced ways that drive the way a company works within itself. 'The way we do things around here' in anecdotal terms. It's a company's best practices, and worst practices, in real time. What the company values and does not. How its people behave; the good, the bad and the ugly.

Which behaviours are rewarded or punished.

I love this description from the late great Ken Robinson:

Culture is about values, ambience, tone and relationships.[vi]

Nanoheal, the automation tech company, poignantly describes culture in its culture code:

Culture is what happens when the boss is not around.

Culture for millennials and Gen Z is a calling card for a company. Young people today want to work in great cultures. Similar research by Futurestep, a division of Korn Ferry, found that nearly two-thirds of the one thousand executives surveyed believe that cultural reputation is the single most important recruitment advantage for global organisations.[vii]

What culture is in tech

Culture in tech is everything. It's a brand. It's a growth driver. It's a lifestyle.

HubSpot proclaims that they don't just care about culture, they obsess over culture.

It's easy to look at tech's culture as slides (looking at you Google) into a canteen brimming with free food from top-end chefs, followed by enjoying a barista-prepared coffee to fuel the table tennis battle royale you are about to have with a colleague.

I personally love how Patreon describes culture:

Culture is a group of people repeating behaviors. When people say they like our culture, they're saying they like the way we treat each other, our visitors, our creators, and our patrons.

Basically people being pleasant to everyone around them. What can be better than that?

Tech workers tend to get swept up in the mission of the company, living and adding to its culture. The company and its culture become their identity to an extent. Zappos knew the power of culture early on:

To all of us in the room, we knew it wasn't just about the money. Together, we had built a business that combined profits, passion, and purpose. And we knew that it wasn't just about building a business. It was about building a lifestyle that was about delivering happiness to everyone, including ourselves.[viii]

Culture in tech is a catalyst for innovation. A study analysing Global Innovation 1000 companies based in Silicon Valley found that 73 per cent of them say their culture supports their innovation strategy while only 51.5 per cent of the highest-spending Global Innovation 1000 companies could say the same. The Silicon Valley companies believe that their internal cultures support their innovation strategy and work hard to accomplish this goal.[ix]

Jocelyn Goldfien, managing director of venture capital firm Zetta Venture Partners, stated that culture is the behaviour you reward and punish. This, especially at the frontline employee level, may be the most accurate description of culture today. Sexy mission statements and saucy cultural values are merely words, it's the actions of people towards other people in a company that set the tone.

If a narcissist bully who spends their day 'managing up' gets promoted over a person who does the right things for the right reasons by their customers and colleagues, that is not a good look. It implicitly says, 'Be a prick to get promoted'; soon everyone will become somewhat prickish.

Netflix succinctly defined and counteracted this sort of thing in their famous culture deck, with a slide saying:

The actual company values, as opposed to the nice-sounding values, are shown by who gets rewarded, promoted, or let go.

Ruthless some may say. But if it weeds out the arseholes, then more power to them.

Speaking of arseholes, although it's not in writing, many tech companies have a 'don't hire arseholes' policy. Even if the candidate being interviewed is the second coming of Bill Gates with game-changing technical and/or business skills, if they are an arsehole, it's a no-hire.

To look outside of tech for a moment, culture is increasingly looked on as the key competitive advantage elsewhere too.

In *Legacy*, James Kerr documented the revitalisation of arguably the greatest sports team to grace a playing field. The New Zealand All Blacks re-established a values-driven, purpose-driven culture. They borrowed from a management technique which begins with questions – the 'Socratic method', so called because Socrates used a type of interrogation to separate his pupils from their prejudices. The goal? To help them find self-knowledge, even if the truth turns out to be uncomfortable.

It is a key technique within the All Blacks' leadership and captured in a Maori proverb:

Waibo kia patai ana, he kaha ui te kaha.

Let the questioning continue; the ability of the person is in asking questions.

Rather than just instruct outwards, the coaches began to ask questions: first of themselves – 'How can we do this better?' and then of their players – 'What do you think?' This interrogative culture, in which the individual makes their own judgements and sets their own internal benchmarks, became increasingly important. The questions the leaders asked of themselves, and of the team, were the beginning of a rugby revolution.

Tech culture is, usually, open

GOOD FENCES MAKE GOOD NEIGHBOURS, BUT TAKE THE FENCE AWAY AND YOU HAVE A BIGGER LAWN. GET A FEW MORE NEIGHBOURS INVOLVED AND SOON YOU'VE GOT A PARK.

— Adam Grant

Hiding best practices. Stealing customers. Sharing nothing. Working in silo from other parts of the company. These are the horrible traits of non- innovative laggard companies. Tech leans towards the opposite, where companies aspire to be as open as possible across their departments, processes and culture at large. And it all stems from a technical approach, which has evolved into a mindset. Open source.

The term *open source* refers to something people can modify and share because its design is publicly accessible. The term originated in the context of software development to designate a specific approach to creating computer programs. Today, however, open source designates a broader set of values – what we call 'the open-source way'. Open-source projects, products or initiatives embrace and celebrate principles of open exchange, collaborative participation, rapid prototyping, transparency, meritocracy and community- oriented development.[x]

Openness and sharing in tech originate from the hacker community, which originated at MIT. John Carmack, the programmer legend behind computer games Doom and Quake, and now leading Meta's metaverse efforts in VR, gushed about the ethos behind hacking on the Lex Fridman podcast:

There is this sense of the hacker ethic. It was about sharing information. Being good. Not keeping it yourself. And that it's not a zero sum game. You can share something with another programmer, and it doesn't take it away from you, you then have somebody else doing something. It's to take joy in somebody else's accomplishments.[xi]

The value of openness is something most of us are only just getting to grips with. Harvard Business School published a report in 2006 that surveyed a range of businesses and concluded that introducing problems to outsiders was the best way to find effective solutions. A European Union report released in 2007 specifically endorsed open-source software, claiming that in 'almost all' cases, long-term costs could be reduced by switching from proprietary software to open-source systems such as Linux. The study also claimed that the number of existing open-source programs already available would have cost firms 12 billion euros (£8 billion) to build, and estimated that the programs available represent the equivalent of 131,000 programmer years, or 'at least 800 million euros (£525 million) in voluntary contributions from programmers alone each year'.[xii]

HubSpot are almost giddy in their explanation of how openly they operate internally:

We share (almost) everything. We make uncommon levels of information available to everyone in the company.

It goes so far that they boast about the quality of their wiki – a wiki being a portal that tech companies build for internal use, where company documents, org structures, FAQs and so on are stored for access by employees. HubSpot claim – this has not been verified – to have 'the most active wiki on the planet', and here is what is shared and discussed in there:

- Financials (cash balance, burn rate, P&L, etc.)
- Board meeting decks
- Management meeting decks
- 'Strategic' topics
- HubSpot lore and mythology

A culture of secrecy exists in some tech companies, primarily due to competitive needs. Apple is notoriously tight-lipped about its product development process, and has even been known to use fake products in its stores to prevent leaks. Jony Ive's design team operated in a studio shut off from every other Apple employee, other than Steve Jobs. Snap, meanwhile, has a strict no-photography policy for employees and is said to be very secretive about its product road map. The point is that culture, be it open or secret, should be purposely considered and optimised for each company and its market conditions.

Culture is coded

As mentioned, there is a lot of value in putting plans to paper. In tech, the culture is analysed, scripted and shouted from the rooftops.

The best coding of culture I've ever seen, and which epitomises the openness of tech culture, is Netflix's Culture deck. Released publicly in 2009, HR head at the time Patty McCord and CEO Reed Hastings hashed it out over several months, culminating in a 124-slide presentation. Netflix's Culture deck has been read by over eighteen million people.

The first slide of their deck presents the yin and yang symbol, with the words 'Netflix Culture: Freedom & Responsibility'. The second slide says, 'We Seek Excellence. Our culture focuses on helping us achieve excellence.'

That deck has been the precursor to other tech companies looking to optimise their own culture, and coding it up is a method they understand. HubSpot's culture code is the operating system that powers the company, and it's open for all to read online. In fact over four million people have read HubSpot's culture code.

Going a step further is Apple University. Steve Jobs wanted a curriculum that would teach Apple newcomers what differentiated the company from its peers. Apple University has classes such as 'Communicating at Apple,' which emphasises clarity and simplicity in products and presentations. There are also case studies on important decisions such as Apple's choice to make the iPod and iTunes compatible with Microsoft Windows.[xiii]

Airbnb, true to form, saw what others did well and went deeper. Execs spent months hashing out the company's six core values:

1. *Be a host*
2. *Every frame matters* ('irrationally paying attention' to every little detail)
3. *Simplify*
4. *Embrace the adventure*
5. *Be a 'cereal' entrepreneur* (as the founders quite literally sold cereal on the side to fund the company early on)
6. *Champion the mission*

The last one proclaimed awkwardly: 'The mission is to live in this world where one day you can feel like you're home anywhere, and not in a home, but truly home, where you belong.' Chesky introduced these values to employees at a company off-site held at the Sonoma estate of sculptors Lucia Eames and Llisa Demetrios, daughter and granddaughter of the famed furniture designer Charles Eames, whom Chesky had idolised in design school. The six values would be used to guide hiring decisions and employee performance reviews and to illustrate Airbnb's ideas about itself to the world.[xiv]

The depth of thought that goes into these companies' codes of culture is fascinating. It's clear that the emphasis on particular language is pointed towards desired behaviours. Simon Sinek explained that for values or guiding principles to be truly effective they need to be verbs. It's not 'integrity,' it's 'always do the right thing.' It's not 'innovation,' it's 'look at the problem from a different angle.' Articulating our values as verbs gives us a clear idea of how to act in any situation.[xv]

Have a look at the culture code for early days Uber, under Travis, in rapid growth mode:

1. *Uber Mission*
2. *Celebrate Cities*
3. *Meritocracy and Toe-Stepping*
4. *Principled Confrontation*
5. *Winning: Champions Mindset*
6. *Let Builders Build*
7. *Always Be Hustlin'*
8. *Customer Obsession*
9. *Make Big, Bold Bets*
10. *Make Magic*
11. *Be an Owner, Not a Renter*
12. *Be Yourself*
13. *Optimistic Leadership*
14. *The Best Idea Wins*[xvi]

This was indicative of hustle culture. Sure, it helped the company get a valuation of $66 billion by 2016, but at a tremendous cost thanks to a lawsuit from former employee Susan Fowler lawsuit that called out bad practices at the company and rightly led to the firing of the company's founder/CEO, Travis Kalanick.

What Uber's new values look like under the leadership of high-EQ possessing CEO Dara Khosrowshahi who took over from Kalanick:

Go get it – Bring the mindset of a champion

Our ambition is what drives us to achieve our mission. How we define a champion mindset isn't based on how we perform on our best days, it's how we respond on the worst days. We hustle, embrace the grind, overcome adversity, and play to win for the people we serve. Because it matters.

Trip obsessed – Make magic in the marketplace

The trip is where the marketplace comes to life. The earner, rider, eater, carrier and merchant are the people who connect in our marketplace – and we see every side. This requires judgment to make difficult trade-offs, blending algorithms with human ingenuity, and the ability to create simplicity from complexity. When we get the balance right for everyone, Uber magic happens.

Build with heart – We care

We work at Uber because our products profoundly affect lives and we care deeply about our impact. Putting ourselves in the shoes of the people who connect in our marketplace helps us build better products that positively impact our communities and partners. Our care drives us to perfect our craft.

Stand for safety – Safety never stops

We embed safety into everything we do. Our relentless pursuit to make Uber safer for everyone using our platform will continue to make us the industry leader for safety. We know the work of safety never stops, yet we can and will challenge ourselves to always be better for the communities we serve.

See the forest and the trees – Know the details that matter

Building for the intersection of the physical and digital worlds at global scale requires seeing the big picture and the details. Knowing the important details can change the approach, and small improvements can compound into enormous impact over time.

One Uber – Bet on something bigger

It's powerful to be a part of something bigger than any one of us, or any one team. That's why we work together to do what's best for Uber, not the individual or team. We actively support our teammates, and they support us – especially when we hit the inevitable bumps in the road. We say what we mean, disagree and commit, and celebrate our progress, together.

Great minds don't think alike – Diversity matters

We seek out diversity. Diversity of ideas. Identity. Ethnicity. Experience. Education. The more diverse we become, the more we can adapt and ultimately achieve our mission. When we reflect the incredible diversity of the people who connect on our platform, we make better decisions that benefit the world.

Do the right thing – Period

Returning to Apple, the spirit of the company is captured in their Cupertino campus in California:

- *Stay Hungry. Stay Foolish.*
- *Why Join the Navy When You Can Be a Pirate?*
- *Insanely Great*
- *Think Different*
- *'Click. Boom. Amazing!'*

You know you have the culture down when your company's culture exists as an adjective, spoken across tongues, across the globe. At Amazon, one has to be seen and heard as being 'Amazonian'. A 'Googler' can be identified in a crowd (they are usually wearing some piece of clothing or branded backpack from the company giving them away a mile off). According to Google's 2004 IPO letter, employees named themselves 'Googlers'.

The danger with getting your cultural values and memes on paper is that you assume the job is done. In reality, you are just getting started, according to Jeff Bezos:

You can write down your corporate culture, but when you do so, you're discovering it, uncovering it – not creating it.[xvii]

Tech's set of values

Every successful tech company nowadays has not only its mission and vision enshrined on the office walls and psyche of its employees, it also tabulates the company values. These values are the guideposts, the *how* if you will, to get towards the mission successfully. It's the code of behaviours and decision- making processes expected from employees.

Buffer, the social media management tech company, demonstrates their values in a compelling way, as they describe their values as 'words to live and do business by', which implies that they look for people to live greatly both inside and outside work. Here are their values:

- *Choose positivity*
- *Default to transparency*
- *Focus on self-improvement*
- *Be a no-ego doer*
- *Listen first, then listen more*
- *Communicate with clarity*
- *Make time to reflect*
- *Live smarter, not harder*

- *Show gratitude*
- *Do the right thing*

A rather refreshing approach to how a company thinks you should go about your day, particularly with such a focus on personal development, respectful relationships and attitude. When it comes to cultural values, tech tries to take a 360-degree view of its people.

Netflix of course take a deeper, albeit more clinical, view on values. They say: 'Actual company values are the behaviours and skills that are valued in fellow employees.' They continue, with an air of self-policing, to say:

At Netflix, we particularly value the following nice behaviours and skills in our colleagues…

1. *Judgement*
2. *Productivity*
3. *Creativity*
4. *Intelligence*
5. *Honesty*
6. *Communication*
7. *Selflessness*
8. *Reliability*
9. *Passion*

…meaning we hire and promote people who demonstrate these nine.

Blockbuster (the Netflix before Netflix) on the other hand espoused to be 'the global leader in rentable home entertainment by providing outstanding service, selection, convenience and value.'[xviii] It's hard to live that mantra when in reality its approach to customers was one of punishment through extortionate late fees for the return of movie rentals. Look where Blockbuster is today compared to Netflix.

Over in China, the e-commerce giant Alibaba espouses the following nine values:

- *Passion*
- *Innovation*
- *Teach and learn*
- *Openness*
- *Simplicity*
- *Teamwork*
- *Focus*
- *Quality*
- *Customer first*

Stripe espouse one of the most thoughtful and positively directional values of all the tech conglomerate. Stripe employees are encouraged to be a 'Macro optimist, but micro pessimist'. Meaning they are visionary and bullish on their mission to increase the GDP of the internet, but really sweat the day-to-day details and decision-making.

Another Irish-bred tech company, Tines, the no-code automation for business provider, have three succinct and powerful values, conveyed even more beautifully by a lovely dollop of alliteration:

Simplicity – We strive for our product, processes, and customer interactions to be as simple, straightforward, and understandable as possible. In everything we do, we try to remove the unnecessary barriers and friction, focusing on the most important and impactful work.

Speed – We are quick to ship, to respond, and to act. Speed is critical, however, it's irrelevant if applied in a haphazard way. We must take ownership, execute with purpose, collect feedback, and iterate. In this way, speed becomes velocity and momentum.

Soundness – We're determined to achieve our mission and goals, but we want to be proud of HOW we achieve them. Doing the right thing for our customers and teammates is what truly sets Tines apart. We believe in giving people the benefit of the doubt. We demonstrate transparency, honesty and integrity at all times.[xix]

Outside of tech, industry leaders have found their own culture codes to drive scalable success. Award-winning restauranteur Danny Meyer, of Union Square Cafe, Gramercy Tavern and Shake Shack, has cracked his own codes. Meyer attempted to name the specific behaviours and interactions he wanted to create at his restaurants. He already had an assortment of catchphrases that he used informally in training – he had a knack for distilling ideas into handy maxims. But then he started paying deeper attention to these phrases, thinking about them as tools. Here are a few:

- *Read the guest*
- *Athletic hospitality*
- *Writing a great final chapter*
- *Turning up the home dial*
- *Loving problems*
- *Finding the yes*
- *Collecting the dots and connecting the dots*
- *Creating raves for guests*
- *One size fits one*
- *Put us out of business with your generosity*
- *Are you an agent or a gatekeeper?*

On the surface, these look like garden-variety corporate aphorisms. In fact, each of them functions as a small narrative in itself, providing a vivid mental model for solving the routine problems the staff faced. Making the charitable assumption means that when someone behaves poorly, you should avoid judging them and instead give them the benefit of the doubt. Collecting the dots means gathering information about guests; connecting the dots is using that information to create happiness.[xx]

Champion diversity and inclusion

Values work best when they are aligned with the vision of the company and its strengths. Amazon strives to be the everything store, ensuring its products are cheap and convenient. One value it cherishes is frugality. It is defined as: Accomplish more with less. Constraints breed resourcefulness, self-sufficiency, and invention. There are no extra points for growing head count, budget size, or fixed expenses.[xxi]

Start working at Amazon in Seattle and you may find your desk is a door from Home Depot. Why? Cheaper than standard office desk furniture of course.

Values live out in the open, in a company that really optimises culture.

Culture is optimised, and scaled

Reed Hastings, in his recent tell-all book on the Netflix culture, *No Rules Rules: Netflix and the Culture of Reinvention*, explained that the business he had before Netflix failed as it could not adapt to changes in its industry because company culture wasn't optimised either for innovation or for flexibility.

He wasn't going to make the same mistake twice; culture was about to be optimised:

With my next company, Netflix, I hoped to promote flexibility, employee freedom, and innovation, instead of error prevention and rule adherence. At the same time, I understood that as a company grows, if you don't manage it with policies or control processes, the organization is likely to descend into chaos.[xxii]

And that insight paid off, in spades. Blockbuster who?:

It was not obvious at the time, even to me, but we had one thing that Blockbuster did not: a culture that valued people over process, emphasized innovation over efficiency, and had very few controls. Our culture, which focused on achieving top performance with talent density and leading employees with context not control, has allowed us to continually grow and change as the world, and our members' needs, have likewise morphed around us.

Back in the 2000s, culture optimisation was pretty profound thinking. It was also shared by Tony Hsieh, founder of Zappos, who incorporated culture optimisation into their business strategy:

Looking back, a big reason we hit our goal early was that we decided to invest our time, money, and resources into three key areas: customer service (which would build our brand and drive word of mouth), culture (which would lead to the formation of our core values), and employee training and development (which would eventually lead to the creation of our Pipeline Team). Even today, our belief is that our Brand, our Culture, and our Pipeline (which we internally refer to as 'BCP') are the only competitive advantages that we will have in the long run. Everything else can and will eventually be copied.[xxiii]

Looking around at the tech companies today, many have taken the baton of optimising culture and running along nicely. There is one company out there, of ex-Facebook leaders, who to my mind learnt what was great and not so great at Facebook, and optimised it further for their own company.

The hypergrowth tech company Asana is built on the notions of mindfulness and intentionality. 'Most companies end up with a culture as an emergent phenomenon,' says co-founder Justin Rosenstein. 'We decided to treat culture as a product.' Co-founder Dustin Moskovitz (who was also a co-founder of Facebook) adds: 'From the beginning we were intentional about wanting to be intentional. A lot of companies have that conversation several years into their existence. We'd already had it in the first couple of weeks. Then we went about trying to manifest it and keep it extensive.' Asana works to regularly reassess and redesign its core values, and when the company makes a change, it launches the new value throughout the organisation in the same way it would launch any other kind of product. Then it goes through the process of feedback and iteration on the road to resolution. Asana calls these problems 'cultural bugs' and works to eradicate them the same way it would a problematic piece of software. When some junior employees came to management saying they felt 'falsely empowered' –

they had decision-making power, but their decisions were too frequently overridden by higher-ups – the company launched a process to restructure the way that power was allocated. Asana was started by some of the best founders in the world. This is what can happen when they turn their entrepreneurial talents beyond products: to the structure of the corporation itself.[xxiv]

At Zappos, right from the very beginning of the hiring process with interviewer calls, to an employee's first day and week, everything is looked at to bolster the culture. Anyone from a warehouse worker to a director has to go through what Christa Foley, the senior manager of human resources at Zappos, calls 'boot camp'. For four weeks each employee is brought up to speed on how the company works, but also on how the company's culture works. It is really the second screening within the Zappos hiring process. Even after getting the job offer, you have to prove that you can absorb the culture.[xxv]

Airbnb furnishes each new manager with a set of online tools to monitor the health of the business and something Brian Chesky called an 'office in a box'. It contained a guidebook to setting up an Airbnb-like working environment and included various props, like a portable ping-pong table and the books *Delivering Happiness* by Zappos founder Tony Hsieh and *Oh, the Places You'll Go* by Dr Seuss. 'Brian was always worried about how do we scale our culture – how does every Airbnb office feel?' says Dubost, who became Airbnb's vice president of business travel and left the company in 2016.[xxvi]

For toy manufacturer turned tech-like LEGO, scaling can simply mean marketing: LEGO has an internal culture marketing division. Responsible for leading the company's internal culture strategy, which is focused on ensuring that LEGO's values, purpose, and mission are communicated, understood and lived throughout the organisation, this division engages with LEGO's employees and stakeholders to ensure that they are aligned with the company's vision and values and are empowered to contribute to a culture of openness, trust, collaboration, and creativity. Additionally, this division is responsible for creating and managing various internal communications and engagement initiatives, such as employee surveys, recognition programs, and events, to foster a culture of learning and development.

Culture is dynamic

IT'S JAZZ, NOT A SYMPHONY.

— Reed Hastings

Apple is an anomaly in tech land in that it's not an open culture. Due to the nature of their slower-moving, high-bar design and need for big-bang product launches, it breeds a secretive culture. The majority of people working at Apple wouldn't have a clue which new features are coming to your next iPhone. Something changed recently, however, and it tells the tale that culture is ever-changing.

Apple CEO Tim Cook made a big announcement internally that they're going to require employees to return to the office three days a week. He rolled this out as a hybrid work model, and they're going to test it out. It's a pilot program.

They're going to ask people to come in Mondays, Wednesdays and Thursdays, I believe. And they can work from home twice a week, which is a huge change for Apple. Previously, working from home was okay in one-off instances, but largely people were required to come in all the time.

A Slack group was created on this topic. It's a channel called Remote Work Advocacy. People immediately started pushing back against the return to the office, saying, 'The world has changed. We've moved on. A lot of tech companies are pushing models where anyone who wants to work from home can all the time. We've had a really successful year working from home. We don't want to be forced to come back.'[xxvii]

This was just the start. Other issues started bubbling up to the press in time, which has completely flipped the lid on Apple's secretive space in tech, that's been coveted for over four decades.

Usually significant changes to the cultural fabric of tech companies don't come from new tools or lawsuits, but from speed of growth and scale. Hiroshi Mikitani, founder and CEO of Rakuten talks about the rule of '3 and 10'. Start a company as one person, then decision-making is straightforward. Get to three people in the company, that's different. Get to ten people, communication and process breaks down a bit more. This happens again at one hundred people.

Then three hundred people, so different. And then one thousand, totally different.

His insight is [that] a lot of companies get into trouble because of this. When you're a quickly growing startup, you get into huge trouble because you blow right through a few of these triplings without really realizing it. And then, you turn around, and you realize ... we're at 400 people now, but some of our processes and systems we set in place when we were 30 ... You should constantly, perpetually be thinking about how to reinvent yourself and how to treat the culture.[xxviii]

WE ENJOY A CONSTANT PARANOIA ABOUT LOSING THE CULTURE, AND A CONSTANT, CREEPING SENSE OF DISSATISFACTION WITH THE CURRENT CULTURE. THIS IS A GOOD SIGN! THIS FEELING OF TEETERING ON THE BRINK OF LOSING OUR CULTURE CAUSES PEOPLE TO BE VIGILANT ABOUT THREATS TO IT. I'D BE CONCERNED IF PEOPLE STOPPED WORRYING.[xxix]

— Laszlo Bock, Google

This dynamism within culture in tech means the coding and values are fair game to adaptation over time. Values are open to change as a company evolves. Facebook had certain values, and now in its new cloak, Meta, the company refreshed its values. Zuckerberg has said that 'values are concepts that you program into the culture', and in order to reorientate the mindset of the business as it matures, he has adapted values:

I think part of this is that good values, you need to be able to give something up in order to get them. So around Move Fast, we've always had this question, you can't just tell people to move fast. The question is: what's the deal? What are you willing to give up? And famously, it used to be Move Fast and Break Things. And the idea was that we tolerated some amount of bugs in the software in order to encourage people to move quickly. Because moving fast, I think, is the key to learning. You want to increase the iteration cycle so that way you can get feedback from the people you serve quickly, and then incorporate that into the product. So we would literally get into situations where competitors of us would ship once a year, once every six months, and we'd ship code every day.

Of course we're going to learn faster, and we're going to build something better if you're shipping something every day. So the question is: what are you willing to give up?

And so it used to be we would tolerate some amount of defects in the product. It got to the point as the company grew that we were producing so many bugs that going back and fixing them was actually slowing us down more than we were speeding up. So I still thought, okay, moving fast, this is still a really important thing. We've got to change how we do it. So we kind of evolved to building a somewhat less sexy phrase: Move Fast with Stable Infrastructure. And basically the new bet was we were going to invest disproportionately in building up good infrastructure and abstractions inside our companies. So that way the average engineer who comes here is going to be much faster and more productive at getting things done than in other places. And at a scale of almost a hundred thousand people, what this really means now, companies just add process over time.[xxx]

Not only have Meta adapted values, they have added more, according to Zuck:

We added that we call Build Awesome Things. And the idea here is that – I actually think that there's a pretty big difference between things that are valuable and things that are awe inspiring and amazing. And I kind of think that our company has been pretty good at building things that a lot of people use and like.

But for a combination of reasons, we just haven't focused quite as much until the last few years, especially as we've worked on a lot of this metaverse work and virtual reality and things like that, we haven't focused as much on things that are just awe-inspiring. And I actually think that there's this balance where you need to do both. You can't do things that are just all inspiration and no substance. But I also think you can go too far in the other direction of just doing things that are useful, but I think a lot of what the world needs right now is inspiration. There are a lot of things in our lives in modern day that work pretty well, but a lot of what we sort of lack is a positive vision for the future.

Culture is diverse

IF YOU'RE GOING TO BUILD A STRONG CULTURE, IT'S PARAMOUNT TO MAKE DIVERSITY ONE OF YOUR CORE VALUES. THIS IS WHAT SEPARATES BRIDGEWATER'S STRONG CULTURE FROM A CULT: THE COMMITMENT IS TO PROMOTING DISSENT.[xxxi]

— **Ray Dalio**

In the tech industry there are diverse cultures, more than in other industries. The tech industry is well known for its diversity. From its early days in Silicon Valley, the industry has always been open to people from all backgrounds and cultures. This diversity is one of the key strengths of the tech industry, and it is one of the reasons why it has been so successful.

There are a number of factors that have contributed to the diversity of the tech industry. One is the fact that the industry is relatively new, and so it has not had time to develop the same kind of entrenched prejudices that can be found in other industries. Another factor is the global nature of the industry, which has allowed people from all over the world to come together and work towards common goals.

The diversity of the tech industry is one of its greatest strengths, and it is something that should be celebrated. The industry is a much richer place for it, and it is one of the things that makes it such an exciting and vibrant sector.

Tech has the highest percentage of non-Caucasian employees compared to other industries. A 2016 survey shows that the percentage of non-Caucasian employees in tech is 44 per cent compared to 31 per cent in other industries and 21 per cent in financial services.

Silicon Valley is home to more than 50 per cent of companies founded by immigrants. In addition, the region has over two thousand start-ups that were started by foreigners.

In fact, there are so many foreign-born entrepreneurs that they make up 20 per cent of all tech CEOs in Silicon Valley.

Immigration wins. Eat shit, Donald Trump.

Culture is toxic

I am going to pause on specifically talking about culture in tech for a moment, and bring our discussion back to a general viewpoint. Toxic cultures exist everywhere. The arseholes often reign supreme. People doing the right things for the right reasons don't get rewarded. Or worse, they get punished. Cultures where teams don't work well with other teams. Cultures where there is an undercurrent of bullying and harassment.

Horrible environments to be in. You have most likely had the unfortunate pleasure of being in one or more. We know the feeling. But what about the actual cost, in numbers? First, healthcare expenditure at high-pressure companies is nearly 50 per cent greater than at other organisations. The American Psychological Association estimates that more than $500 billion is siphoned off from the US economy because of workplace stress, and 550 million workdays are lost each year due to stress on the job. Sixty per cent to 80 per cent of workplace accidents are attributed to stress, and it's estimated that more than 80 per cent of doctor visits are due to stress. Workplace stress has been linked to health problems ranging from metabolic syndrome to cardiovascular disease and mortality.

The stress of belonging to hierarchies itself is linked to disease and death. One study showed that the lower someone's rank in a hierarchy, the higher their chances of cardiovascular disease and death from heart attacks. In a large-scale study of over three thousand employees conducted by Anna Nyberg at the Karolinska Institute, results showed a strong link between leadership behaviour and heart disease in employees. Stress-producing bosses are literally bad for the heart.

Second is the cost of disengagement. While a cut-throat environment and a culture of fear can ensure engagement (and sometimes even excitement for the hardy few) for some time, research suggests that the inevitable stress it creates will likely lead to disengagement over the long term. Engagement in work – which is associated with feeling valued, secure, supported, and respected – is generally negatively associated with a high-stress, cut-throat culture.

And disengagement is costly. In studies mentioned earlier by the Queens School of Business and by the Gallup Organisation, disengaged workers had 37 per cent higher absenteeism, 49 per cent more accidents and 60 per cent more errors and defects. In organisations with low employee engagement scores, they experienced 18 per cent lower productivity, 16 per cent lower profitability, 37 per cent lower job growth and 65 per cent lower share price over time. Importantly, businesses with highly engaged employees enjoyed 100 per cent more job applications.

Lack of loyalty is a third cost. Research shows that workplace stress leads to an increase of almost 50 per cent in voluntary turnover. People sniff around the job market, decline promotions or resign. The turnover costs associated with recruiting, training, lowered productivity, lost expertise, and so forth, are significant. The Center for American Progress estimates that replacing a single employee costs approximately 20 per cent of that employee's salary.[xxxii]

The numbers speak for themselves. What I love about tech is its view that culture can be optimised. However it misses a lot of the human phenomena that crop up. Bad actors can live in supposedly great cultural environments. Tech is doing a good job in trying to weed out the bad actors and bad behaviours. It still has a long way to go though.

Culture can be fixed

One of the biggest under-told stories in tech is the culture transformation at Microsoft and the result, an almost eightfold increase in the company's stock price in less than a decade. All thanks to a changing of the guard. From the bullish CEO Steve Ballmer to the wise and pragmatic Satya Nadella.

Microsoft CEO Satya Nadella spent the first few years focused on transforming Microsoft into a 'learn-it-all' culture, believing that the 'learn-it-all' perspective and growth mindset will always perform better.

It wasn't just about transforming culture. It was about driving digital transformation. During a recent visit to India, Satya Nadella predicted that by 2030, there will be fifty billion connected devices and 175 zettabytes of data. For a company to succeed in that world, the Microsoft CEO argues they must embrace tech intensity, where you not only have to adopt new technologies, but also build leading-edge capabilities to use them. The company has simplified this as a formula (tech intensity = tech adoption + tech capability) that holds the secret to future success for companies in the age of digital transformation.

Ongoing, proactive upskilling of its own employees is a key factor in building capabilities within.

While the culture itself likely existed before 2014, it was in that year that Microsoft CEO Satya Nadella coined the term and made clear that it was the future for Microsoft's operations. A learning culture embraces trying new, innovative ideas, encouraging invention, and learning from the inevitable mistakes that arise. These concepts are centred on a growth mindset, an idea advocated by psychologist Carol Dweck in her book *Mindset*, and further expounded on by psychologist Angela Duckworth in *Grit*.

Learning cultures unite employees through curiosity and a desire to progress in their professional development; innovation and adventure are encouraged through a creative staff base. One company that has long held a 'learn-it-all' culture is Tesla. From the beginning, Elon Musk has welcomed innovative ideas from all members of staff. He famously once said there was no hierarchy within Tesla, that all staff should speak to whoever they require at the time to speed up innovation. Today Tesla is viewed as one of the most forward-thinking companies across all industries.[xxxiii]

In *Time, Talent, Energy: Overcome Organizational Drag and Unleash Your Team's Productive Power*, Michael Mankins gives three clear ways to build or restore a winning culture:

Raise the strategic ambition and recentre your company's purpose in a customer- or socially-focused mission. Ask yourself whether you can see your company's purpose come to life every day in your employees' actions.

Reawaken the ownership mindset and performance orientation through 'constructive disruptions' at moments of truth, both the symbolic and the routine. Reinforce the behaviours you want with feedback systems and consequence-based performance management systems.

Reset the company's operating model, especially its ways of working and talent systems, to embed the change. Renew your talent acquisition strategy, leadership behavioural signature and talent-management systems to attract difference-makers. Ask yourself whether you are encouraging culture-strengthening or culture-weakening behaviours.[xxxiv]

Customer-first cultures

BUSINESSES OFTEN FORGET ABOUT THE CULTURE, AND ULTIMATELY, THEY SUFFER FOR IT BECAUSE YOU CAN'T DELIVER GOOD SERVICE FROM UNHAPPY EMPLOYEES.

— Tony Hsieh, Zappos

One clear common trait in the cultures of tech companies is that they all direct the culture towards serving the customer or end user. The customer is the reason they are in business. The customer pays employees. The customers are the reason behind tech companies' values, how useful a company is to customers today and in the future.

Twilio's Jeff Lawson believes the goal of their culture is to build an army of empowered, truth-seeking, good-decision-making leaders. The more they enable their frontline teams to ask the right questions, put aside politics and titles, and come to the best answers, the greater chance they have of solving hard problems and serving their customers.[xxxv]

Another way to think about this customer-first culture is to look at it in terms of service. The best tech companies have a service and hospitality mentality. A mentality that Twilio and Lawson lead with:

Service is the technical delivery of a product. Hospitality is how the delivery of that product makes its recipient feel. Service is a monologue – we decide how we want to do things and set our own standards for service. Hospitality, on the other hand, is a dialogue. To be on a guest's side requires listening to that person with every sense, and following up with a thoughtful, gracious, appropriate response. It takes both great service and great hospitality to rise to the top.[xxxvi]

Amazon founder and CEO Jeff Bezos described the role of his corporate innovation teams very well when he stated:

We're a company of builders. Of pioneers. It's our job to make bold bets, and we get our energy from investing on behalf of customers.' A good example of this in action is Amazon Prime Now. Amazon customers had expressed a desire for faster deliveries ever since the company was first founded. Taken to an extreme, Amazon decided to see what the fastest possible delivery time might be. Within 111 days they created and launched a pilot, first in Manhattan and now in several cities in the US and in London, UK, whereby customers can place an order and receive delivery of selected goods within an hour. Two-hour delivery is free and one-hour delivery is $7.99.[xxxvii]

This customer-first approach to culture optimisation might be seen as a fluffy nice-to-have and not something that exists on a balance sheet (sorry, accountants, not on yer watch) but when worked right, it's a growth driver. Tony Hsieh explains:

Even though it would hurt our growth, we decided to cut most of our marketing expenses, and refocused our efforts on trying to get the customers who had already bought from us to purchase again and more frequently. Little did we know that this was actually a blessing in disguise, as it forced us to focus more on delivering better customer service. In 2003, we would decide to make customer service the focus of the company.[xxxviii]

I truly admire (again) Patreon's approach here. Going beyond 'customers' or 'users', getting to the human level:

Put creators first. Deliver <u>unusual</u> care to creators

Our business is creators' income and rent checks, so we do not take our responsibility lightly. We exist because of, and in service of, creators.

There is a creator behind every text, email, call, request, bug and payment issue, and we treat them as humans, not users

We will fight to keep the human spark in our relationships as we scale. As a business we invest in teams like Community Happiness and Creator Care who are on the front lines taking care of our creators. We revere these teammates on the front line

Defining a human first culture like that takes a buffet of thoughtfulness. Bravo to Patreon.

Culture comes from the top and bottom

Who is responsible for creating and nurturing culture? Where are the culture drivers or culture ambassadors in a company? Who 'owns' the culture?

In tech, at its optimum, it's everyone. Which is easier said than done. A fresh graduate out of college will likely find it daunting to carry the culture torch with regard to decision-making, communication and actions. All they see above them are seasoned leaders.

People around Google and other corners of Silicon Valley often refer to this as the HiPPO phenomenon. That is, the highest paid person's opinion (HiPPO) usually dominates how people make decisions inside most organisations.

People look to the HiPPO to make decisions. People equate status and money with intelligence and insight, when often there's little correlation.[xxxix]

Tech companies fight against this HiPPO phenomenon. Usually this is by bringing things back to the customer (hello, major theme in the book, nice to see you again). Bring it back to the customer and let employees figure it out. Innovative companies create a culture in which everyone, regardless of their mandate to innovate, is tasked with understanding the customer and seeking ways for the company to do a better job in serving them, both with today's products and services and in the future.

Jeff Lawson broke it down further with regard to the company's developers:

The most important thing is to give developers problems, not solutions. While Ping-Pong tables and tricycles are nice, I'm convinced the key to building a world-class engineering culture is bringing developers into the big problems you're trying to solve, and leveraging their full brains. It's not too hard to tell if that's happening in your company. When you see a developer, ask what they're working on, and what customer problem it's going to solve. Do they know? Ask when they last interacted with a customer, and how it made them feel. Did it motivate them? Ask what they learned that surprised them. Based on their answers, you'll get a sense for whether developers are truly brought into customer problems, or whether they're just asked to implement solutions.[xl]

Tech's politics leans towards meritocracy. This is one of the most widely held beliefs in the start-up and tech movement: good ideas can come from anywhere, and people should be given resources, and a safe space platform, to bring their ideas to the fore.

Culture can be measured

What can be coded, can be measured. So is the belief of tech. I'll talk more about how tech companies measure themselves by internal means later in the book, but for now, culture, at a high level can be analysed in a few clicks.

Just visit Glassdoor, one of the largest job and recruiting sites in the world. Since its launch in 2008, Glassdoor has collected more than forty-nine million reviews and employee insights, covering approximately nine hundred thousand organisations. Employees submit anonymous reviews, which means they can offer their candid opinions without fear of reprisal. Companies, moreover, cannot remove critical reviews. By aggregating these reviews, we can construct a comprehensive picture of a company's culture that moves beyond the anecdotes and personal observations that managers often rely on to understand their corporate culture.

On Glassdoor, employees rate their company's culture and values on a five- point scale, but these quantitative scores alone shed little insight into the specifics of a company's culture. The real value for understanding and measuring culture lies in the free-text responses that each reviewer provides. Here, employees describe – in their own words – the pros and cons of working at a particular company and offer advice to management. By analysing this textual data, we can assess how well a company is doing on critical dimensions of culture – including diversity, collaboration or integrity – in the eyes of employees' lived experience.

Policies scale the culture

At the same time, I understood that as a company grows, if you don't manage it with policies or control processes, the organization is likely to descend into chaos.[xli]

So what did Reed Hastings and Patty McCord do to keep Netflix's culture roaming with autonomous, creative, driven employees flourishing, whilst also not losing the run of the shop? Some very clever policies.

One such policy was for travel and expenses (T&E). Usually this policy at companies allows for a maximum spend per day for food and drinks, along with restrictions on business class travel and hotel rates. And for anything beyond board, approvals are needed. Even when fairly priced expenses are submitted, managers at companies still trawl through the expenses, line by line, to approve. Netflix deemed this not a good use of time, somewhat disrespectful to the adults they hired and counterintuitive to their culture optimisation.

The entirety of the travel and expense policy consists of these five simple words:

Act in Netflix's best interest.

Such a policy plays itself pitch perfectly to the aforementioned ethos they set out to achieve when optimising Netflix's culture:

If your goal is to build a more inventive, fast, and flexible organization, develop a culture of freedom and responsibility by establishing the necessary conditions so you can remove these rules and processes too.

Tech is famed for its free food. I adored going to work at Facebook each morning for the breakfast; on days off I often popped in to get a nosh in. We are talking eight different types of eggs here, people. Lunch and dinner were provided too, along with micro kitchens on every floor just in case you wanted snacks around the clock. To the untrained eye these are an exorbitant luxury.

However, Facebook's culture prided itself on moving fast and focusing on people's strengths, so removing the need for staff to leave the building to fend for food allowed them to focus on the job at hand. Also having colleagues sit for three meals a day had the added benefit of enhancing relationships and therefore collaboration.

The language of the culture

Google's former Head of People Operations, Laslo Bock, was on the money when he said that language affects thinking, thinking affects behaviour and companies must change how people speak if they are to change how people behave.[xlii]

Tech's mindset is clearly different from other industries, and as a result tech talks much more differently than industries.

Look at Hootsuite who have the delightful acronym 'BSU', or #BSU as it would be shown in their internal communications. It stands for 'Blow Shit Up', a motivational mantra from their founder Ryan Holmes. It may seem very Varsity Blues American Pow Wow-ey, but it works for their culture for four reasons:

(1) It exists as a unique pillar of their language and culture, (2) it has a lot of energy behind it, (3) it's limitless in scope, and (4) it's inherently disruptive in its nature.

It can go much, much further than acronyms. At Amazon they have a famed six-page process for submitting new ideas and plans – more on that to come later. For that piece of communication, and pretty much everything else you would be expected to type at Amazon as an 'Amazonian', a set of guidelines exist to get your communication as concise and impactful as possible, under the banner of 'How to write like an Amazonian':

Use less than 30 words per sentence
E.g.: Due to the fact that – because
Totally lacked the ability to – could not

Replace adjectives with data
E.g.: We made the performance much faster – We reduced server side tp90 latency from 10ms to 1ms

Eliminate weasel words
E.g.: Nearly all customers – 87% of Prime members
Significantly better – +25 basis points

Does your writing pass the 'so what' test?
If you get a question, reply with one of four Amazon answers:

1. *Yes*
2. *No*
3. *A number*
4. *I don't know (and will follow up when I do)*

Throughout the walls, emails, Slacks and Zooms of tech companies, you are going to hear the word 'scale' fifty million times. 'Can we scale it?', 'Is there adequate scalability?'

At Meta, in meetings, 'Let's move fast' was uttered probably every other meeting.

Other gems of the tech vernacular? 'Pivot', 'disrupt', 'hack'. Language fuels culture. Language fuels speed of understanding. Language fuels growth.

Culture gets physical

I remember working in my first tech job in London, in an office of thirty or so people, which had free tea and coffee. I did the milk run, submitting my three- pound sterling expense every week to finance. Sitting at my desk with a coffee, I came across an article on Google's offices on the computer screen, and my mind exploded. There in front of me was a huge slide that ran into their cafeteria!

I knew there and then that offices could be so much more, and tech was showing the world what workplaces could be, dare we say it, fun. Or purposely enjoyable at least.

Thoughtfully looking at a space and deliberately designing it to nudge humans towards certain thinking and behaviours is documented, yet underutilised.

In *Atomic Habits*, James Clear points out that despite our unique personalities, certain behaviours tend to arise again and again under certain environmental conditions. In church, people tend to talk in whispers. On a dark street, people act wary and guarded. In this way, the most common form of change is not internal, but external: we are changed by the world around us. Every habit is context dependant.[xliii]

So taking this insight, organisations have looked to engineer environments to unlock certain behaviours. In Schiphol Airport, cleaning staff put stickers resembling a fly near the centre of each urinal. Men going for a hefty piss after coming off their transatlantic flight aimed for what they thought was a bug.

The stickers improved their aim and significantly reduced 'spillage' around the urinals. Bathroom cleaning costs fell by 8 per cent a year as a result.

The design of tech's physical spaces follows its leaders' mantra to lead with context. The make-up of the spaces informs employees as to the space and values. It goes deeper than the free lunches and slides in the office. Slides alone don't make culture; look at Ryanair, who famously put a slide in their office to mimic Google. Those two cultures couldn't be further apart. It wasn't too long ago staff at Ryanair had to bring their own stationery to work.

At Meta, with its hacker culture and openness to autonomy, employees are encouraged to 'hack the offices'. At Meta, we built our own bars – yes you heard that right. Each team had their own bar, stocked with booze, paid for by the company. Culture building, yeah? Our Northern Europe team (that's UK/Ireland and the Nordics) built a bar stocked with a Guinness tap, craft beers and sauna-like seating. We called the space 'Aurora Barealis'.

Going further, staff got to vote on the names of meeting rooms. Entire floors would have themes. There were 'Local Pubs' and 'Simpsons Quotes'. My personal favourite was the floor with 'Irish Mammies (Mothers) Sayings', with this particular gem of a room: 'Not angry, just disappointed'.

In the name of speed, each Meta office has an IT helpdesk, with several tech experts on hand to fix (or replace lost) phones or laptops, the tools of work. Their goal is speed of service, no hanging about.

Have you ever gone through the mental agony of trying to find a set of batteries or get another working mouse when at work, and it takes up an hour or more scrambling around the place like a lunatic to find them? Not so in tech land. They have vending machines on each floor housing keyboards, batteries, headphones, cables, USB drives and more. For free. Just scan your employee badge (to discourage people taking the piss and grabbing loads of tech for family Christmas presents, which I never did. Those Sennheiser headphones went down a treat with my siblings though) and pick out whatever you needed.

Indeed the offices at Meta look unfinished. Each office sports consciously exposed concrete pillars and wires on the roof, meant to reflect its start-up roots and the idea that the 'journey is 1% finished'.

Meta's open culture is physically practised at CEO level – Mark Zuckerberg's meeting room, known as the 'aquarium' or 'fishbowl,' is open to everyone – literally. The glass walls allow everyone inside to see and hear what's happening in the meeting, and vice versa.

If you're not already picturing this scene from *Office Space*, we'll help: A sea of cubicles with one guy sitting at a desk behind a partition that doesn't reach the ceiling. He's eating something crunchy in a bag and looking nervous as he listens to his boss drone on about something boring that he doesn't care about.

The difference is that instead of being alone in your cube, surrounded by co- workers who don't care about you either, you are surrounded by people who are excited about what you have to say because they can see it. You're part of something bigger than yourself; it's not just 'the company'.

Steve Jobs was a pioneer in the value of optimising space for culture.

While working on the design of Pixar's new headquarters, he insisted that it include an open space where anyone could drop in and work on any project they were interested in. This free-flowing workspace was designed to foster creativity and productivity in employees while also creating a sense of community among them. Serendipity and relationships thrive there.

Jobs also enforced strict rules on how employees could decorate their offices. He wanted everyone's space to be unique. Jobs believed that employees should be able to personalize their workspaces to make them feel like their own. In fact he ruled that employees decorate their offices with whatever inspired them, whether that was family photos, toys, or posters.

These rules had the effect of making each employee feel like they had their own special place within the company – like they belonged there.

Apple's brand-new Cupertino headquarters, seen as his swansong project, bears the name 'One Infinite Loop'. One Infinite Loop is a loop that has no end. It is infinite in nature and will continue to go on forever without ever ending.

This is a perfect metaphor for Apple's vision of the future. The company believes that one day it will eventually make technology so advanced that it becomes part of our lives and can be used to improve our lives in countless ways.

Culture needs trust and respect

Melissa Daimler has led Global Learning & Organizational Development at Adobe, Twitter and WeWork so has seen it all in terms of culture greatness, and poorness, in tech.

She found that in great tech cultures there are three elements: behaviours, systems, and practices, all guided by an overarching set of values. A great culture is what you get when all three of these are aligned, and line up with the organisation's espoused values. When gaps start to appear, that's when you start to see problems – and see great employees leave.

These gaps can take many forms. A company might espouse 'work-life balance' but expect people to stay late consistently every night or not offer paid parental leave (a behaviours-system gap). They might espouse being a learning organisation that develops people, but then not give people the time to actually take classes or learn on the job (system-behaviours gap). Maybe the company tells people to be consensus-builders, but promotes people who are solely authoritative decision makers (behaviour-practices gap).[xliv]

It's so easy for leadership to miss the mark with a decision or policy and for it to have an adverse effect on the culture. Culture is so sensitive. In order to counteract that sensitivity, leadership have to truly care. To look at employees with the trust and respect they deserve, and then some.

Because if that happens, everything rises. A positive workplace is more successful over time because it increases positive emotions and well-being. This, in turn, improves people's relationships with each other and amplifies their abilities and their creativity. It buffers against negative experiences such as stress, thus improving employees' ability to bounce back from challenges and difficulties while bolstering their health. It also attracts employees, fostering loyalty to both the leader and the organisation as well as bringing out their best strengths. When organisations develop positive, virtuous cultures, they achieve significantly higher levels of organisational effectiveness – including financial performance, customer satisfaction, productivity and employee engagement.[xlv]

What we've learned is that in order to integrate your corporate culture around the world, above all you have to be humble, you have to be curious, and you have to remember to listen before you speak and to learn before you teach.

WITH THIS APPROACH, YOU CAN'T HELP BUT BECOME MORE EFFECTIVE EVERY DAY IN THIS EVER-FASCINATING MULTICULTURAL WORLD.[xlvi]

— Reed Hasting

It's people. Be fucking sound.

New studies are finding that the depth and meaningfulness of a person's relationships is the strongest indicator of their level of happiness.[xlvii] If you think about the amount of time we spend at work in a given week, those relationships we have are paramount to our happiness. Forty hours spent with the same colleagues week in week out. Why do we not try to make workplaces as happy as they can possibly be?

If we don't, if we keep going as we are, not looking at the culture and relationships in a business as crucial, it's a merry-go-round of shit, frankly. Further research by Sarah Pressman at the University of California, Irvine, found that the probability of dying early is 20 per cent higher for obese people, 30 per cent higher for excessive drinkers, 50 per cent higher for smokers, but a whopping 70 per cent higher for people with poor social relationships. Toxic, stress-filled workplaces affect social relationships and, consequently, life expectancy.[xlviii]

So be kind and giving to yourself and your colleagues, and hold the leadership accountable to making the workplace a happy place. Or else we can keep killing ourselves, one nine-to-fiver at a time.

People make the world, and business, go round. Never forget that.

Chapter 4
GROWTH IS GOD

OUR INDUSTRY DOES NOT RESPECT TRADITION – IT ONLY RESPECTS INNOVATION.

— Satya Nadella, CEO Microsoft

For centuries we have seen religion take hold in influencing and chaperoning humans. Giving them a compass with which to live by. Religion guided behaviour, both good and bad. And in tech, there is a new religion in town – growth.

Growth is the pure mindset of these companies. Be it exponential or incremental growth. The most innovative companies appear to make innovation the theme and don't worry quite so much about whether it is incremental or disruptive.[i] Every Hail Mary, every inch, of growth, is progress and is rewarded. This spirit of growth at all costs has had adverse effects, like over-eager reporting of growth (WeWork) to dangerously mislabelling product attributes (Theranos) in order to show growth.

Indeed Wall Street gets a hard-on for growth. Look at how these companies report business intentions to investors. In particular the master of annual shareholder letters, Jeff Bezos. His annual state of the Amazon nation to shareholders is prescribed reading for anyone interested in tech and/or business. His very first letter, from 1997, is so compelling he has attached it to every other shareholder letter as a reference point. Here is a juicy sample:

It's All About the Long Term

We believe that a fundamental measure of our success will be the shareholder value we create over the long term. This value will be a direct result of our ability to extend and solidify our current market leadership position. The stronger our market leadership, the more powerful our economic model.

Market leadership can translate directly to higher revenue, higher profitability, greater capital velocity, and correspondingly stronger returns on invested capital.

Our decisions have consistently reflected this focus. We first measure ourselves in terms of the metrics most indicative of our market leadership: customer and revenue growth, the degree to which our customers continue to purchase from us on a repeat basis, and the strength of our brand. We have invested and will continue to invest aggressively to expand and leverage our customer base, brand, and infrastructure as we move to establish an enduring franchise.

Because of our emphasis on the long term, we may make decisions and weigh tradeoffs differently than some companies. Accordingly, we want to share with you our fundamental management and decision-making approach so that you, our shareholders, may confirm that it is consistent with your investment philosophy:

- *We will continue to focus relentlessly on our customers.*
- *We will continue to make investment decisions in light of long-term market leadership considerations rather than short-term profitability considerations or short-term Wall Street reactions.*

- *We will continue to measure our programs and the effectiveness of our investments analytically, to jettison those that do not provide acceptable returns, and to step up our investment in those that work best. We will continue to learn from both our successes and our failures.*
- *We will make bold rather than timid investment decisions where we see a sufficient probability of gaining market leadership advantages. Some of these investments will pay off, others will not, and we will have learned another valuable lesson in either case.*
- *When forced to choose between optimizing the appearance of our GAAP accounting and maximizing the present value of future cash flows, we'll take the cash flows.*
- *We will share our strategic thought processes with you when we make bold choices (to the extent competitive pressures allow), so that you may evaluate for yourselves whether we are making rational long-term leadership investments.*
- *We will work hard to spend wisely and maintain our lean culture. We understand the importance of continually reinforcing a cost-conscious culture, particularly in a business incurring net losses.*
- *We will balance our focus on growth with emphasis on long-term profitability and capital management. At this stage, we choose to prioritize growth because we believe that scale is central to achieving the potential of our business model.*
- *We will continue to focus on hiring and retaining versatile and talented employees, and continue to weight their compensation to stock options rather than cash. We know our success will be largely affected by our ability to attract and retain a motivated employee base, each of whom must think like, and therefore must actually be, an owner.*

We aren't so bold as to claim that the above is the 'right' investment philosophy, but it's ours, and we would be remiss if we weren't clear in the approach we have taken and will continue to take.

Let's go under the hood of this religion, even cult, of growth. First, there are a range of principles applied to it. Then there is how they measure growth. All of which can be adapted to your business, work or even daily life.

Scale, scale, scale

If there was one word that is most commonly heard in the brainstorms and Slack channels of tech workers, it's scale. It's the verb of choice for every person in tech, from engineering to sales. The more scalable the better. If it can't scale, fuck it, throw it in the bin.

What does scale mean in the context of tech, I hear you say. Well, a blunt answer would be AI, a means to produce a product or fulfil a service by computing and with no human involvement (humans cost a lot more money to resource a product/service than a juicy algorithm).

Digging deeper, it's a path to doing a task faster, more easily and on a bigger scale each time. As the task grows in volume and complexity, the means of completing that task can effectively still be achieved. Whether the task is being done ten times or ten million times, the same outcome results.

Back to Bezos, his weapon of scale is the 'flywheel'. In *The Everything Store: Jeff Bezos and the Age of Amazon*, journalist Brad Stone explains that the 'flywheel effect' in the company's early stages worked like this: 'Lower prices led to more customer visits. More customers increased the volume of sales and attracted more commission-paying third-party sellers to the site. That allowed Amazon to get more out of fixed costs like the fulfilment centres and the servers needed to run the website. This greater efficiency then enabled it to lower prices further. Feed any part of this flywheel, they reasoned, and it should accelerate the loop.'

It is a way of thinking, a mental model that influences the behaviour of Amazonians. Amazon innovates better than most other companies because its flywheel generates continuous improvement up and down the organisation.

Everyone is expected to innovate – not just a handful of scientists in white lab coats.[ii] Innovation that scales, is everyone's job at Amazon.

For any wannabe entrepreneurs reading this, a key distinction with successful tech companies is they think and look globally from the get-go, and then adapt to market and cultural nuances. Most take the 'Go global, adapt local' approach.

Coinbase laid this path out:

Coinbase is adopting a go broad and go deep approach to scale globally in order to further its mission of bringing more economic freedom to each and every individual and business around the world:

- *Go Broad: launch foundational products that are a gateway to Web3 and crypto in every country*
- *Go Deep: launch localized infrastructure and public facing products with a full suite of services*[iii]

Being lean

IT'S NOT ABOUT WORKING HARDER; IT'S ABOUT WORKING THE SYSTEM.

— **Evan Spiegel, CEO Snapchat**

'Let's bootstrap this bitch,' I once overheard in a café known to harbour techies. In this case, this chap was a cut and paste of what mainstream culture has come to know as the tech, bro.

What does bootstrapping mean? Bootstrapping is a process whereby an entrepreneur starts a self-sustaining business, markets it, and grows the business by using limited resources or money. This is accomplished without the use of venture capital firms or even significant angel investment.[iv]

It's the garage entrepreneur. Prototyping a product and putting it in customers' hands, as quickly and cheaply as possible. And it's a mindset that pervades tech, to work in as lean a manner as possible. It's become the path most travelled in tech. Amazon, Google and Apple were famously started in actual garages. Their lead is followed every day.

It's a mindset that challenges us to look at what is necessary or important. The business world is now asking itself whether they need to be in an office nine to five, Monday to Friday. Tests are being carried out, and the results are promising.

The fintech company Atom Bank recently announced its move to a four-day work week without cutting pay, becoming the UK's largest company to make the shift. It expects Friday to be the default day off.

It cited an increase in efficiency and productivity, saying:

Atom bank is a business that's built on efficiency – it's exactly what allows us to be more agile and customer-focused than traditional banks. So, naturally, we're always excited to try new ways of doing things if it will help us become even more efficient.

Switching to a four-day week has not just been a case of giving everyone an extra day off; it's been an exercise in reviewing how we operate and deciding what's really necessary. It's a bit like packing light when you're used to bringing a whole suitcase – with a bit of thought, you can still enjoy all your essentials while leaving the extras at home, whether those are unnecessary meetings or overlong procedures.

Note that 'it's a bit like packing light' – lean, lean, lean.

Estonian mobility tech company Bolt also ran a three-month experiment for a four-day work week, which proved their core thesis, showing improvements in:

1. Productivity

2. Engagement
3. Wellness

A lean mindset means finding the path of least resistance to impact and results. Like tech's bias to openness, this mindset stems from the engineering community.

Finding the shortest technical path in context is what engineers do for a living. It's what they're trained to do in computer science classes. There's actually something called Dijkstra's algorithm, which finds the shortest path between multiple nodes – and tech/engineers all learned it. But instead of harnessing that short-path-finding brainpower, most companies tell developers (and staff at large) to turn off that part of their brain.[v]

Another way to frame this mindset is around the effort impact matrix, quite possibly my favourite mental framework ever, one I learned from Facebook engineers. It's all about working smarter, not harder. Simply ask yourself, what is the easiest way to have the most impact?

Speaking of making life easier for ourselves …

Lean on AI and automation. Let the machines do the heavy lifting. Let the machines automate as many minuscule tasks as possible. Such is the attitude of tech.

The simple question 'What can be automated?' is nearing the status of default in meeting rooms in tech nowadays. Automation equals scale.

In a later chapter we will delve into data and AI further. But for now, ponder the role data and AI played for the science community with regard to Covid. Against the odds and in record time, pharmaceutical companies produced groundbreaking vaccines and therapeutics that promise a sustainable recovery from the coronavirus pandemic. It's been a truly remarkable accomplishment, and their use of data and artificial intelligence to accelerate progress holds important lessons for every sector and company.

First and foremost is the imperative to embrace these rapid technological advances that are driving the fourth industrial revolution. For any company that wants to position itself for growth, betting on this agenda is an insurance policy for long-term success. Big data and AI radically improve innovation, speed and agility, which are the lifeblood of all effective organisations.[vi]

In tech, data bears truth. The more data, the more insightful truths are uncovered. And also more opportunity to automate tasks to scale the truths.

Ruthless prioritisation

Ruthless prioritisation is another sizeable dose of vernacular uttered across tech. It comes as a verb, and screams of lean, an impact over effort mindset.

Ruthless prioritising allows us to counteract a human flaw innate in us, something we hold on to as a total fallacy. Multitasking. Bounce between one activity and another and you lose time as your brain reorients to the new task. Those milliseconds add up. Researchers estimate we lose 28 per cent of an average workday to multitasking ineffectiveness.[vii]

Barack Obama in his presidency exuded ruthless prioritisation, even in the seemingly banal, such as his suit wear.

'You'll see I wear only grey or blue suits,' Barack Obama claimed back in his POTUS days. 'I'm trying to pare down decisions. I don't want to make decisions about what I'm eating or wearing. Because I have too many other decisions to make.' He mentioned research that shows the simple act of making decisions degrades one's ability to make further decisions. It's why shopping is so exhausting. 'You need to focus your decision-making energy. You need to routinize yourself. You can't be going through the day distracted by trivia.'[viii]

This focus on what matters most is the essence of ruthless prioritisation. Mark Zuckerberg does the exact same thing with his clothing decisions, or lack thereof. Same jeans, same grey T-shirt. So his finite decision-making capabilities each day go to his mission of connecting the world.

Jeff Bezos is probably the most 'ruthless' of the tech leaders. His decision- making principles, that are executed with speed and precision by hundreds of thousands of 'Amazonians' are famous. The 'two-pizza team', 'Amazon flywheel' and 'Day 1' mentality being the most famous, and dealt with in more detail throughout the book.

Hope is not a strategy

When it comes to thinking and planning for future endeavours, tech doesn't lean on that bastion of human positivity, and frankly, comfort – hope. It's a term we all fall back on in conversation when talking up the future. 'X will be done, then Y, and we hope we will get there'. It ranges from psychological safety net to full-on cop-out.

'Hope is not a strategy' is yet another meme that travelled the meeting rooms and micro-kitchens of Facebook. In practice it meant that Facebookers needed to apply best practices, instead of just letting the product do the work, waiting on new features to launch and trusting that all will be rosy. It was a crucial counterpoint in mindset, as it was easy to watch the tech giant grow around them and yet they would still feel at ease, knowing that they didn't need to be hungry and honest.

Test and learn

Chris Rock, that legendary comedian who got a slap off Will Smith, has an approach to writing for the big stage that surprises many. When preparing fresh material, he will first appear at small nightclubs like the Comedy Store in LA dozens of times and test hundreds of jokes. He brings a notepad on stage and records which bits go over well and where he needs to make adjustments. The few killer lines that survive will form the backbone of his new show, likely an HBO or Netflix special.

I once saw Judd Apatow play at the Comedy Store in LA. He came on stage with sheets of paper and just started riffing off his notes. There were no jokes, just scenarios. After a while you could tell these were the test plots for future films a la *Superbad, Knocked Up*, and so on.

Satya Nadella's culture pivot within Microsoft to a 'learn it all culture' spoke volumes to the crucial attitude needed to survive and thrive in tech. Nothing is fully known. Nothing is guaranteed. Testing for understanding, to understand what works and doesn't, learning what will scale – that is the muscle of tech. To test and learn.

A more academic slant would be to call it validated learning, which is the process of demonstrating empirically that a team has discovered valuable truths about a start-up's present and future business prospects. It is more concrete, more accurate and faster than market forecasting or classical business planning. It is the principal antidote to the lethal problem of achieving failure: successfully executing a plan that leads nowhere.[ix]

Next time you are with a friend or family member, check out their Facebook or Instagram app, and compare it to yours. The features, buttons, colours, and so on. There is a strong chance there will be differences. Why? Facebook is renowned for constantly running thousands of different tests of minor changes to improve the overall experience for users.

Building around experimentation is what has helped Netflix build such an insanely sticky product. Netflix researchers estimate that if a typical user doesn't find something to watch in the app within sixty to ninety seconds, they run the risk of getting bored and moving on to something else. The company fanatically A/B tests (also known as split testing) everything from the content that a user sees when they open the app, to loading speeds in order to fanatically optimise the user experience.

As one company blog post from Netflix wrote:

By following an empirical approach, we ensure that product changes are not driven by the most opinionated and vocal Netflix employees, but instead by actual data, allowing our members themselves to guide us toward the experiences they love.[x]

Measure what matters

Measuring something is the first step to improving it. Peter Drucker famously opined, 'What gets measured gets managed.' It's true. If you don't know how much money your business is collecting or spending, it's difficult to know whether or not any change you make to your business system is actually an improvement. If you want to lose weight, you first must know how much you weigh right now, then track how any changes you make affect your weight.

Without data, you're blind. If you want to improve anything, you must measure it first.[xi]

Why? What? How? When? All the questions that need to be asked when measuring business performance.

A common pitfall is choosing the right lens of measurement. James Clear explained that we focus on working long hours instead of getting meaningful work done. We are more about getting ten thousand steps than we are about being healthy. We teach for standardised tests instead of emphasising learning, curiosity and critical thinking. We optimise for what we measure.

When we choose the wrong measurement, we get the wrong behaviour.

This stems from Goodhart's law, which states, 'When a measure becomes a target, it ceases to be a good measure.' Measurement is only useful when it guides you and adds context to a larger picture, not when it consumes you. Each measure is simply one piece of feedback in the overall system.[xii]

Markets matter

Market matters most; neither a stellar team nor fantastic product will redeem a bad market. Markets that don't exist don't care how smart you are. – Marc Andreessen, venture capitalist

TAM. What's the TAM? The words on the lips of every investor in tech land.

TAM means total addressable market. It, somewhat crudely, works out the overall customer and revenue potential a product or service may have.

The ideal TAM is a big blue ocean, or 'greenfield' market, which comes with caution according to Google's Eric Schmidt when he commented that many entrepreneurs dream of entering 'greenfield' markets that are brand new and have no competition. But usually there's a reason the market is empty: it's not big enough to sustain a growing venture. It still may be a good business opportunity – someone must make money from all of those niche products we see in the SkyMall catalogue – but if you want to create an environment of innovation, it's better to look for big markets with huge growth potential.[xiii]

Tech prides itself not so much on finding these beastly TAMs, but creating the new categories for products and services in general, and benefitting from first- mover advantage into new TAMs. Look at Peloton, creating an entire new workout from home category. Peloton revolutionized the fitness industry by creating a new category of workout equipment for home use. Peloton has successfully made it possible for fitness enthusiasts to enjoy a gym-like experience from the comfort of their homes. By combining high-quality hardware, interactive software, and a vast library of workout classes, Peloton has created an engaging and immersive workout experience that has never been seen before.

Size does matter

Peter Thiel, founder of PayPal and investor in Facebook, teaches a class at Stanford in which he advocates that students not think in terms of competing in a marketplace, but in terms of defining a position they can 'monopolise'.[xiv] Monopolisation is the economic holy grail in tech, never uttered publicly by tech leaders of course for fear of anti-competition regulators pulling down their chinos.

With great size comes great power, power to dominate not just one industry but several. Such is the size of Amazon, it can merely mention it is considering entering into a new category, and the category leaders will lose value overnight. When it announced it would join JPMorgan Chase and Berkshire Hathaway for a healthcare initiative, healthcare stocks sank. When Amazon announced the launch of its own delivery service, something called 'Shipping with Amazon', stocks of FedEx and UPS fell over 5 per cent.

Moats in tech are the conceptual weapons of fortifying size, and giving further runway to scale. Moats are the lily pads to monopolies. And increasingly, data is becoming the key lever to moat building, due to the speed of change in business and society, as Scott Galloway attests to:

Firms try to build higher and higher walls to keep enemies (upstarts and competitors) from invasion. Business theorists call these structures 'barriers to entry'. They are nice in theory, but, increasingly, traditional walls are showing cracks, even crumbling – especially in tech. The plummeting price of processing power (Moore's law again), coupled with an increase in bandwidth and a new generation of leadership that has digital in their DNA, has produced bigger ladders than anyone ever expected. ESPN, J. Crew, and Jeb Bush ... all unassailable, no? No. Digital ladders (over-the-top video, fast fashion, and @realdonaldtrump) can vault almost any wall.[xv]

Speed is everything

MOVE FAST AND BREAK THINGS.

— Mark Zuckerberg, 2009

MOVE FAST WITH STABLE INFRA.

— Mark Zuckerberg, 2014

There's a brilliance to Zuckerberg's original motto: 'Move fast and break things.' It's all to do with urgency and taking risks. 'Moving fast' is something I must have said in the hundreds at my time at Facebook, and I heard it in meetings in the thousands. Zuckerberg also acknowledges that moving fast incurs a cost – things won't be perfect – and he's okay with that. He's saying, 'If you break something, I have your back as long as you were pushing the envelope to invent something for our customers.' By doing this, he ensures that the innovation directive will prevail.

Facebook had created a culture where engineers were encouraged to ship, or deliver, products as quickly as possible. 'Fuck it, ship it' was a popular expression across the company.[xvi]

2014 was a time of maturation for the company, and an acknowledgement that a scrappy mantra in 'breaking things' didn't translate well in public opinion, a public who expected a tech giant to have its shit together. Hence the pivot to 'stable' talk and practice.

Facebook's success with Instagram has a lot to do with its speed in adjusting to the market. Its ability to punch out new features is unrivalled. Some of them work (Messenger, mobile app, News Feed), and some fall flat (the snoopy, short-lived Beacon, which would share our purchases with our friends, and the failed 'Buy' button as part of a shift to commerce). The birthing, and killing, of new products makes Facebook the most innovative big company on earth.[xvii]

Speed in tech has seen a new leader in recent years – in China, in a phenomenon dubbed 'Shenzhen speed'. What underpins this need for speed with Chinese tech companies is an unforgiving work culture dubbed 996: working from nine in the morning until nine at night, six days a week. Chinese tech companies are now the leaders in innovating at speed.

DESPERATION SOMETIMES DRIVES INNOVATION.

— Dara Khosrowshahi, Uber

Bias for action

WE HAVE A 'BIAS FOR ACTION' AT FACEBOOK. MANY COMPANIES TALK ABOUT BEING WILLING TO TAKE RISKS, BUT FEW ACTUALLY DO IT.

— Mark Zuckerberg

Leonardo da Vinci once observed, 'It has long since come to my attention that people of accomplishment rarely sat back and let things happen to them. They went out and happened to things.' That is the artist's way. To happen to things. To turn nothings into somethings.[xviii]

It's quite simple. Tech is brimming with doers. Builders. Creators. Experimenters. Crafters.

Software code is pushed to the platforms and apps of tech companies at an accelerating rate. Code is pushed to cars, yes cars, at a daily rate now. Like Teslas. The company that famously built a massive battery factory in just thirteen months, despite the project being estimated to take several years.

All talk, all action.

Platform play

A platform business gets techies giddy with glee. They are the pinnacle of scalability.

A platform is a foundation created by a company that lets other companies build products and services upon it. It is neither market nor company, but something new. A platform, like a department store, offers stuff it did not create. One of the first widely successful platforms was Microsoft's operating system (OS). Anyone with ambition could build and sell a software program that ran on the OS that Microsoft owned. Many did. Some, like the first spreadsheet, Lotus 1-2-3, prospered hugely and became mini platforms in themselves, birthing integrations from third parties for other features, thereby creating an ecosystem of interdependent products and services.

This spawned a second generation of platforms that acquired more of the attributes of markets. iTunes being one of the first when launched for the iPhone. Apple owned the platform, which also became a marketplace for phone apps. Vendors pitched a virtual stall and sold their apps on iTunes. Apple regulated the market, weeding out junky, exploitative or buggy (shitty) applications. iTunes was an entire ecosystem of apps constructed on the capabilities built into the phone, and it boomed. Apple kept adding ingenious new ways to interact with the phone, including new sensors such as a camera, GPS and accelerometer; thousands of novel species of innovations deepened the iPhone ecology.

And they still get away with charging apps on the store with a 30 per cent transaction fee for payments made by users on another company's app. Not bad rent to be getting in the bank.

It's no wonder the wealthiest and most disruptive organisations today are almost all multisided platforms – Apple, Microsoft, Google and Facebook. All these giants employ APIs (more on these later) extensively that facilitate and encourage others to play with their platforms. Uber, Alibaba, Airbnb, PayPal, Square, WeChat and Android are the newer wildly successful multi-side markets, run by a single company, that enable robust ecosystems of derivative yet interdependent products and services.[xix]

User/customer first

CUSTOMERS SHOULD BE NUMBER ONE, EMPLOYEES NUMBER TWO, AND THEN ONLY YOUR SHAREHOLDERS COME AT NUMBER THREE.

— Jack Ma, founder, Alibaba

Amazon, the 'most customer-centric company in the world', is renowned for its mindset of obsessing over customers. Yes, obsessing. Jeff Bezos is the thought leader of thought leaders in this area:

Our customers have made our business what it is, they are the ones with whom we have a great relationship, and they are the ones to whom we owe a great obligation. And we consider them to be loyal to us – right up until the second that someone else offers them a better service.[xx]

He once remarked, when comparing Amazon to their direct competitor at the time, the largest book retailer in the US:

I can roam the floors of Barnes & Noble for hours on end, and not one assistant will make a recommendation to me because they have no idea what kinds of books I might be interested in. Amazon's business model is built on knowing exactly what I want and giving me as many shortcuts to that as possible.[xxi]

Thanks to a customer-first attitude to growth, Amazon took off. In 1999 the company had fourteen million clients, reaching up to twenty million clients by the year 2000. In 1999 more than 4,700,000 books could be found in its catalogue, with an average of $375,000 turnover per employee. At that time traditional booksellers had an average of $27,000 turnover per employee.

In the year 2000 Amazon had a turnover of $700 million, whereas Barnes & Noble had a turnover of $320 million. The rest is history.

One advantage of a customer-driven focus is that it aids a certain type of proactivity. Back to you, Jeff:

When we're at our best, we don't wait for internal pressures. We are internally driven to improve our services, adding benefits and features, before we have to. We invent before we have to. These investments are motivated by customer focus rather than by reaction to competition. This approach earns more trust with customers and drives rapid improvements in customer experience.

Amazon's foray into India is a testament to this approach, which Bezos explains:

India is another example of how we globalise an offering like Amazon Marketplace through customer obsession and a passion for invent. Last year we ran a program called Amazon Chai Cart where we deployed three wheeled mobile carts to navigate in a city's business districts, serve tea, water and lemon juice to small business owners and teach them about selling online. In a period of four months, the team travelled 15,280 kilometres across thirty-one cities, served 37,200 cups of tea and engaged with over 10,000 sellers. Through the program and other conversations with sellers, we found out there was a lot of interest in selling online but that sellers struggled with the belief that the process was time-consuming, tedious, and complex. So, we invented Amazon Tatkal, which enables small businesses to get online in less than 60 minutes.

Amazon Tatkal is a specially designed studio-on-wheels offering a suit of launch

services including registration, imaging, and cataloguing services, as well as basic seller-training mechanisms.

Zappos, which Amazon acquired, also had a customer-first approach to growth, and had these learnings to share:

Dave Morrissey

Top 10 Ways to Instill Customer Service into Your Company

1. Make customer service a priority for the whole company, not just a department. A customer service attitude needs to come from the top.
2. Make WOW a verb that is part of your company's everyday vocabulary.
3. Empower and trust your customer service reps. Trust that they want to provide great service ... because they actually do. Escalations to a supervisor should be rare.
4. Realize that it's okay to fire customers who are insatiable or abuse your employees.
5. Don't measure call times, don't force employees to upsell, and don't use scripts.
6. Don't hide your 1-800 number (excuse the dated reference, who makes calls to companies anymore?). It's a message not just to your customers, but to your employees as well.
7. View each call as an investment in building a customer service brand, not as an expense you're seeking to minimize.
8. Have the entire company celebrate great service. Tell stories of WOW experiences to everyone in the company.
9. Find and hire people who are already passionate about customer service.
10. Give great service to everyone: customers, employees, and vendors.[xxii]

Amazon takes customer first thinking to such a grand level, that in company meetings, there is always an empty chair. It represented *The Customer*: "the most important person in the room"

Optimise money

FOCUS ON THE USER ... AND THE MONEY WILL FOLLOW.[xxiii]

— Eric Schmidt

Profits? As mentioned earlier, tech gags in its mouth at the thought of having to produce profits in the first few years of operation. To fuel unprecedented business growth, tech has come at financing in completely new ways.

Scott Galloway nailed their attitude and approach when looking at Amazon:

Amazon has had more access to cheaper capital for a longer period than any firm in modern times. Most successful VC-backed tech companies in the nineties raised less than $50 million before showing a return to investors. By comparison, Amazon raised $2.1 billion in investors' money before the company (sort of) broke even.

Normal business thinking: If we can borrow money at historically low rates, buy back stock, and see the value of management's options increase, why invest in growth and the jobs that come with it? That's risky. Amazon business thinking: if we can borrow money at historically low rates, why don't we invest that money in extraordinarily expensive control delivery systems? That way we secure an impregnable position in retail and asphyxiate our competitors. Then we can get really big, fast.[xxiv]

Which is a great time for all when economies are in good nick, and interest rates are in the favourable to almost zero spectrum. When the financial shit hits the fan, tech does pivot, towards 'efficiency'. Marc Benioff, CEO of Salesforce, has been an evangelist for growth over profit in the tech era, and open to a pivot:

We've never had an efficiency focus at the company before because we've had 24 years of just grow, grow, grow ... we're looking at this moment to reassess.

A lot of this is posturing to Wall Street, saying we are looking at costs. Within tech, a growth mindset still oozes through the fibre cables. They are hardly counting pennies hoping that's what will improve the financials. The accountants can stay in their colourless corner playing Solitaire.

Big bets

WHEN I HAVE A GOOD QUARTERLY CONFERENCE CALL WITH WALL STREET, PEOPLE WILL STOP ME AND SAY 'CONGRATULATIONS ON YOUR QUARTER,' AND I SAY 'THANK YOU,' BUT WHAT I'M REALLY THINKING IS THAT QUARTER WAS BAKED THREE YEARS AGO. RIGHT NOW I'M WORKING ON A QUARTER THAT'S GOING TO REVEAL ITSELF IN 2023 SOMETIME, AND THAT'S WHAT YOU NEED TO BE DOING.

— **Jeff Bezos**

Amazon has shown that focusing on the long term allows the interests of your customers, who want better and faster services cheaper, and the interests of your shareholders, who want a return on investment, to come into alignment. That's not always true in the short term.[xxv]

As Jeff Bezos wrote in Amazon's first annual letter, in 1997, 'Given a 10 percent chance of a hundred times pay-out, you should take that bet every time.' It's in tech's DNA to future-gaze and aspire to conquer whole new worlds, be it digital markets or the space-based aspirations of Bezos and Elon Musk.

Betting big has big pay-offs. As Marty Bryde said in *Ozark*, 'Like tech, break big, win big'. Tech looks to different time horizons and visions of scale than other industries. Often calling them 'moonshots,' tech's idea of breaking new ground is to create entire new categories (Amazon Web Services and cloud computing) or upending existing categories (Uber and mobility). All done with a mishmash of data analysis, beta testing and good old gut instinct.

Some tech companies are better than others at big betting, or at least look the part more. Point in case, Google X. Google X is 'The Moonshot Factory'.

Essentially a research and development lab for Google's big bets. Or as they say, 'We create radical new technologies to solve some of the world's hardest problems.'[xxvi]

One of its very first big bets since its founding in 2010 is nearing the mainstream, the self-driving car. The project officially graduated in July 2018 and is known as Waymo. Waymo logged more than two million miles on public roads, has conducted the world's first self-driving ride on public roads, and is currently conducting a public trial in Phoenix, Arizona. Waymo's self-driving cars are equipped with sensors, cameras, and software to detect and respond to pedestrians, bicyclists, and other cars. Waymo's goal, is to make transportation safer and easier for everyone. 'Look, no hands' car driving jokes are soon to be extinct thanks to techs' big betting.

Incremental/marginal gains

In preparation for the 2012 Olympics, Team GB's cycling team followed a now famous detail-oriented plan in order to unlock marginal gains to achieve victory:

- Customised aerodynamic helmets
- 'Hot pants' – worn to keep thigh muscles warm between races
- Sweat-resistant clothing
- Alcohol sprayed on wheels to enhance traction at the start
- Hypoallergenic pillows to prevent riders catching colds

Team Sky took it even further for Bradley Wiggins, transporting his bed throughout the 2,173-mile, twenty-three-day course of the Tour de France and then on to London for the Olympics. Costly, but worth it for two gold medals for Wiggins.[xxvii]

What are marginal gains, in a nutshell? One hundred things done 1 per cent better to deliver cumulative competitive advantage. They're the result of applying the concept of '1% better' to one hundred different areas of your business. Each 1 per cent improvement, when compounded over time, leads to a significant competitive advantage for your company.

Amazon is an example of this in action – they've created algorithms for everything from recommending products based on past purchases to sorting packages based on how customers want them delivered. They even had an algorithm for how fast their employees could walk from one place to another! This kind of thing might seem like overkill for some companies – but for Amazon, it's part of their success story.

Airbnb's founders wanted to make sure their hosts were able to provide guests with fresh towels every time they stayed at an Airbnb property; Google made sure its search results were more accurate than those of competitors because even if only one out of every ten users clicked on one result over another, that would mean millions more clicks than competitors would receive if their results weren't as accurate as Google's.

Pivot for growth

The almighty pivot. Second only to the failure-to-success story in tech, in terms of searing storylines.

What does a pivot mean in tech and business? Well, it's a structured course correction designed to test a new fundamental hypothesis about the product, strategy and engine of growth. Successful pivots put companies on a path towards growing a sustainable business. It's a re-growth play.[xxviii]

Tech is brimming with pivot stories. Slack is the current story in vogue. CEO Stewart Butterfield's company, Tiny Speck, began developing a game called Glitch. After a brief launch in 2011, Glitch was returned to beta (testing mode) and by 2012, Butterfield declared the concept wasn't viable. However, the internal communications platform Tiny Speck had created to communicate between US and Canadian offices turned out to be the real opportunity. The messaging app Slack officially launched in 2014 and became a unicorn ($1 billion-plus valuation) the same year.[xxix]

Other notable pivots can be seen everywhere. Netflix changed from mail order to streaming. Shopify was originally called 'Snow Devil', an e-commerce site for snowboarders, which morphed into an e-commerce platform for every business. YouTube moved from a dating site to online video. Twitter pivoted from podcast platform to social media.

A pivot requires a willingness to change. It takes balls to change course. And it falls on leaders to call the shots and ensure the entire company is aligned.

Why and when to pivot is worth diving into. Eric Ries, in his must-read for anyone aspiring to start a business or work in tech, *The Lean Startup*, outlines the different pivots that can be approached.

First there is the zoom-in pivot, refocusing the product on what previously had been considered just one feature of a larger whole. Then there is the zoom-out pivot. In this reverse situation, sometimes a single feature is insufficient to support a whole product. In this type of pivot, what was considered the whole product becomes a single feature of a much larger product.

A common pivot is the customer segment pivot. In this pivot, the company realises that the product it's building solves a real problem for real customers but that they are not the customers it originally planned to serve. In other words, the product hypothesis is confirmed only partially.

It's a mindset, fixed or growth

Tech companies, at their best, take a holistic view of the whole business and its people. Everything can be improved. Everything can be optimised. Everything can, and should, grow, like never seen before.

Going above and beyond to grow, to go that extra step, permeates success in society, not just tech. The late great Hunter S. Thompson, when a young *Time* magazine journalist, copied out entire texts of Scott Fitzgerald's *The Great Gatsby* and Hemingway's *Farewell to Arms*, twice. Johnny Depp told *The Guardian* that Thompson 'wanted to know what it felt like to write a masterpiece.'

It's a total and utter mindset. It's the mindset for growth on steroids. It's an exciting and inspiring way to believe. A fixed mindset makes it hard to maintain confidence because difficulty, effort and other people who are perceived to be better all pose threats. But, in a growth mindset, the same things are opportunities.

But such a mindset on steroids can be hazardous, as the basic plumbing of businesses might get ignored. Many entrepreneurs become frustrated when their business seems to hit a 'plateau' and growth appears to stop. Spending time on maintenance or consolidation seems like a waste, or a flaw in the business idea. That's not the case at all: these phases are necessary to ensure the business succeeds, and they should be respected. A business that fixates on expansion but short-changes maintenance and consolidation will experience the commercial equivalent of cancerous growth.[xxx]

So move fast and ~~break things~~ build stable infrastructure.

Chapter 5
DATA IS THE NEW GOLD

WE NEED A HELL OF A LOT OF LITTLE FOLKS RUNNING AROUND SHITTING US DATA, YOU KNOW, FOR THE EYEBALLS, FOR THE REVENUE, FOR THE SCALE.[1]

— Lukas Mattson, aka 'Hans Christian Anderfuck', Succession

San Francisco has had two beautiful booms in wealth accumulation in its short lifetime. The first being the California Gold Rush in 1848.

The second boom has been in more recent times, with the explosion of innovation and cultural cachet that has come from its production of silicon chips in the 1960s right up to today. In those chips is, today's gold rush, data.

The ones who create and control the information that pours out of society are the ones who amass power and wealth. The Information Age has quite a few barons, and billions of serfs.

Data accumulation is one thing, how it's understood and how its insights are scaled for effective usage across millions to billions of touchpoints is a bigger thing, which is where AI comes in. Data is the oxygen for AI; without it, it ceases to exist. AI simply broken down is a learning machine. AI is access to more minds than was ever possible in human history. Lest we forget that knowledge is power.

Artificial intelligence is the future of business

IT SEEMS PROBABLE THAT ONCE THE MACHINE THINKING METHOD HAD STARTED, IT WOULD NOT TAKE LONG TO OUTSTRIP OUR FEEBLE POWERS. THEY WOULD BE ABLE TO CONVERSE WITH EACH OTHER TO SHARPEN THEIR WITS. AT SOME STAGE THEREFORE, WE SHOULD HAVE TO EXPECT THE MACHINES TO TAKE CONTROL.

— Alan Turing

The power to automate processes, optimise operations and streamline workflows is so powerful that it can change your business as we know it. And if you're not using AI yet, you probably should be.

But what exactly do we mean by 'artificial intelligence'? Well, it's a technology that allows computers to learn from experience and then make decisions based on what they've learned. These decisions can be anything from the way a computer plays chess or poker to how well it can recognise images or understand human speech.

So what does this mean for your business? Here are just a few of the ways that artificial intelligence can help your company grow:

- It will save you time by automating processes and eliminating repetitive tasks so that you can focus on more important things like growing revenue and generating new ideas.
- It will help improve customer experience by allowing your business to provide customers with smarter recommendations based on their tastes or purchase history.

- It will allow businesses to scale up or down based on demand without needing additional staff members.

Against this 'knowledge is power' backdrop, it's alarming that 76 per cent of C- suite executives say they struggle with how to scale AI, according to research from Accenture, even though 84 per cent believe it is critical to their business objectives. But perhaps we shouldn't be so quick to judge. After all, 90 per cent of the data in the world was created in the past two years, and forecasts suggest 175 zettabytes of data will be produced by 2025.[ii]

Here are some more incredible stats for the volume of communication we send out every minute:

- We send 16 million text messages.
- There are 1,100,000 Tinder swipes.
- 149,513 million emails are sent through Gmail.
- 5,900,000 searches are conducted on Google.
- There are 103,447,520 spam emails sent.
- There are 1,700,000 pieces of content shared on Facebook.[iii]

Data and AI are turning non-tech companies into tech leaders. Paddy Power built a high-powered quants system that, coupled with bombastically brilliant marketing plays, led it to be a world-leading gambling company.

The adoption of data and algorithmic modelling in particular put the company at the top of the global gambling food chain. Paddy Power set tech on a practice that was inherently driven by thumb-in-the-air decision-making. 'The mindset was that gambling was innate,' Simon Moore, a statistician come quantitative analyst at Paddy Power, remembers. 'People would actually say in the trading room, "I can feel a goal coming on here." How do you explain that you can codify that "feeling"? Or we would hear things like "that horse was class", so how could you convince someone that you had put a mathematical model around it?'

Moore and his colleagues began building models for football and tennis, which were both relatively simple to distil down to their mathematical principles.

What started as a mid-level player in the UK and Ireland gambling market in the '90s has become a leading global behemoth, thanks to the focus on data and working algorithms around it.

The impact that AI is going to have on all of our lives is real and profound. Amazon Rekognition said they were observing AI compute double every five months. To help put this into context, consider that we've spent our entire lives in a world where everything that touched technology was governed by Moore's law – doubling in capability every eighteen months. Doubling every five months is 2x at five months, 4x at ten months, 8x at fifteen months, and so on. Put simply, society is supercharging in ways that would give a Duracell bunny a heart attack.

A Chinese game company appointed an AI to be the company CEO. You read that right. NetDragon named Tang Yu, an 'AI-powered virtual humanoid robot,' as CEO of Fujian NetDragon Websoft. The company claimed that Tang Yu would ensure a 'fair workplace for all employees' and increase efficiency, risk management, and decision-making. In a press release, NetDragon Chairman Dejian Liu stated:

We believe AI is the future of corporate management, and our appointment of Ms. Tang Yu represents our commitment to truly embrace the use of AI to transform the way we operate our business and ultimately drive our future strategic growth.

Why data is so valuable

What has heralded data as the new tool of influence? Data gets you closer to the truth of what is happening, at immense scale. This leads to exceedingly better decision-making. Better decision-making, in business, unlocks key strategic initiatives and enables better relationships with customers and other stakeholders. It's also the fuel for AI, the weapon of efficiency today, and most certainly tomorrow.

Data creates insight and changes behaviours, for the better ideally. Take the Heart app on an iPhone for instance. It logs one's step count, distance travelled and flights of stairs climbed. It has evolved further to measure sleep rates.

Apple is the guardian angel of health you didn't know you had.

Features that have just landed in ChatGPT catalyse data to be a Swiss army knife for your everyday needs. That butler you always wanted, empowers you to Batman your life, in a sense, I suppose. Get a load of this power at your fingertips with a cheeky prompt or two of ChatGPT:

- Browse thousands of stores
- Generate videos using AI
- Create and manage to-do lists
- View live sports scores, stats and other data
- Book and organise any holiday
- Interact with numerous web applications (Gmail, Trello, Google Sheets)
- Search for and reserve restaurants
- Explore magazine articles
- Engage in gaming
- Order from local businesses
- Monitor cryptocurrency prices
- Learn new languages
- Create, manage, and store notes
- Solve complex mathematical problems
- Locate and generate documents

In business ~~practice~~ dominance, Scott Galloway explained that a trillion-dollar company (read big tech) must have technology that can learn from human input and register data algorithmically – Himalayas of data that can be fed into algorithms to improve the offering. The technology then uses mathematical optimisation that, in a millisecond, not only calibrates the product to customers' personal, immediate needs but improves the product incrementally every time a user is on the platform for other concurrent and future customers.[iv]

In short, you have much better information about your business with which to adapt to the accelerating changes in society.

We should target cutting-edge technology and mobilize prime resources to make breakthroughs in developing core big data technology, and accelerate building an independent and controllable industrial chain, value chain and ecosystem of big data.[v]

China's Xi Jinping underscored the importance of building a digital economy with data as a key factor, highlighting the fact that research on and use of big data is indispensable in building a modern economy.

The internet, big data and artificial intelligence are the real economy and all ought to be interconnected, the president said, adding that industrialisation and the use of information should be integrated deeper.

Data and AI create huge opportunities. They can maximise efficiencies, reduce manufacturing costs, create new products and services, improve customer satisfaction, meet regulatory and compliance requirements, enhance brand loyalty and improve profitability.[vi]

Research by Goldman Sachs indicates that AI could eventually increase annual global GDP by 7 per cent over a 10-year period: driven by a combination of significant labour cost savings, new job creation and higher productivity for non-displaced workers. Generative AI will raise annual US labour productivity growth by approximately 1.5 per cent over a ten-year period.[vii]

Data drives understanding and decisions in tech

In the past decade, the world's most important companies have become experts in data – its capture, its analytics and its use. The power of big data and AI is that it signals the end of sampling and statistics – now you can just track the shopping pattern of every customer in every one of your stores around the world, and then respond almost instantly with discounts, changes in inventory, store layouts, and so on ... and do so 24/7/365. Or better yet, you can build in the technology to respond every second, automatically.[viii]

The amassing of data by big tech allows for a plethora of permutations of insights, which could never be surfaced by a human. More insight means more opportunity to build and create.

The intense focus on numbers and data has been one of the key motivations for many a digital-first business. Look at Graze, the healthy snack e-commerce business. According to the former CEO, Anthony Fletcher, data-focused decision-making was imperative to their success:

One of the things which really helped us was our attitude to data. Very early on in the business, we put a lot of effort into how data was stored and how it could be accessed. It wasn't just performance marketing. It was everything from finance data, product review data, any data that could help our customer service team respond to queries. It helped that we have a pretty geeky company culture.[ix] Being a DTC company built on constant iteration and using data turned out to be a huge advantage when it came to retail. Our retail customers were blown away when six weeks after launching our range, we showed them the data to convince them to de-list a third of the range and replace them with new products. This approach was totally radical, given the normal NPD (new product development) cycle of 24–36 months of traditional FMCG brands. The retailers were really impressed that we were able to be proactive and react so fast.

We are entering what lead Google economist Hal Varian calls a new period of 'combinatorial innovation':

This occurs when there is a great availability of different component parts that can be combined or recombined to create new inventions. For example, in the 1800s, the standardisation of the design of mechanical devices such as gears, pulleys, chains and cams led to a manufacturing boom. In the 1900s, the gasoline engine led to innovations in automobiles, motorcycles and airplanes. By the 1950s, it was the integrated circuit proliferating in numerous applications. In each of these cases, the development of complementary components led to a wave of inventions. Today the components are all about information, connectivity and computing. Would-be inventors have all the world's information, global reach and practically infinite computing power.

They have open-source software and abundant APIs that allow them to build easily on each other's work. They can use standard protocols and languages.

They can access information platforms with data about things ranging from traffic to weather to economic transactions to human genetics.[x]

In short – it's never been easier to put things together to create something of value to someone else. And data is becoming the glue that unites these elements. Knowledge is power, I must repeat.

Efficiency gains

London's cabbies (taxi drivers for those from other cities) famously have to do a four-year course that ensures they know every street name and route in one of the world's few megacities. Pass the test after four years of training and you get your taxi license. It's an impressive feat, quaint even. But wait, doesn't Google Maps do that very thing these days?

Data sure hasn't been a sexy part of society at large. Data originally came largely in the form of spreadsheets. Data was talked about by professors and academics. Data was black and white numbers, with no colour to it. The past two decades have seen a shift in perception when it comes to data, and not because of the growth of talk around 'big data'.

Organisations that excel at distilling data into insights (data intelligence) and activating these in real time in their operations (data reflexes) will achieve a competitive advantage.[xi]

Data's existence in the world has a new swagger thanks to it being made interesting and famous. Brad Pitt and Jonah Hill became the face of sexy data, thanks to the 2011 film *Moneyball* based on Michael Lewis's book *Moneyball: The Art of Winning an Unfair Game*. Taking a pragmatic, analytical look at baseball players' performance across a range of data points gave the Oakland As an advantage to succeed that was disproportionate to the dollars they had to play with each year compared to other teams in the league like the New York Yankees.

Moneyball was data's eureka moment in sport and a catalyst in its perception in culture. In business, data means efficiency gains. And techies were early adopters of taking data-led approaches to decision-making and execution to deliver efficiency gains unseen in business.

The most techy sport is Formula 1, which utilises data as an essential muscle for marginal gains. Their attention to detail rips a new arsehole in most human endeavours that lean into data for successful execution. 'When I first started in F1, we recorded eight channels of data. Now we have 16,000 from every single parameter on the car. And we derive another 50,000 channels from that data,' said Paddy Lowe, a Cambridge-educated engineer, who is currently the technical leader of Mercedes F1. 'Each channel provides information on a small aspect of performance. It takes us into the detail, but it also enables us to isolate key metrics that help us to improve.'[xii] That is a hell of a lot of thousands in ways to look at performance.

Imagine trying out different shades of a colour in your logo, looking at the data to see what worked best, then releasing the logo in that winning shade (not colour change, shade alone!) and gaining another $200 million in your bank account at the end of the year? Google did so, under Marissa Mayer's, then Google's head of product, famed '50 shades of blue experiment'. Essentially, they A/B tested a range of shades on 1 per cent of users and then analysed the click metrics that followed to determine the winners. Over forty experiments later, a purplish shade of blue won the contest and resulted in two hundred more smackers in a lift in Google ad revenue.

Full disclosure, I got in on the AI game towards the end of finishing this book. I wish I had done it earlier to be honest; writing a book is the Mount-fucking- Everest of procrastination, bringing a hefty dollop of mental turmoil. Thanks to AI-driven editing tools like Copy.ai, I could pop in some ideas I was bouncing around into the tool, a few keywords would suffice, and just like that thirty iterations of paragraphs would come back at me. I'd select the one most fitting to my idea and tone, adjust a word or turn of phrase, and into the final draft it goes.

And then ChatGPT came out towards the finishing stages of this book. Had it come out a year earlier, I'd have 'written' this whole bloody book with the thing if possible.

The human creative spark is needed, but the AI editor helps with the heavy lifting. Impact over effort. Back of the net.

Products get more valuable with use

With these efficiency gains comes a game-changing phenomenon in modern- day business – products are now getting more valuable with use, not depreciating in value like a car or phone.

Modern products absorb and process information, data, at an accelerated clip thanks to Moore's law. Faster chips in products make for more effective dissemination of data, which in turn is used by the product to become more useful for the end user.

Look at Alexa (or feel free to give her a holler). Alexa is the epitome of a modern-day product, getting better with each use. Why? It is learning how to respond to the user's requests and questions. It's learning different skills like ordering you batteries. It's learning new accents, like my thick exasperated Limerick accent, asking her to 'play BBC 6 Music', the only thing I ask of her, ever. It gets better for, other, customers every day.

Amazon's Alexa-powered products, Go and Echo, suggest that the company is headed towards zero-click ordering across its operations. Leveraging big data and unrivalled knowledge of consumer purchasing patterns, Amazon will soon meet your need for stuff, without the friction of deciding or manual ordering.[xiii] It's Amazon's flywheel strategy in full flow. Which we will dig into in later chapters.

The Cinematch algorithm represents the marriage of marketing and technology that conferred such extraordinary success on Netflix. Because consumers found what they wanted among a limited DVD library, they left the video store and followed Netflix online. The trust they placed in the company – fostered by co-founder Marc Randolph's intuitive user interface and peerless customer service coupled with Hastings's beautiful algorithms – allowed it to smoothly shift the movie rental paradigm to streaming, where so many others had failed.[xiv]

Data-led products open up the possibility of real-time consumer decisions. The closer businesses are to a customer's motivations and purchase decisions, the quicker they can adapt to their needs, and therefore add more value than their competitors.

Look at self-driving cars as they come online in the coming years, they will get smarter and ultimately safer. I'd bet that after five years of mass consumption use, self-driving cars will bring road accidents down to single figures, by country.

Going back to OpenAI, they are making unprecedented leaps in value creation thanks to their leadership in AI with tools like ChatGPT, Dall-

E and more. A balance between deployment and discovery, OpenAI ensures their tools update in real time in the hands of users across the world, adapting based on real-time feedback. Iterative deployment and iterative discovery are two key principles that guide the development and deployment of AI systems at OpenAI.

Iterative deployment refers to the process of continuously improving and updating an AI system based on feedback from users and other stakeholders. This involves deploying a version of the system to users, collecting feedback on its performance, and then using that feedback to inform further development and updates. The goal is to gradually improve the system over time, making it more accurate, efficient, and useful.

At OpenAI, iterative deployment is achieved through a combination of rigorous testing, continuous integration and deployment, and close collaboration with users and other stakeholders. The development team works closely with users to understand their needs and to collect feedback on the system's performance. This feedback is used to identify areas for improvement and to prioritize development efforts.

Iterative discovery, on the other hand, refers to the process of using AI systems to generate new insights and discoveries in a particular field or domain. This involves training AI systems on large datasets and using them to identify patterns and relationships that may not be immediately apparent to human analysts.

Iterative discovery is achieved through a combination of deep learning techniques, large-scale data processing, and collaboration with domain experts. The goal is to use AI to accelerate scientific discovery and to help researchers make new breakthroughs in fields such as medicine, materials science, and climate science.

Overall, the principles of iterative deployment and iterative discovery are central to OpenAI's approach to AI development and deployment, as they enable the organization to continuously improve its systems and to make new discoveries that can benefit society as a whole. Value being supercharged, in real time, in unison with the end user. A brave new world, indeed.

It's cheaper

What goes up, must come down. Data gathering and processing are certainly on the up, and consequently costs are going way down. Thanks to the efficiency gains from data and better tools for its capture and use, doing business is much cheaper and savings can be passed on.

Starting a digital business today is a breeze compared to say ten years ago, as Twilio's Jeff Lawson explains:

The same thing is happening for another group of creative artists – software developers. Software infrastructure used to be incredibly expensive, but now it's cheap or even free to get started. You don't need to buy massive servers or rent space in a data center anymore. There's a whole toolkit that you can take down off the shelf and use to build your apps – Amazon or Microsoft for servers and storage, Google for Maps, Twilio for communications, Stripe for payments. Any kid has access to the same core building blocks as the largest corporations in the world. The same goes for distribution. Developers no longer have to strike a deal with a software publisher, get shelf space at CompUSA, or land a coveted spot preinstalled on a mobile phone. Anyone can put their app on an app store, just like anyone can put their video on YouTube. A web developer can buy ads on Google using their credit card, for as little as pennies a click.[xv]

Every one of those products and tools has benefited from data making them better and cheaper with use.

Source of truth, that humans can't find

We humans are wonderful creatures, but terribly flawed. A key flaw is that of bias. We have a limited capacity to ingest and process information, so our brains have to use a myriad of shortcuts to help us make sense of the world around us. This limitation announces itself as a blind spot, or bias. Of which we have tons.

I implore you to read Daniel Kahneman's *Thinking Fast and Slow*, a landmark publication that documented his findings from Nobel Prize winning work around human psychology. It's a bit of a mind-bender of a read, but worth it. You will go on a journey through your own blindness.

Bias in business is a dangerous game. Believing one's own hype. Believing that what worked last week will work this week. Believing that your tastes are those of your customers. Bias kills business. And data can be the remedy, as data is the closest tool we have with which to treat truth appropriately. Let's look at one such bias that pollutes the world of business.

Modal bias is the automatic assumption that our idea or approach is best. Most of us like to assume we have everything together – that we know what we're talking about, we know what we're doing and our way of doing things is optimal. Very often, we are quite mistaken. There is always more than one way to get something done, and good ideas can come from anywhere. The HiPPO rules as mentioned – decisions made according to the 'highest paid person's opinion' was coined by Avinash Kaushik in *Web Analytics: An Hour a Day* in order to explain why it's critically important to support business proposals and decisions with data. In the absence of data, you'll ultimately be forced to do things the boss's way: modal bias ensures that the bosses think that their way is best, unless you can prove otherwise. In a battle of opinions, the HiPPO always wins. The best way to avoid modal bias is to use inhibition to temporarily suspend judgement. Part of the value of understanding cognitive biases is the knowledge that you're not immune to them, and simply knowing they exist doesn't make them any less influential. Modal bias is automatic – we have to use willpower to overcome it. If you're a leader or manager, it pays to consciously suspend your judgement long enough to thoroughly consider the perspectives and suggestions of the people you work with.

Otherwise, you're very likely to miss important information. Remind yourself to keep an open mind, and you'll enhance your ability to make wise decisions.[xvi]

It is impossible for us to comprehend true realities given the number of signals thrown at us every waking second (thanks, tech, for greatly adding to the pile) and our deep blind spots make truthful navigation challenging to say the least. Data can be our guardian angel, when collected and used right.

Data reduces cognitive loads. Data streamlines decision-making. Data bolsters precision and accuracy.

The source of truth with regard to data has nuances, however, which brings us to the big data versus small data debate: big data can explain what is happening. But it cannot explain why. Correlation is not causation.[xvii] Melinda Gates said:

We have been forced to rethink some of the way we use data. At the beginning there was a lot of excitement about Big Data, and we still firmly believe that getting better statistics is very important and technology can do amazing things. But we cannot be naïve – understanding the social context matters.

To overcome big data's discrepancies, the likes of Meta, Uber, Amazon and Google are known to embrace ethnography for user research.

An anthropologist named Grant McCracken observed how people consume Netflix, suggesting that the company talk about 'feasting' on shows, not 'bingeing', since that had more positive connotations of control. Again, there is nuance in the data, that needs to be adhered to.

Hard to become data-driven

Data and AI are upending the business world; decision makers and executives are struggling to bring this change into the core of their companies. What's at the root of this slow progress? According to findings from a newly released executive survey from NewVantage Partners for the fifth consecutive year, executives report that cultural challenges – not technological ones – represent the biggest impediment around data initiatives. In the 2021 survey, 92.2 per cent of mainstream companies reported that they continue to struggle with cultural challenges relating to organisational alignment, business processes, change management, communication, people skill sets and resistance or lack of understanding to enable change. This represents an increase from an already high percentage of 80.9 per cent of firms that named cultural challenges as the greatest impediment to success just four years ago.

Like tech at large, the data side of it requires a growth mindset and a culture that prides itself on curiosity and learning. Fostering an environment where everyone is open to new ideas and is data literate is key. Easier said than done of course, but put simply there has to be an understanding and willingness to be data-driven.

Everyone is in the data game

Seemingly 'non-tech' areas of business and society are cottoning on to the benefit of getting into the data game.

The New York Times has been one of the best-known success stories not only for a successful digital transformation strategy, but for business adaptability and sustainability.

The 'Newspaper of Record' used data and analytics to drive key subscription- based decision-making. There needed to be a complete revamp of how data was deployed and how intelligent insights could play a major role in increasing revenues. For this to fructify, the NYT had to transform itself into a data and analytics company and view subscriptions much like how a SaaS entity looks at renewals. By structuring its data and analytics infrastructure into a modern, technologically enhanced environment, it was able to assimilate consumer demographics, understand consumer behaviour and actions and leverage analytics, which enabled the firm to predict what it took for users to renew their subscriptions.

It should be noted that the NYT put proper focus on this data-led digital segment of the media organisation by the establishment of the New York Times Digital (NYTD) in 1999, a separate business unit consisting of all the digital operations.

Kate Swanborg, DreamWorks CEO, said at the 2021 Web Summit:

So here's the secret: Yes. We make movies that we hope viewers will love ... But, behind the scenes, DreamWorks is a digital manufacturer. We make data. Lots and lots of data.

Football star of Manchester City fame Kevin De Bruyne was recently in the midst of contract negotiations to extend his stay at the club for another two years. Unusually, De Bruyne did not use an agent to broker the new deal, conducting negotiations with Man City himself, with his father and lawyer – both in Belgium – assisting remotely. He went data-first. De Bruyne commissioned data analysts to assess his influence at Man City and how well they are set up for success in the coming years, based on the age and qualities of the current squad.

De Bruyne was able to show Man City, through data collected, his enduring value to the team as their most influential player, and used this to negotiate a significant pay rise under the terms of the new deal.[xviii] His weekly pay went up $50,000, from $350,000 per week to $400,000. Not bad for a footballer who upskilled his mindset to keep ahead of the game. He did a *Moneyball* (Michael Lewis's enlightening book, and film, on how the Oakland As utilise data to defy the sporting odds) on himself.

For the third consecutive year, investment in data and AI initiatives has been nearly universal, with 99 per cent of firms reporting investment in these technologies.[xix] Data is as vital to modern-day business as capital and talent.

Look around at home, you buy and consume things. Films, you go to Netflix. Through your and everyone else's use of their platform, it can recommend the films most suited to your taste and interest thanks to its incredible recommendation algorithm. Music, just listen to Spotify's

Discover Weekly, and you can hear the richness of data being used. It's hard not to hit 'Love' on every track. Wine, go to Vivino, to select wines like you might know what you are talking about.

Data and AI are transforming, or on the precipice of transformation at least, industries across human society. Kevin Kelly, in his phenomenal read *The Inevitable: Understanding the 12 Technological Forces That Will Shape Our Future*, forecasts ahead:

Take chemistry. Another physical endeavour requiring laboratories of glassware and bottles brimming with solutions. Move atoms – what could be more physical? By adding AI to chemistry, scientists can perform virtual chemical experiments. They can smartly search through astronomical numbers of chemical combinations to reduce them to a few promising compounds worth examining in a lab.

That was chemistry, what about interior design?:

Add utility AI to a system that matches levels of interest of clients as they walk through simulations of interiors. The design details are altered and tweaked by pattern-finding AI based on customer response, then inserted back into new interiors for further testing. Through constant iterations, optimal personal designs emerge from the AI.

What a world that is right in front of us, thanks to data and AI doing the tango. One more from the *Wired* magazine co-founder, this time regarding the field of law:

You could also apply AI to law, using it to uncover evidence from mountains of paper to discern inconsistencies between cases, and then have it suggest lines of legal arguments.

Gymshark, the apparel e-commerce brand, and one of the most exciting new brands in decades, in my biased opinion having worked with them, got to a happy place of best practices for data. Simple, succinct lessons and applicable to every business:

1. *Respect users' privacy:* Build brand-loyalty and trust with your customers by using first-party data responsibly.
2. *Let your data lead you:* When it comes to building a roadmap for growth, make the shift from "I reckon" to data-informed decision-making.
3. *Partner for efficiency:* Keep your focus on what matters, utilising expert partners for one-off tasks and quicker implementation.
4. *Reassess your KPIs:* Seek a more holistic view of performance, prioritising and measuring user-level data over one-off sessions.
5. *Identify pain points:* Analyse purchase journey data to spot possible gaps, and use problem statements to find a solution.
6. *Optimise for motivations:* Explore how consumer behaviour and needs differ across touchpoints and optimise accordingly.[xx]

Money in them hills

The companies that have grown the most in the past decade are the ones that have data at the heart of their business. They collect it, at scale, analyse the hell out of it and adapt their product or service offering to what they learnt about thousands to millions of customers.

Amazon, Meta and Google have experienced the largest market cap growth in this time. They are data companies. You don't hear of your local bank or retailer building data centres, do you?

Just looking at their primary money-making engines (ignoring Amazon's gigantic retail and cloud businesses of course), that being their advertising engines: US digital ad spending soared past $200 billion in 2021, marking 38.3 per cent growth from 2020. The triopoly of Google, Meta and Amazon making up 64.0 per cent of all the spend.

Crypto has seen a wave of hubristic charlatans believing they are financial Svengalis, set on making millions from digital coins that bear no real value of application in everyday society. These crypto cowboys are missing where true value is being generated. AI's contributions to transportation, finance, and media already dwarf any value recognized from crypto.[xxi]

The fashion industry has seen a giant enter the space, in just the past few short years, seemingly out of nowhere, propelled by a data-first approach to design and distribution.

Shein, a Chinese-backed fast fashion app, uses tech such as Google Trends to find out what's trendy in fashion at the moment, designs the products and then combines in-app and user data to forecast what the demand for its items may be while pushing advertising campaigns through a paid acquisition and influencer programme. This culminates in TikTok trends generating hype before the item has even been produced by Shein.

The company is able to produce the item in such little time that it can keep up with the trends while almost popularising them itself.

The Chinese company is covertly the biggest fashion brand in the world and recently overtook Amazon to become the most downloaded shopping app in the US.[xxii]

With great power comes great responsibility

The collection of data has never been so easy thanks to technology. Every log, browse, click, swipe, dwell and purchase is collected and stored, ready almost in real time for analysis. Regardless of recent industry changes that aim to give more privacy to the everyday person, namely Apple's app tracking changes and the EU's GDPR rollout, these have merely acted as speed bumps. Information on customers can still be gathered, and new means to collect it created.

Due to AI in particular, data's usage comes into vital scrutiny. AI to the everyday person can be perceived as another reason for the end of the world being nigh, thanks to pop culture moments like *Minority Report* and Microsoft releasing an AI bot on Twitter, that turned racist, very quickly.

Data and AI aren't evil. The people using and building them can range from the unempathetic to straight-up arseholes though, resulting in AI optimising for negative societal outcomes.

Just be sound with data, people, and all will be rosy.

Chapter 6

BE OPEN

THE ARTIST DOES NOT VALUE SAFETY AND SMALLNESS. REDUCING OUR PALETTE TO FIT THE PERIMETER OF LIMITED BELIEFS SUPPRESSES THE WORK. NEW CREATIVE POSSIBILITIES AND SOURCES OF INSPIRATION ARE BLOCKED FROM VIEW. IF AN ARTIST KEEPS PLAYING THE SAME NOTE, EVENTUALLY THE AUDIENCE LOSES INTEREST.

— Rick Rubin

Openness is quite the virtue in tech. A culture of openness pervades tech. Internal access and flow of information are paramount to the growth story (hyper-secretive Apple aside). Being a good boy or girl within your company is one thing, how about playing nice with others outside the company, even to the extent of being nice to your direct competitors?

Welcome to a brave new world, where the company 'eating your lunch' today is the same company you have to get into bed with tomorrow. That requires a whole mindset shift, a mindset ingrained in the key talent in tech. Being open is the mindset du jour of tech, thanks to the engineering culture around open- source coding.

The value of openness is something most of us are only just getting to grips with. Harvard Business School published a report in 2006 that surveyed a range of businesses and concluded that introducing problems to outsiders was the best way to find effective solutions. A European Union report released in 2007 specifically endorsed open-source software, claiming that in 'almost all' cases, long-term costs could be reduced by switching from proprietary software to open-source systems such as Linux. The study also claimed that the number of existing open-source programs already available would have cost firms 12 billion euros (£8 billion) to build, and estimated that the programs available represent the equivalent of 131,000 programmer years, or 'at least 800 million Euros (£525 million) in voluntary contributions from programmers alone each year.'[i] That was 2007, you could multiply that amount tenfold to reflect the value in more modern times.

Collaborations are all the rage in business and media today. Look at LEGO. LEGO opening up its IP (intellectual property, or brand for use) has brought game-changing growth, making it the world's most valuable brand. Adidas, Sonic the Hedgehog, Star Wars and IKEA are just some of the names LEGO has done a 'LEGO x …' with. Stretching its consumer reach wider and further.

In tech, partnering and laying bare to those who would seem to be competitors is becoming the norm. Elon Musk is now partnering with Google — one (soon-to-be) self-driving car manufacturer collaborating with another, although not partnering in that category in which they directly compete.

Google has partnered with SpaceX to provide cloud services to help deliver internet through the latter's Starlink satellites.

Under the deal, Elon Musk's space development company will install Starlink ground stations at Google data centres that connect to Starlink satellites, with the aim to enable high-speed broadband internet via Google Cloud.

Jeff Bezos is quite the proponent of partnerships. In shareholder letters he has been known to talk up the expansion of Amazon's partnership programs:

Through our platform, we are able to bring tremendous value to our partners, such as drugstore.com. In fact, our experience so far suggests that Amazon.com may easily be the most efficient, effective means for our partners to build their businesses. In many areas, partnering is the best way for us to rapidly expand our store in a customer-focused, cost-effective manner. One point worth emphasising: the quality of customer experience a partner delivers is the single most important criteria in our selection process – we simply won't build a partnership with any company that does not share our passion for serving customers.[ii]

In tech, openness isn't just a nice piece of the culture pie, it's a profound growth driver.

They all partner

It will surprise you, how closely tech companies partner with each other, especially the tech giants who mainstream society deems as mortal enemies. They may look like direct competitors, but there are teams and departments in each company working closely with the 'enemy'.

In sales departments in tech companies, the language is all about partnering. Sales reps look to 'partner' with clients on their growth. It's a subtle but key distinction from solely looking at them as clients, less transactional sounding. It opens up deeper, more collaborative work between the companies.

Partnerships come in a myriad of different forms. Many arrangements of partnerships exist for different purposes. Be it entry to new markets and access to customers, or technical integrations in the name of further scale. A former colleague from my Facebook days, Rich

O'Connell, gave a great breakdown recently of the purpose and formations of various partnerships below:

Channel partnerships

These types of partnerships most commonly involve working with third parties who will SELL or provide SERVICES around your products.

You could work with experts who can help you sell into new GEOGRAPHIES, new INDUSTRIES or specific customer SEGMENTS (SMB, Mid-Market, Enterprise).

Based on the complexity of your product, you might need partners who can help customers implement your solution, manage the solution or run training programs to help them get the most value from the product.

'Distributors and resellers typically drive 70% or more of a tech vendor's revenue,' according to the Boston Consulting Group (BCG).

Resellers / value-added-resellers (VARs)

These are companies that focus on selling your product for you (resellers) and can often add additional value in the form of packaging your product with other complimentary products or provide some services to help customers be more successful (VARs). You often sell your products at a discount to these partners and they can resell for a higher price and keep the difference (their margin).

System integrators (SIs)

These are companies that specialise in helping companies solve hard technical challenges or work through digital transformations. They can be small, local experts or be large, global consulting companies (GSIs) like Accenture. They may help resell your product based on the margin they can make and/or the demand they see from clients.

Managed service providers

These companies can sell, but also manage your product on behalf of customers. This can be of value where the product itself can be very complicated (SAP) or the product is used in a complex, dynamic industry (digital advertising).

Examples of channel partnership programs

Microsoft have one of the oldest and best-known channel programs in the industry, with 95% of their revenue coming via their partners. Stewart Townsend, who built channel programs at Zendesk and DataSift, recommends companies invest in channel sales when they hit 50+ employees and $1+ million in revenue.

Setting the right expectations is key. 'You are not usually going to knock out double-digit millions in revenue from a partnership strategy in year one. You have to get tightly aligned with your executive team and the board as to what they should expect in the short term,' says Sendoso's Brian Jambor.[iii]

Joint ventures (JV)

In this scenario, two or more companies pool resources (money, people, IP) and work towards a shared outcome. They often create a new legal entity to make it easier to share returns and risks.

Strategic JV

This is where companies partner to work towards a larger strategic goal, which would be harder to achieve independently. Sony Ericsson is an example of a JV between two large companies. In this case, they partnered in the early 2000s with the aim of being a world leader in mobile phones. After several years of operating as a JV, the venture eventually became solely owned by Sony.

Another example of a joint venture is the joint venture between the taxi giant UBER and the vehicle manufacturer Volvo. The joint venture goal was to produce driverless cars. The ratio of ownership was 50%-50% and the business worth was $350 million as per the agreement in the joint venture.

Distribution agreement

These JVs often focus on trying to enter a new market or geography. Starbucks frequently utilises joint ventures to enter new, emerging markets; in 2012, it established a joint venture agreement with Tata Global Beverages to own and manage Starbucks stores in India. This joint venture operates over 216 locations.

Project-based JV

Here companies pool resources with a very specific goal in mind, often for shorter periods of time. An example here is GSK and Sanofi, two of the world's biggest pharmaceutical giants, joining forces in 2020 to create a vaccine to stop the spread of COVID-19.

Research-based JV

These partnerships often focus on developing complex, new technology which can give partners a strategic advantage, or have them become table-stakes to stay relevant in a given industry. A good example here is BMW and Toyota co- operating on research into hydrogen fuel cells and ultra-lightweight materials, so they can both remain market leaders in these emerging areas.

Product partnerships

Product, or platform, partnerships usually resolve around building integrations with complimentary products from partners.

They may help fill gaps in your own product portfolio, they may be in response to customer demand or the integrated products may provide a better experience for customers which helps with customer satisfaction (CSAT, NPS) or reduces customer churn.

They may take a little longer to start than other types of partnerships, but once you build solid foundations here, they can be very scalable and add lots of value for your company and your customers.

Strategic integrations

This is where companies work together to deeply integrate their products, in a seamless (native, out-of-the-box) way, that tries to make them feel and act like they are the same product.

The logic here is that the combined products provide more customer value then the siloed products could, and often do, make the combined solution more competitive and attractive.

Some examples of this kind of partnership:

- *In Atlassian's code management product, Bitbucket, you can now use security capabilities from Snyk, a leading application security company.*
- *Salesforce and AWS have partnered to allow their customers to more easily access their data cross-platform, to enable easier app development.*
- *Shopify and Stripe have partnered to allow for easy payment processing for Shopify merchants.*

They are customers of each other

Tech reminds me of the app that was created in Iceland to prevent people hooking up with someone who could be their direct relative due to the small population in the country. All of the tech companies are hooking up with each other in some way or another, and here we see they have no problem paying for the hook-ups.

Apple is reportedly now Google Cloud's largest customer in terms of storage. Cupertino was on track to spend around $300 million on Google Cloud storage in 2021, an increase of around 50 per cent on 2020. Apple's status as the platform's largest customer, reportedly 'dwarfing' other high-profile GCP customers, has led to staff giving Apple the internal code name 'Bigfoot'.

This is fascinating when you think of how directly they compete for mobile market share with iPhone versus Android.

Spotify was Google's next largest customer with about 460 petabytes of data, Twitter after that with 315 petabytes, and Snapchat with about 275 petabytes.[iv]

Amazon's cloud service, Amazon Web Services, counts Snap and Pinterest as some of its largest customers. Snap and Pinterest make their money from advertising, an area Amazon have also entered in recent years. In fact Amazon now comes third in market share for digital ad dollars, after Google and Meta.

APIs and marketplaces

If you think of the code as the TV in your living room, as the object capable of carrying information to you, then APIs (application programming inter-faces) are the channels you flick through to get to the show you want to watch. APIs are the connections between one company and another, used to unlock a certain feature or functionality. APIs are the embodiment of openness between different companies. Almost like a pub and restaurant, with separate owners, sharing staff, who get on well with their customers.

An API is a set of protocols, routines, and tools used for building software applications. APIs provide a way for different software applications to communicate with each other and exchange information, without requiring developers to understand the underlying technology or implementation details.

APIs typically define a set of rules for how different software components can interact with each other. This includes specifying the types of data that can be exchanged, the format of that data, and the specific methods or functions that can be called to access or manipulate that data.

A well-used API, unbeknown to the everyday user, is Google's Maps API. The Google Maps API is an API that allows developers to integrate Google Maps into their own applications. This API provides access to a wide range of features, including displaying maps and satellite imagery, searching for locations, calculating directions, and even providing street-level imagery.

Developers can use this API to build custom applications that integrate Google Maps functionality, such as location-based services, real-time traffic updates, or geospatial analysis tools. The Google Maps API is just one example of the many APIs available that enable developers to build powerful and innovative software applications.

APIs can be used to integrate different software applications, enable third- party developers to build plugins or extensions for existing software, or expose certain functionality of a software application to other applications or services.

Each API supplier provides only a piece of the solution. Amazon Web Services delivers the data centre. Twilio provides communications. Stripe and PayPal enable payments. Modern apps integrate dozens of these small components into a unique value proposition for the customer. This shift to component software is the next big leap in the evolution of the software industry.[v]

Outsource innovation

It takes a certain level of humility for a successful company to admit it may not have all the answers. This is when tech companies tend to look outside for innovation opportunities. By developing and extending external innovation programs broadly, corporate innovators consider tools that allow them to become partners and collaborators with other innovators, thus bringing these breakthroughs into supporting rather than disrupting roles in the plans of the corporation as licensing partners, go-to-market partners and sometimes in joint ventures.

The Netflix Prize is probably the most famous happening of a tech company looking outside for inspiration, and putting up a juicy reward. It was an open competition for the best collaborative filtering algorithm to predict user ratings for films, based on previous ratings without any other information about the users or films, that is without the users or the films being identified except by numbers assigned for the contest.

The prize? A cool $1 million, won by BellKor's Pragmatic Chaos team, which bested Netflix's own algorithm for predicting ratings by 10.06 per cent.

Meaning it improved the possibility of you finding another godforsaken TV show to binge-watch and 'chill' to.

If you can't beat 'em, buy 'em

Mark Zuckerberg will go down in history as one of the most astute acquirers of companies in tech history. Instagram, WhatsApp, Oculus. The first two started life as companies gobbling up user attention and the latter is a VR company that seemed to have cracked how to mainstream virtual reality.

Just look at Instagram. Meta bought Instagram for $1 billion in 2012, a shocking sum at that time for a company with thirteen employees.

Instagram today has well over 1.3 billion users and contributes over $27 billion to Facebook's annual revenue. Bargain, with a capital B.

Zuckerberg realised the threats to his own company, and decided to buy in the competition. A practice all too common in tech, as seen in the land of M&A, mergers and acquisitions. These partnership scenarios range from buying a company outright to making a strategic monetary investment in them to help with alignment and access.

A common trope in tech with regard to innovation is 'build or buy'. And in Meta's case, they have often pushed the 'buy' button. Here are examples of the myriad of ways to buy, acquire, lure and snare other companies:

Direct acquisition

You buy the company and integrate its products, intellectual property (IP) and people into your business. This can often be a good choice if you want to enter a new industry or customer segment quickly. The product you acquire will often live on as a stand-alone offering under your company brand.

Tuck-in

In this scenario, you also buy the company outright, but their products become a *feature* in your existing portfolio and do not live on as a stand-alone offering. This can be a great way to accelerate your road map in specific areas.

Acquire

In this scenario, you acquire another company, but only for the people and their expertise. You often end of life (EOL) their product, but you may highly value the domain expertise these people can bring to your organisation. EOL does exactly what it says on the tin, it gets kicked to the bin.

Strategic funding

Here, you may make an investment in another company. This could be to help increase alignment, and provide more opportunities to partner down the road, or make it easier to work through a full acquisition at a later date. Many large tech companies have investment funds to perform these programs at scale.

Examples of different types of M&A

M&A is far from straightforward. Every season of *Succession* will illuminate such complexities, there is drama and human bias involved. Let's add more types of M&A to the mix to complicate things further shall we?

There is horizontal acquisition, market extension acquisition, vertical acquisition, conglomerate acquisition, congeneric acquisition, and triangular merger. Lost you?

A horizontal acquisition is when two companies of the same size and scope merge together. A market extension acquisition is when a company acquires another company in a different market in order to enter that market. A vertical acquisition is when a company acquires another company at a different stage in the production process. A conglomerate acquisition is when a company acquires a company in a different industry. A congeneric acquisition is when a company acquires a company in a related industry. A triangular merger is when two companies merge and a third company acquires the merged entity.

Google has made a number of different types of mergers and acquisitions over the years. These include horizontal acquisitions, such as the purchase of YouTube in 2006; market extension acquisitions, such as the purchase of DoubleClick (digital ads serving platform) in 2007; vertical acquisitions, such as its purchase of Motorola in 2012; conglomerate acquisitions, such as its purchase of Nest Labs (thermostats and home automation) in 2014; congeneric acquisitions, such as its purchase of DeepMind Technologies (artificial intelligence) in 2014; and triangular mergers, such as its purchase of Apigee (API management) in 2016.

Build, or buy. Google go buy buy.

Ownership and openness tomorrow

In October 2021, Mark Zuckerberg laid down the gauntlet for the next era of computing, the next frontier from the current computing era we are in, which is mobile. Enter, the metaverse.

What the metaverse is, very simply, is a new dawn of the internet where ownership is in the ability of the everyday user. Others are calling it Web 3.0.

Web 1.0 was 'read', in that you just browsed websites when 'surfing the web'. Web 2.0 was 'read and write', where we users became creators. Blogging, posting selfies, ice bucket challenges, and so on. We contributed.

Web 3.0, or the metaverse, is 'read, write and own'. We will have digital properties akin to the real world. The goal of Web 3.0 is to create a more open, transparent, and user-centric web that empowers individuals and communities, rather than large corporations and centralized authorities.

How it fully plays out is five to ten years away really. I could sit here and speculate what it will look like with you but such predictions are futile for now. What I can say is the key implication of the metaverse to businesses is that openness will be paramount to survival.

Everything's getting more digital. The line of ownership will get blurred initially. Those open to change and partnership with other businesses, and indeed their customers (who could own God-knows-what digital stuff), are best prepared to ride the new wave of digital disruption.

Grow Like Tech

What worked last week won't work this week.

Chapter 7
FAIL FAST

WHAT WOULD YOU DO IF YOU WEREN'T AFRAID?

— Meta poster motto

This is a poignant dollop of text that adorned posters around Meta's offices. A chin scratcher. A question designed to reframe your thinking, particularly when it comes to failure.

Few words are more polarising in the world of business than failure. In Silicon Valley, there's this strange fetishization of failure. People talk openly about celebrating failure. Investors talk about rewarding a founder who fails by funding their next company. There's a zealotry towards failure that's baked so deep into the DNA of Silicon Valley that you'd almost imagine highly successful entrepreneurs walking around sulking, with dreams of eventual failure dancing in their heads. But it's not the failure that's celebrated, it's the deep learnings that advance the mission. Failure is merely accepted as a natural consequence of the learning. When people talk about accepting failure, they're talking about accepting the journey, or adventure rather, of discovery.[i]

Tech's modus operandi is innovation. Failure is the most vital electrical current of innovation. Tech aspires to create environments safe for failure. Some even brag about it, most notably Jeff Bezos on Amazon: 'We are the best place in the world to fail.' Bezos continues:

Failure needs to scale too. As a company grows, everything needs to scale, including the size of your failed experiments. If the size of your failures isn't growing, you're not going to be inventing at a size that can actually move the needle.[ii]

Research by Amy Edmondson of Harvard Business School demonstrates, in her work on psychological safety, that a culture of safety – where leaders are inclusive, humble and encourage their staff to speak up or ask for help – leads to better learning and performance outcomes. Rather than creating a culture of fear of negative consequences, feeling safe in the workplace helps encourage the spirit of experimentation so critical for innovation. 'What would you do if you are not afraid?' nukes the workplace fear of failure.

Successful innovators know that the path to success may be lined with failed attempts. Thomas Edison once said, 'I have not failed. I've just found ten thousand ways that won't work.' Winston Churchill noted, 'Success is stumbling from failure to failure with no loss of enthusiasm.'

But my favourite take on failure and experimentation comes from Jeff Bezos. In his 2015 letter to Amazon shareholders, Bezos reminded investors that three of Amazon's biggest successes – Marketplace, Prime and Amazon Web Services – began as experiments, and that, when they were conceived, nobody knew whether they would work or not. After all, most of the company's experiments fail. Bezos used a baseball analogy to explain why he pushes his developers to keep running as many experiments as possible: 'If you swing for the fences, you're going to strike out a lot, but you're also going to hit some home runs.' He went on to note that in baseball, the very best outcome from swinging the bat is a grand slam, scoring four runs. However, 'in business, every once in a while, when you step up to the plate, you can score 1,000 runs.'

Fail fast, fail hard, fail well

Tech's take on failure is that it embraces it with open arms, and like an adult who hugs their upset child, seeks to comfort that little ball of failure, and help it learn lessons for the future. Tech loves to optimise failure. How it fails is crucial.

Let's step away from tech for a wee moment, and look at how two other industries look at failure and optimise it. Or in the case of one industry, optimises failure like an ostrich with its head so far in the sand that it's reached Australia. Our example comes from *Black Box Thinking: The Surprising Truth About Success*, Matthew Syed's absolutely phenomenal book on failure that I can't recommend enough.

He looked at the make-up of two critical industries to understand how their cultures ticked, those industries being healthcare and aviation. He found that these organisations have differences in psychology, culture and institutional change. But the most profound difference is in their divergent approaches to failure. In the airline industry the attitude is striking and unusual. Every aircraft is equipped with two almost-indestructible black boxes, one of which records instructions sent to the onboard electronic systems, and another that records the conversations and sounds in the cockpit. If there is an accident, the boxes are opened, the data is analysed, and the reason for the accident excavated. This ensures that procedures can be changed so that the same error never happens again.

On the other side of the industry divide, healthcare has a very different attitude regarding failure. In 1999, the American Institute of Medicine published a landmark investigation called 'To Err Is Human'. It reported that between 44,000 and 98,000 Americans die each year as a result of preventable medical errors. In a separate investigation, Lucian Leape, a Harvard University professor, put the overall numbers higher.

In a comprehensive study, he estimated that a million patients are injured by errors during hospital treatment and that 120,000 die each year in America alone. But these statistics, while shocking, almost certainly underestimate the true scale of the problem. In 2013 a study published in the *Journal of Patient Safety* put the number of premature deaths associated with preventable harm at more than 400,000 per year. (Categories of avoidable harm include misdiagnosis, dispensing the wrong drugs, injuring the patient during surgery, operating on the wrong part of the body, improper transfusions, falls, burns, pressure ulcers and postoperative complications.) Testifying to a Senate hearing in the summer of 2014, Peter J. Pronovost, MD, professor at the Johns Hopkins University School of Medicine and one of the most respected clinicians in the world, pointed out that this is the equivalent of two jumbo jets falling out of the sky every twenty-four hours.

Why is this the case? Historically, healthcare institutions have not routinely collected data on how accidents happen, and so cannot detect meaningful patterns, let alone learn from them. Also if a doctor scuffles a diagnosis or procedure, they are at risk of a legal challenge, particularly in the US with its residents' ravenous love for suing one another. With healthcare, the culture is one of evasion. Accidents are described as 'one-offs' or 'one of those things'. Doctors say, 'We did the best we could.' This is the most common response to failure in the world today. In aviation, things are radically different: learning from failure is hard-wired into the system.

Learning from failure literally saves lives as seen in these two industries. Tech is more like aviation. Just with thousands upon thousands of black boxes, or alpha and beta tests as tech likes to call them. And learning from failure saves businesses from dying.

To innovate, you must learn to fail well. Learn from your mistakes: any failed project should yield valuable technical, user and market insights that can help inform the next effort. Morph ideas, don't kill them: most of the world's great innovations started out with entirely different applications, so when you end a project, look carefully at its components to see how they might be reapplied elsewhere. As Larry Page says, "If you are thinking big enough it is very hard to fail completely. There is usually something very valuable left."[iii]

How tech fails is also a point of fascination. It spreads the risk. A muscle built for iterative experimentation allows tech to fail regularly and lightly. But add up the multitude of learnings, and 'magic' can come. Pixar's Ed Catmull said, 'Early on, all of our movies suck. That's a blunt assessment, I know, but I … choose that phrasing because saying it in a softer way fails to convey how bad the first versions of our films really are. I'm not trying to be modest or self-effacing by saying this. Pixar films are not good at first, and our job is to make them go … from suck to non-suck … We are true believers in the power of bracing, candid feedback and the iterative process – reworking, reworking and reworking again, until a flawed story finds its throughline or a hollow character finds its soul.'

This process was at the forefront during the *Finding Nemo* film. Realising the need to fail and move forward, bit by bit, Pixar reverted to disciplined iteration. First they adapted the narrative to a more chronological approach – and it began to align. The tale of the Tank Gang became a subplot. Other changes, smaller, but cumulatively significant, began to emerge. By the end, the film had gone from suck to non-suck. Catmull writes: 'Despite our hopes that *Finding Nemo* would be the film that changed the way we did business, we ended up making as many adjustments during production as we had on any other film we had made. The result, of course, was a movie we're incredibly proud of, one that went on to become the highest grossing animated film ever. The only thing it didn't do was transform our production process'.[iv]

Framing failure – feedback is a gift

Nobody wants to be told they are shit. The essence of failure in our society – that failure is profoundly negative, something to be ashamed of in ourselves and judgemental about in others – has deep cultural and psychological roots. According to Sidney Dekker, a psychologist and systems expert at Griffith University, Australia, the tendency to stigmatise errors is at least 2,500 years old.

So it's a touchy subject. How it is communicated and felt by the recipient is something that must be carefully approached. Tech to the rescue. 'Feedback is a gift' was another poster that dotted the walls of Facebook's offices around the world. It works so well in disarming the negative connotation of feedback. Making it virtuous to give and receive feedback.

There are two types of failure according to Jeff Bezos:

There's experimental failure – that's the kind of failure you should be happy with. And there's operational failure. We've built hundreds of fulfilment centres at Amazon over the years, and we know how to do that. If we build a new fulfilment center and it's a disaster, that's just bad execution. That's not good failure. But when we are developing a new product or service or experimenting in some way, and it doesn't work, that's okay. That's great failure. And you need to distinguish between those two types of failure and really be seeking invention and innovation.[v]

At Netflix, employees are encouraged to get on the front foot with failure, to lean right into critiques. In verb form too. Netflix employees are driven to 'farm for dissent'. If you are a Netflix employee with a proposal, you create a shared memo explaining the idea and invite dozens of your colleagues for input. They will then leave comments electronically in the margin of your document, which everyone can view. Simply glancing through the comments can give you a feeling for the variety of dissenting and supporting viewpoints.

The more actively employees farm for dissent, and the more you encourage a culture of expressing disagreement openly, the better the decisions that will be made in your company. This is true for any company of any size in any industry.[vi]

Some companies wrap tech around their quest for feedback. E-commerce company NextJump have an app for that. An actual feedback app for employees to log feedback for each other quickly and succinctly. Quicker feedback, quicker learning.

Soundstripe, the music royalty tech platform, say, 'Fail quickly and cheaply'. The only stipulations they have for failures are:

1. *If your idea fails, be self-aware and humble, quickly move on to the next project.*
2. *That failure shouldn't break the bank. Test ideas as cheaply as you can. If they work, we can scale them later.*

At Patreon, it's explicit that feedback is crucial to their mission:

If one falls short of our high expectations, they will know about it because we give and receive candid feedback constantly. We help our teammates through tough times, just as we expect our teammates to stick with Patreon through tough times – to the extent that it serves our mission. We don't expect anyone to stay with Patreon if we aren't the best way to fund the creative class. And Patreon won't retain someone if having them on our team is not the best way to achieve our mission.

Be open about failings

Framing failure is only the beginning. The consistent broadcasting of failure is another trait of tech that's to be admired.

One way of communicating attitudes to failure is the actions taken against those who fail. Eric Schmidt understood this greatly when building Google:

Don't stigmatize the team that failed: Make sure they land good internal jobs. The next innovators will be watching to see if the failed team is punished. Their failure shouldn't be celebrated, but it is a badge of honor of sorts. At least they tried.[vii]

Reed Hastings brought rays of sunshine to failure. Well, not really, but at Netflix he called it 'sunshining' failure. That is, shining a light on failure and taking the good from it, the good being the learning, which means talking openly and publicly about things that go wrong. And he leads on communicating the sunshine:

Every time I feel I've made a mistake, I talk about it fully, publicly, and frequently. I quickly came to see the biggest advantage of sunshining a leader's errors is to encourage everyone to think of making mistakes as normal. This in turn encourages employees to take risks when success is uncertain ... which leads to greater innovation across the company. Self-disclosure builds trust, seeking help boosts learning, admitting mistakes fosters forgiveness, and broadcasting failures encourages your people to act courageously. We want all employees taking bets they believe in and trying new things, even when the boss or others think the ideas are dumb. When some of those bets don't pay off, we just fix the problems that arise as quickly as possible and discuss what we've learned. In our creative business, rapid recovery is the best model.[viii]

When failure crops up, Asana takes an interestingly pragmatic approach, softening the blow whilst also extracting as much understanding as possible. Asana has an "Ask 5 Whys" exercise embedded in the culture:

We treat 'failures' as opportunities for growth. When things don't go according to plan, we run a 5 Whys exercise. By the time we reach our fifth 'Why' we reach the root of the problem and can better avoid the same issues in the future.

Win or learn

FAILURE AND INVENTION ARE INSEPERABLE TWINS. TO INVENT YOU HAVE TO EXPERIMENT, AND IF YOU KNOW IN ADVANCE THAT IT'S GOING TO WORK, IT'S NOT AN EXPERIMENT.

— Jeff Bezos

'What were the learnings?' is one of the most progressive things the fresh Facebook-er in me heard when starting at the company. It opened up new pathways in my brain. To look at trying things out and talking about them afterwards in a completely new way. No 'ostriching' with one's head in the sand. Getting learnings was a mark of achievement, quite often at least.

In a sense, tech takes a scientific mindset into failure. One of the most important lessons of the scientific method is that if you cannot fail, you cannot learn. Trial and error is the name of the game. I'll also argue taking action in itself enables better learnings. A bias for action accelerates the opportunity to win or learn. And tech cleverly, with prototyping and beta testing as we will chat more about later, sets the platform to play to that old adage, 'Practice makes perfect.'

In effect, practice is about harnessing the benefits of learning from failure while reducing its cost. It is better to fail during practice in preparation for the big stage than on the big stage itself. This is true of organisations, too, which conduct pilot schemes (and in the case of aviation and other safety-critical industries test ideas in simulators) in order to learn, before rolling out new ideas or procedures. The more we can fail in practice, the more we can learn, enabling us to succeed when it really matters.[ix]

The notion of getting into the trial-and-error process early informs one of the most elegant ideas to have emerged from the high-tech revolution: the lean start-up. This approach contains a great deal of jargon, but is based on a simple insight: the value of testing and adapting. High-tech entrepreneurs are often brilliant theorists. They can perform complex mathematics in their sleep. But the lean start-up approach forces them to fuse these skills with what they can discover from failure.[x]

Resilience as a trait to think and hire

Failure at company level is open to change. How it is viewed. How it is rewarded, or punished. Tech looks to optimise failure. But what about at an individual level? That's where we step into the wibbly wobbly world of humans and their jolly biases.

When we are confronted with evidence that challenges our deeply held beliefs, we are more likely to reframe the evidence than we are to alter our beliefs. We simply invent new reasons, new justifications, new explanations. Sometimes we ignore the evidence altogether.

In his seminal book *Why Smart Executives Fail: And What You Can Learn from Their Mistakes*, Sydney Finkelstein, a management professor at Dartmouth College, investigated major failures at over fifty corporate institutions. He found that error-denial increases as you go up the pecking order. Ironically enough, the higher people are in the management hierarchy, the more they tend to supplement their perfectionism with blanket excuses, with CEOs usually being the worst of all. For example, in one organisation they studied, the CEO spent the entire forty-five-minute interview explaining all the reasons why others were to blame for the calamity that hit his company. Regulators, customers, the government, and even other executives within the firm – all were responsible. No mention was made, however, of personal culpability.[xi]

There is a range of biases and blind spots to be aware of to counteract unnecessary failures. Let's look at the most crucial ones that affect business practice, which, by the way, tech also suffers from.

'Cognitive dissonance' occurs when mistakes are too threatening to admit to, so they are reframed or ignored. This can be thought of as the internal fear of failure: how we struggle to admit mistakes to ourselves.

Then there is 'confirmation bias'. The philosopher Karl Popper wrote:

For if we are uncritical we shall always find what we want: we shall look for, and find, confirmations, and we shall look away from, and not see, whatever might be dangerous to our pet theories. In this way it is only too easy to obtain ... overwhelming evidence in favour of a theory which, if approached critically, would have been refuted. Confirmation bias in action, and it is eerily reminiscent of early medicine (where doctors interpreted any outcome in their patients as an affirmation of bloodletting). It provides another reason why the scientific mindset, with a healthy emphasis on falsification, is so vital. It acts as a corrective to our tendency to spend our time confirming what we think we already know, rather than seeking to discover what we don't know.[xii]

We also have a tendency to underestimate the complexity around us, which is now a well-studied aspect of human psychology and it is underpinned, in part, by the so-called 'narrative fallacy'. We are so eager to impose patterns on what we see, so hardwired to provide explanations, that we are capable of 'explaining' opposite outcomes with the same cause without noticing the inconsistency. Daniel Kahneman has said:

Narrative fallacies arise inevitably from our continuous attempt to make sense of the world. The explanatory stories that people find compelling are simple; are concrete rather than abstract; assign a larger role to talent, stupidity, and intentions than to luck; and focus on a few striking events that happened rather than on the countless events that failed to happen. Any recent salient event is a candidate to become the kernel of a causal narrative.[xiii]

Last but not least, the desire for perfection rests on two fallacies. The first resides in the miscalculation that you can create the optimal solution sitting in a bedroom or ivory tower and thinking things through rather than getting out into the real world and testing assumptions, thus finding their flaws. It is the problem of valuing top-down over bottom-up. The second fallacy is the fear of failure. Earlier on we looked at situations where people fail and then proceed to either ignore or conceal those failures. Perfectionism is, in many ways, more extreme. You spend so much time designing and strategising that you don't get a chance to fail at all, at least until it is too late. It is pre-closed loop behaviour. You are so worried about messing up that you never even get on to the field of play.

So when looking at an individual level, it's important to take an objective view as far as possible, accounting for biases at an unconscious level.

And then you need people with a significant amount of resilience, or grit, to deal with failure. Without that in the individuals in a company, cultural processes and beliefs only go so far.

The deepest and most overlooked truth is that innovation cannot happen without failure. Indeed, the aversion to failure is the single largest obstacle to creative change, not just in business but beyond.

Tech start-ups create experiments to try things out without causing financial ruin. This is key to inspiring a culture of trust. When a start-up is set up properly, there's no incentive to cover up failure; the whole idea is to search for truth.

After all, feedback is a gift. Push for truth, even when it challenges you to your core.

IT'S FINE TO CELEBRATE SUCCESS BUT IT'S MORE IMPORTANT TO HEED THE LESSONS OF FAILURE.

— Bill Gates

Chapter 8

LEADERSHIP

GOOD LEADERS BUILD PRODUCTS. GREAT LEADERS BUILD CULTURES. GOOD LEADERS DELIVER RESULTS. GREAT LEADERS DEVELOP PEOPLE. GOOD LEADERS HAVE VISION. GREAT LEADERS HAVE VALUES. GOOD LEADERS ARE ROLE MODELS AT WORK. GREAT LEADERS ARE ROLE MODELS IN LIFE.

— Adam Grant

Steve Jobs, Bill Gates, Mark Zuckerberg, Sundar Pichai, Melissa Mayer, Elon Musk, Susan Wojcicki, Jeff Bezos, Whitney Wolfe, Satya Nadella, Brian Chesky, Reed Hastings. Just some of the names of lore in modern tech. Their names carry with them semblances of greatness, of genius. They are the leaders.

Some view tech cultures as, well, cults. And any good cult has itself a powerful, enigmatic leader or two. Tech certainly has its leaders put on pedestals. Tech leaders are brands nowadays, like popular musicians or athletes. The nerds are the cool kids.

And it all started with Steve.

We need to talk about Steve

AGAIN AND AGAIN OVER THE LAST FOUR DECADES, STEVE JOBS SAW THE FUTURE AND BROUGHT IT TO LIFE LONG BEFORE MOST PEOPLE COULD EVEN SEE THE HORIZON.

— James Dyson

Steve Jobs redefined how a tech exec looks and acts, going further, how any person in business looks and acts. Such is the mystique surrounding Apple's co- founder and CEO of the company at the time of his passing in 2011, he has been idolised in modern culture. The man is basically seen as the Jesus Christ of tech.

Such is his influence that there have been ten, and counting, books written on him, as well as two major Hollywood films (nice job, Michael Fassbender; Ashton Kutcher, not so much) and a character in the Simpsons. He is the poster boy for tech. An entire person and company was modelled on his spirit and aesthetic with Elizabeth Holmes and Theranos, albeit with dire consequences. Check out the documentary *The Inventor: Out for Blood in Silicon Valley* for a good look at pretty wild levels of mimicry.

There was charisma. There was daring. He was an acid-taking buck coupled with relentless focus. That perfect hybrid of curiosity and persistence. His vision and relentless pursuit of perfection to realise the vision is something else.

Eric Schmidt and Jonathan Rosenberg had this to say about him:

Steve Jobs saw this future with great clarity. There is no better example of the impact a smart creative can have on the world than him. He embodied a combination of technical depth, artistic and creative talent, and business savvy that allowed him to create computing products with which people actually fell in love. He merged beauty and science in a tech community that had a lot of nerds and business people, but very few artists. The two of us learned a lot about smart creatives from working with and observing Steve, about how much personal style can influence company culture and about how that culture is directly tied to success.[i]

Jobs's impact on the world wasn't just the iPhone. His impact was felt across generations, from revolutionising personal computers with the introduction of the Macintosh in 1984. The original Macintosh is the first successful mass- market all-in-one desktop personal computer to have featured a graphical user interface, built-in screen and mouse.[ii]

After being controversially ousted from his company only to return in 1997 to save it from the brink of bankruptcy, he brought to the world the iPod and iPhone, which became the most valuable consumer products in history. Not only that, he brought beautiful design to the masses and the spirit of 'Think Different'.

He has left behind a legacy where he is the gold standard in tech leadership, which isn't necessarily a good thing as he was infamous for his manipulative, dogged ways at times. He is emulated in some shape or form by most in tech. Everyone in tech refers to him and his lessons. Here are a few of his finest musings; it's hard not to get overwhelmingly inspired by his words:

Your time is limited, so don't waste it living someone else's life.

We're here to put a dent in the universe. Otherwise why else even be here?

My model for business is The Beatles: They were four guys that kept each other's negative tendencies in check; they balanced each other. And the total was greater than the sum of the parts.

Be a yardstick of quality. Some people aren't used to an environment where excellence is expected.

I'm convinced that about half of what separates successful entrepreneurs from the non-successful ones is pure perseverance.

Principles, principles, principles

Like tech's coded values and behaviours, its leaders get a thoughtful playbook to work with in the form of leadership principles, designed to show leaders what great looks like for the betterment of the culture and company values.

Amazon has the following leadership principles:

Customer Obsession

Leaders start with the customer and work backwards. They work vigorously to earn and keep customer trust. Although leaders pay attention to competitors, they obsess over customers.

Ownership

Leaders are owners. They think long term and don't sacrifice long-term value for short-term results. They act on behalf of the entire company, beyond just their own team. They never say 'that's not my job'.

Invent and Simplify

Leaders expect and require innovation and invention from their teams and always find ways to simplify. They are externally aware, look for new ideas from everywhere and are not limited by 'not invented here'. As we do new things, we accept that we may be misunderstood for long periods of time.

Are Right, a Lot

Leaders are right a lot. They have strong judgment and good instincts. They seek diverse perspectives and work to disconfirm their beliefs.

Learn and Be Curious

Leaders are never done learning and always seek to improve themselves. They are curious about new possibilities and act to explore them.

Hire and Develop the Best

Leaders raise the performance bar with every hire and promotion. They recognise exceptional talent, and willingly move them throughout the organisation. Leaders develop leaders and take their role in coaching others seriously. We work on behalf of our people to invent mechanisms for developments like Career Choice.

Insist on the Highest Standards

Leaders have relentlessly high standards – many people may think these standards are unreasonably high. Leaders are continually raising the bar and drive their teams to deliver high quality products, services, and processes.

Leaders ensure that defects do not get sent down the line and that problems are fixed so they stay fixed.

Think Big

Thinking small is a self-fulfilling prophecy. Leaders create and communicate a bold direction that inspires results. They think differently and look around corners for ways to serve customers.

Bias for Action

Speed matters in business. Many decisions and actions are reversible and do not need extensive study. We value calculated risk taking.

Frugality

Accomplish more with less. Constraints breed resourcefulness, self-sufficiency, and invention. There are no extra points for growing headcount, budget size or fixed expense.

Earn Trust

Leaders listen attentively, speak candidly, and treat others respectfully. They are vocally self-critical, even when doing so is awkward or embarrassing.

Leaders do not believe their or their team's body odor smells of perfume. They benchmark themselves and their teams against the best.

Dive Deep

Leaders operate at all levels, stay connected to the details, audit frequently, and are sceptical when metrics and anecdotes differ. No task is beneath them.

Have Backbone; Disagree and Commit

Leaders are obligated to respectfully challenge decisions when they disagree, even when doing so is uncomfortable or exhausting. Leaders have conviction and are tenacious. They do not compromise for the sake of social cohesion.

Once a decision is determined, they commit wholly.

Deliver Results

Leaders focus on the key inputs for their business and deliver them with the right quality and in a timely fashion. Despite setbacks, they rise to the occasion and never settle.

Strive to Be Earth's Best Employer

Leaders work every day to create a safer, more productive, higher performing, more diverse and more just work environment. They lead with empathy, have fun at work and make it easy for others to have fun. Leaders ask themselves: Are my fellow employees growing? Are they empowered? Are they ready for what's next? Leaders have a vision for and commitment to their employees' personal success, whether that be at Amazon or elsewhere.

Success and Scale Bring Broad Responsibility

We started in a garage, but we're not there anymore. We are big, we impact the world, and we are far from perfect. We must be humble and thoughtful about even the secondary effects of our actions. Our local communities, planet, and future generations need us to be better every day. We must begin each day with a determination to make better, do better, and be better for our customers, our employees, our partners, and the world at large. And we must end every day knowing we can do even more tomorrow. Leaders create more than they consume and always leave things better than how they found them.[iii]

As a point of contrast, Google's leadership principles are succinct and very directly aimed at you, the leader:

- *You are a good coach.*
- *You can empower a team without micromanaging.*
- *You create an inclusive team environment and show concern for success and well-being. You are productive and results-oriented. You are a good communicator.*
- *You support career development and discuss performance. You have a clear vision/strategy for the team.*
- *You possess key technical skills to help the team. You can collaborate across Google.*
- *You are a strong decision-maker.*[iv]

The language used in both sets of principles is deliberate. One can imagine leaders, HR and communications teams spent an inordinate amount of time crafting them. For values or guiding principles to be truly effective they have to be verbs. It's not 'integrity,' it's 'always do the right thing'. It's not 'innovation,' it's 'look at the problem from a different angle'. Articulating values as verbs gives a clear idea and context ... with a clear idea and context of how to act in any situation.[v]

Once the principles are nailed down, great leadership has a playbook to thrive. But what does great leadership look like in practice, particularly in tech?

Lived the product

> **SUCCESSFUL LEADERS IN TECH MORE OFTEN THAN NOT SHARE A COMMON CHARACTERISTIC, THEY ARE PRODUCT PEOPLE. TECH OBVIOUSLY CARRIES WITH IT A STRICT NEED FOR PEOPLE WITH TECHNICAL SKILLS. CODING AND DATA ANALYSIS ARE TWO KEY COMPETENCIES IN TECH. LEADERS OF TECH COMPANIES NATURALLY NEED A SOLID UNDERSTANDING OF THESE COMPETENCIES, THEIR FUNCTION AND POTENTIAL.**
>
> **ONE OF THE THINGS THAT STRUCK ME AT AMAZON WAS HOW MUCH INFLUENCE AND DECISION-MAKING ABILITY DEVELOPERS HAD. THE MOST SENIOR LEADERS ON MANY OF THESE PROJECTS AT THE TIME WEREN'T BUSINESS LEADERS, BUT TECHNICAL LEADERS.**[vi]
>
> — **Jeff Lawson**

What's common in tech goes beyond merely understanding the technical. Tech leaders have played a part in the actual building of the product. So many are engineers early on, coding up the very products of companies they are the CEO of. It's often said that leadership is earned, not given. By virtue of all the bricks they laid, tech leaders earn their stripes early on.

Not only do they help build the product in the early days, when they graduate to full-time CEO, the best ones stay close to the product and its core work.

Mark Zuckerberg famously devotes one day a month to building code for the Facebook platform.

Tech CEOs are so technical that innovation and product development are core to their role in the company. They are the futurologists in the company, or stealthy chief innovation officers.

In the most innovative and valuable companies in the world, the chief innovation officer is the CEO. We see this latter model in place at the most innovative companies: Apple (Steve Jobs now replaced by Tim Cook), Alphabet/Google (Larry Page and Sergey Brin), Amazon (Jeff Bezos), Facebook (Mark Zuckerberg), and Microsoft (Bill Gates, then Steve Ballmer, and now Satya Nadella).[vii]

Pixar's Ed Catmull saw this devotion to the product from tech leaders as key to success, due to its top-down influence:

To ensure quality, then, excellence must be an earned word, attributed by others to us, not proclaimed by us about ourselves. It is the responsibility of good leaders to make sure that words remain attached to the meanings and ideals they represent.[viii]

Mark Zuckerberg takes it a step further. Every year Zuck will take on a new project, and publicise his intention and progress. One year it was to read twenty-five books. Another year was very interesting: as AI was becoming the topic du jour of tech, it was becoming clear people and companies who master AI will succeed most. So Zuck decided as a project to research AI and build it into his home, himself. So he essentially coded his own butler into his house. Walk the walk.

Bring it back to the *why*

IT STARTS WITH MISSION, IT ENDS WITH CULTURE, AND IN BETWEEN [THERE IS] WHAT'S OUR WORLDVIEW, WHAT'S OUR STRATEGY. I THINK OF THE THINGS THAT ARE CONSTANT AS THAT SENSE OF PURPOSE AND MISSION AND CULTURE, AND THE THINGS THAT ARE TEMPORAL ARE WORLDVIEWS AND STRATEGIES.

— Satya Nadella

The most common behaviour of tech leaders is they keep the organisation tracking towards the North Star, the company's *why*. As Jeff Bezos would say, 'Be stubborn on the vision, flexible on the details.'

Leaders forever have their eye on the prize, and communicate at length the nature and value of that prize. It's compelling, such are the visions they espouse. Mind you, talking up the vision and mission can cover up the charisma cracks. Hello, Jack Dorsey, just watch interviews with him on YouTube.

And research from cognitive science tells us that repetition has value.

First, brain scans show that repetition causes the brain to physically change. New connections are formed between neurons (think of neurons as information messengers). And the connections between neurons are thicker, stronger and more hard-wired.[ix]

According to leadership psychologist Colin Wilford, 'All behaviour is made possible by a myriad of electrical pathways in the brain. As we learn new tasks and make them habits we create a new sequence of electrical impulses in the brain that continue to follow the same pathway in the same order. Changing the pathways/habits once set is not easy, but it is refreshingly possible as we overcome our failings and turn them into strengths.'

Up ahead is Slack's Stewart Butterfield communicating the 'Why of Slack' to staff, a masterclass in shaping ambition with context:

Dave Morrissey

Why?

There's no point doing this to be small. We should go big, if only because there are a lot of people in the world who deserve Slack. Going big also means that it will have to be really, really good. But that's convenient, since there's also no point doing it if it is not really, really good. Life is too short to do mediocre work and it is definitely too short to build shitty things.

To do this well, we need to take a holistic approach and not just think about a long list of individual tasks we are supposed to get through in a given week. We get 0 points for just getting a feature out the door if it is not actually contributing to making the experience better for users, or helping them to understand Slack, or helping us understand them. None of the work we are doing to develop the product is an end in itself; it all must be squarely aimed at the larger purpose.

Consider the teams you see in action at great restaurants, and the totality of their effort: the room, the vibe, the timing, the presentation, the attention, the anticipation of your needs (and, of course, the food itself); nothing can be off. There is a great nobility in being of service to others, and well-run restaurants (or hotels, or software companies) serve with a quality that is measured by its attention to detail. This is a perfect model for us to emulate.

Ensuring that the pieces all come together is not someone else's job. It is your job, no matter what your title is and no matter what role you play. The pursuit of that purpose should permeate everything we do.

But Slack is a bit more complicated than a restaurant (at least in some ways). Since it is new and less familiar, we are less able to fall back on well-established best practices. That means we need to listen, watch & analyze carefully. We'll need to build tools to capture users' behaviour and reactions. And then we'll need to take all that information and our best instincts and be continuously improving.

We are an exceptional software development team. But, we now also need be an excellent customer development team. That's why, in the first section of this doc, I said 'build a customer base' rather than 'gain market share': the nature of the task is different, and we will work together to understand, anticipate and better serve the people who trust us with their teams' communications, one customer at a time.

The answer to 'Why?' is 'because why the fuck else would you even want to be alive but to do things as well as you can?'. Now: let's do this.[x]

Porter Erisman's book *Alibaba's World: How One Remarkable Chinese Company Is Changing the Face of Global Business* gives a great insight into Jack Ma communicating the *why* of Alibaba at a critical time in the company:

It was the first time we'd all gathered since the IPO, and the staff surely felt Alibaba was poised for global dominance. As the day of performances and celebrations came to an end, Jack took the round stage in the centre of the arena to address the employees who surrounded him. Ever the contrarian, Jack's message was a sobering one, meant to both inspire and humble the staff.

We need to be looking out ten years. In ten years people won't be talking about 'the Internet' or 'e-commerce.' It will be a part of our daily lives. We have only ten years to make Alibaba great, because in ten years the infrastructure for e-commerce will already be built. After that it will be too late. So many companies rise and fall quickly. The environment changes so quickly. A few years ago Yahoo! was our hero. Who would have ever imagined that it would fall from its pedestal to be where it is today? So many of our heroes from yesterday have come and gone. In ten years, when people talk about e-commerce, we want them to be talking about Alibaba. We don't want people to look back and say, 'Alibaba was once a great company.' We must stick to our promises. Today you've begun to have a little money. You've begun to have a little prestige. Don't change because other people see you differently. Don't change because you have money in your pocket. Because there is one thing that can never change: our dreams, our values, and our promises.

2007 was a great year for Alibaba, ending with the exclamation mark of our B2B IPO. Alibaba's social impact is huge. But we have to remember that we are still a small company, not a big company. We are small, but I already notice we are sometimes wasteful. We are small but sometimes we move too slowly. We should prepare for any crisis, and if that crisis comes, we all need to ask, 'What can we do to help the company?' We want it to be the case that if you have a business, no matter where you are, you can plug into Alibaba's ecosystem. We need to be bigger than Walmart someday. Some of you think that is crazy. But one thing is for sure: if you don't imagine it, it will never happen. Maybe you think that our outlook is great, the economy is great, the stock market is great, and Alibaba is doing really well. But I want to tell you that 2008 is going to be a difficult year. Why did we go public last year? Because we sense that a winter is coming and we have to prepare.

In 2008 Alibaba is going to lie low and prepare for a new winter. And during this winter we have to remember our goals from long ago – to be the last man standing. No matter what, we must be the last man standing.[xi]

Stay close to the customer

IF YOU'RE COMPETITOR-FOCUSED, YOU HAVE TO WAIT UNTIL THERE IS A COMPETITOR DOING SOMETHING. BEING CUSTOMER-FOCUSED ALLOWS YOU TO BE MORE PIONEERING.

— Jeff Bezos

Talking the *why* of the company all day every day isn't a good use of leaders' time either, because people will get bored of the same old yarn coming their way. Apathy sets in. Business declines.

The trick is to always bring words and actions back to who the mission is looking to serve, the customer.

Bezos had an email for customer complaints, customers could raise an issue with the delivery or product quality to jeff@amazon.com, which he did look at in the early years, and act on to be 'flagging a fire' with the relevant department. The CEO wanted to stay that close to the customers.

He even proofread any customer service emails that dealt with any new topic.[xii] The CEO wanted to ensure the customers were communicated to perfectly.

The UK e-commerce darling HUEL, which delivers delicious meal replacement drinks directly online, prides itself on putting the customer first, and has it ingrained in the culture. Their founder Julian Hearn explains:

It was always essential to me that we looked after our customers incredibly well. This goes right back to the early days when I hand-signed a thank you note in the first 1000 orders, to when I switched our delivery company when I began to receive complaints about the crappy delivery experience our customers were getting. It may cost a bit more, but if your customers are unhappy, they will not come back. I have two things that resonate with me; the first is to make sure customers are happy. Everyone in the company has that mindset. The second is don't be a dick and be nice. It's pretty straightforward.[xiii]

Be authentic

BE YOURSELF. EVERYONE ELSE IS TAKEN.

— Oscar Wilde

When it comes to great leadership, authenticity is vital, although rare in its purest form.

People aren't stupid. They can spot a fraud pretty easily. Reed Hastings will tell you from his experience leading Netflix since 1997: 'Spinning the truth is one of the most common ways leaders erode trust. I can't say this clearly enough: don't do this. Your people are not stupid. When you try to spin them, they see it, and it makes you look like a fraud.'[xiv]

You see, authenticity doesn't mean coming to work talking like you would in the pub and dressing like you have come out of hibernation thanks to a binge on a season of *Succession* in a darkened bedroom. Authentic leaders ooze an aura of doing the right things for the right reasons. And that means being truthful in intent, and purposeful in action.

Back to the wise sage, Mr Hastings:

Every time I feel I've made a mistake, I talk about it fully, publicly, and frequently. I quickly came to see the biggest advantage of sunshining a leader's errors is to encourage everyone to think of making mistakes as normal. This in turn encourages employees to take risks when success is uncertain ... which leads to greater innovation across the company. Self-disclosure builds trust, seeking help boosts learning, admitting mistakes fosters forgiveness, and broadcasting failures encourages your people to act courageously.[xv]

Laszlo Bock, former head of People Analytics at Google, recommends that leaders ask their people three questions:

What is one thing that I currently do that you'd like me to continue to do?

What is one thing that I don't currently do frequently enough that you think I should do more often?

What can I do to make you more effective?[xvi]

Lead with context

LEAD WITH CONTEXT, NOT CONTROL, AND COACHING YOUR EMPLOYEES USING SUCH GUIDELINES AS, 'DON'T SEEK TO PLEASE YOUR BOSS.'

— Reed Hastings

Overbearing micro-management? Yes please, all of it. Said absolutely no fucking one, ever.

Good to great leadership in tech is not seen with cracking the whip. It's a far cry from the top-down leadership of more traditional companies.

It is worth noting that staff at tech companies are highly self-motivated and talented, making this sort of leadership much more effective in the culture. The intrinsic motivation of staff is one to ponder for all you current and future leaders. Teach to fish, or cast out the trawler nets yourself?

Netflix promotes a culture of openness and the idea that everyone's idea carries merit. A lot of companies have this ambition, but in practice it doesn't happen. Reed Hasting's own actions give context to the desired culture:

I don't have my own office or even a cubicle with drawers that close. During the day, I might grab a conference room for some discussions, but my assistant knows to book most of my meetings in other people's work spaces. I always try to go to the work spot of the person I'm seeing, instead of making them come to me. One of my preferences is to hold walking meetings, where I often come across other employees meeting out in the open.[xvii]

Elon Musk's mission with Tesla is 'to accelerate the advent of sustainable transport by bringing compelling mass-market electric cars to market as soon as possible', so in order to fulfil that mission, big, bold and speedy decision- making is needed throughout the company. What Musk asks of his staff enforces the tone of daring urgency needed in the culture.

There can be no question that Musk has mastered the art of getting the most out of his employees. Interview three dozen SpaceX engineers and each one of them will have picked up on a managerial nuance that Musk has used to get people to meet his deadlines. One example from Brogan: Where a typical manager may set the deadline for the employee, Musk guides his engineers into taking ownership of their own delivery dates. 'He doesn't say, "You have to do this by Friday at two P.M.,"' an engineer at Tesla said. 'He says, "I need the impossible done by Friday at two P.M. Can you do it?" Then, when you say yes, you are not working hard because he told you to. You're working hard for yourself. It's a distinction you can feel. You have signed up to do your own work.'[xviii]

Danny Meyer has a range of micro-sayings, or culture memes as I like to call them, as mentioned earlier in the 'Culture' chapter. It is where Meyer excels in his leadership style. He approaches his catchphrase-creating process with the focused verve of a pop songwriter. He generates constantly, testing which ones work. He seeks snappy, visceral phrases that use vivid images to help team members connect. Studies on him have noted, 'The most powerful thing about all those phrases is the way Danny embodies them. What he's exceptional at is realizing that people are looking at him every second, and he's delivering those messages every second, every day. He's like a powerful Wi-Fi signal. Some people send three bars, but Danny is at ten bars, and he never goes below nine.'[xix]

Ed Catmull at Pixar, on the flip side, is wary of mottoes and catchphrases, as he believes they can easily distort reality. Nonetheless a handful of 'Ed-isms' are heard in Pixar's corridors. Here are a few:

- *Hire people smarter than you.*
- *Fail early, fail often.*
- *Listen to everyone's ideas.*
- *Face toward the problems.*
- *B-level work is bad for your soul.*
- *It's more important to invest in good people than in good ideas.*

You'll notice that, in contrast to Danny Meyer's vivid, specific language, these are defiantly un-catchy, almost zen-like in their normalness and universality.

This reflects the fundamental difference between leading for proficiency and leading for creativity: Meyer needs people to know and feel exactly what to do, while Catmull needs people to discover that for themselves. Food for thought for your own business, and the purpose of your leadership.

Be brave with big bets

Speaking of Elon Musk and his big betting, Google's Larry Page holds Musk up as a model he wishes others would emulate – a figure who should be replicated during a time in which the business community and politicians have fixated on short-term, inconsequential goals. 'I don't think we're doing a good job as a society deciding what things are really important to do,' Page said. 'I think like we're just not educating people in this kind of general way. You should have a pretty broad engineering and scientific background. You should have some leadership training and a bit of MBA training or knowledge of how to run things, organize stuff, and raise money. I don't think most people are doing that, and it's a big problem. Engineers are usually trained in a very fixed area. When you're able to think about all of these disciplines together, you kind of think differently and can dream of much crazier things and how they might work. I think that's really an important thing for the world. That's how we make progress.'[xx]

Tech leaders often start by asking what could be true in five years, and beyond. Larry Page often says that the job of a CEO is not only to think about the core business, but also the future; most companies fail because they get too comfortable doing what they have always done, making only incremental changes. And that is especially fatal today, when technology-driven change is rampant. So the question to ask isn't what will be true, but what could be true? Asking what will be true entails making a prediction, which is folly in a fast-moving world. Asking what could be true entails imagination: what thing that is unimaginable when abiding by conventional wisdom is in fact imaginable?[xxi]

At Meta, Mark Zuckerberg and the leadership team have defined an innovation strategy that focuses on three future innovation domains which they believe are fundamental to achieving their mission to 'Give people the power to share and make the world more open and connected.' These three innovation domains are:

- Connectivity – including terrestrial solutions, telco infrastructure, free basics, satellites, drones and lasers
- Artificial intelligence – including vision, language, reasoning and planning
- VR/AR – including social VR, mobile VR, Oculus Rift, touch and AR technologies

This list of innovation domains is well understood by the entire Meta management team and board who are actively exploring and communicating about these exciting topics.

Mark Zuckerberg himself is a thought leader in these coming areas of innovation; when he speaks both within the company and to external audiences about them, he also discusses their collective impact on the coming digital future and the resulting connected world. He has also been a visionary around the risks of not enabling all of humanity to access such benefits and most recently has needed to address the risks of communities that become disconnected or unsafe to everyone.[xxii]

Drive for standards most high

Those with leadership potential are motivated by a deeply embedded desire to achieve for the sake of achievement.[xxiii] – Harvard Business School Press

Bob Iger, in his autobiography about his tenure as Disney CEO, *The Ride of a Lifetime,*' talks a lot about 'the relentless pursuit of perfection'. He explains this to mean a mindset more than a specific set of rules. It's not about perfectionism at all costs. It's about creating an environment in which people refuse to accept mediocrity. It's about pushing back against the urge to say that 'good enough' is good enough.[xxiv]

Ed Catmull spends his days roving around Pixar and Disney (where he also acts as president of Walt Disney Animation Studios following Disney's acquisition of Pixar) watching. He helps onboard new employees and observes BrainTrust meetings (more on these later), observing the interactions for signs of incipient trouble or success. He cultivates back-channel conversations to find out what's going on behind the scenes. He worries when he sees awkward silences or people avoiding each other; he celebrates when a group takes initiative without asking permission (such as when a group of animators organised an impromptu Boy Scout–themed sleepover on Pixar's lawn). He defends teams when they make mistakes (and they have been known to make some extremely expensive mistakes). Catmull has been described like the engineer of a ship. He doesn't steer the ship – he roves around below decks, checking the hull for leaks, changing out a piston, adding a little oil here and there. 'For me, managing is a creative act,' he says. 'It's problem solving, and I love doing that.'[xxv]

Decision-making and prioritisation

Tech's leaders in such fast-paced environments have been adept decision makers. Making decisions for others to keep the ball rolling with their tasks and projects is a key skill. Somewhat understated is a leader's own time management. Every meeting, every minute counts.

Where they spend their time and energy is vital. Not just in the office but outside (tech bosses love a good hike or cycle, ironically to shut off from some of their addictive creations on the mobile screen), where they get their inputs for thinking and action. It's all very thoughtful and deliberate.

For instance, here is how Brian Chesky, CEO of Airbnb, prioritises his workdays:

Dave Morrissey

Because we're more functional and more integrated (from a company restructure spurned by Covid), I don't have per se two or three focus areas. I'm connected to every part of the company. If we're launching a new product, I see myself as the orchestra conductor. I'm not a specialist, but I have to understand every instrument and every part of the sound – how it all works.

The areas that I'm particularly focused on are product design. If I had a job at a large corporation, I would probably be either a designer, a marketer, or a product marketer. I spend a lot of time on design and product marketing, product management, and marketing communication. I use those terms interchangeably. That's probably my big area. I spend quite a lot of time on people, talent, and hiring.

The third bucket is telling the Airbnb story. I don't mean the same old story over and over again. It's a continuous story that evolves every single minute of every single day. I'm probably a little more hands-on than the average CEO because of the way I've chosen to run the company. When things are functional, they all kind of roll up to you. I do focus more on product, design, culture.[xxvi]

That's where he spends his time. Now hear how he decides on whether to get close to the customer and code, or not:

The areas that I'm less involved in – we talked about a technology stack, like application layer, to the kind of atomic components, or the processor chips. The same thing is true in a company. I'm kind of more in the top half of the layer.

The financial accounting, the technology infrastructure, the data warehouse, and the hardcore underlying payments to infrastructure, I'm not as involved in.

I would consider that below the operating system of the company. That's considered like the microprocessor, the graphics card – the very bottom of the stack. I'm involved in payments at the consumer and host level: what do we want to be able to offer in which countries, and what are the benefits?

I don't micromanage. I trust the team understands the trade-offs and is able to deliver. I'm pretty involved in trying to understand what new benefits we want to be able to deliver to guests and hosts from a payment standpoint, but payments is highly technical. I try to not go too far into the stack.[xxvii]

Microsoft's Satya Nadella prioritises by value to people and the world at large:

Anything we do has to be aligned with that first question, which is: is this something that makes sense given who we are as a company? And more importantly, if we go about doing that, does it add unique value in the world? Is that something that both differentiates us competitively and is that something that's useful for people? That's, to me, the most helpful way to [run] the businesses we are in.[xxviii]

Meanwhile Jeff Bezos told Fast Company in very prescriptive form:

There are two types of decisions. There are decisions that are irreversible and highly consequential; we call them one-way doors, or Type 2 decisions. They need to be made slowly and carefully. I often find myself at Amazon acting as the chief slowdown officer: 'Whoa, I want to see that decision analyzed seventeen more ways because it's highly consequential and irreversible.' The problem is that most decisions aren't like that. Most decisions are two-way doors.

You can make the decision, and you step through. It turns out to have been the wrong decision; you can back up. And what happens in large organizations – not in start-up companies but in large organizations – is that all decisions end up using the heavyweight process that is really intended only for irreversible, highly consequential decisions. And that's a disaster.

When there's a decision that needs to be made, you need to ask, 'Is it a one-way door or a two-way door?' If it's a two-way door, make the decision with a small team or even one high-judgment individual. Make the decision. If it's wrong, it's wrong. You'll change it. But if it's a one-way door, analyze it five different ways. Be careful, because that is where slow is smooth and smooth is fast.

You do not want to make one-way-door decisions quickly. You want to get consensus or at least drive a lot of thought and debate.[xxix]

Bezos also has a mental exercise that is part of his risk-calculation process, called the 'regret minimisation framework'. He would imagine what he would feel when he turned eighty and thought back to the decision:

I want to have minimised the number of regrets I have, I knew that when I was eighty, I was not going to regret having tried this. I was not going to regret trying to participate in this thing called the internet that I thought was going to be a really big deal. I knew that if I failed, I would regret that, but I knew the one thing I might regret is not having ever tried. I knew that that would haunt me every day.

The foundation of Amazon's decision-making philosophy was laid out in its 1997 letter to shareholders:

We will continue to focus relentlessly on our customers.

We will continue to make investment decisions in light of long-term market leadership considerations rather than short-term profitability considerations or short-term Wall Street reactions.

We will continue to measure our programs and the effectiveness of our investments analytically, to jettison those that do not provide acceptable returns, and to step up our investment in those that work best. We will continue to learn from both our successes and our failures.

We will make bold rather than timid investment decisions where we see a sufficient probability of gaining market leadership advantages. Some of these investments will pay off, others will not, and we will have learned another valuable lesson in either case.

You can count on us to combine a strong quantitative and analytical culture with a willingness to make bold decisions. As we do so, we'll start with the customer and work backward. In our judgement, that is the best way to create shareholder value.

Empathy matters

ANY FOOL CAN KNOW. THE POINT IS TO UNDERSTAND.[xxx]

— **Albert Einstein**

Empathy is particularly important today as a component of leadership for at least three reasons: the increasing use of teams, the rapid pace of globalisation and the growing need to retain talent.[xxxi] Leadership, in every industry, will need a heightened level of EQ, emotional intelligence, going forward. In fact *Harvard Business Review* has proclaimed empathy to be the most important leadership principle.

Empathy requires a high degree of openness and diversity. There is a building body of research that shows that when leadership teams are more diverse, they bring more ideas, perspectives and points of view, which can very positively impact the creativity and innovation of the combined team. This is true for leadership teams, boards of directors and functional and divisional teams. Catalyst, the leading US non-profit organisation with a mission to accelerate progress for women through workplace inclusion, in summarising the case for more women on executive teams and boards, shows through a synthesis of the academic and scientific research on gender diversity and its impact on performance that four important drivers are all positively impacted:

- Financial performance is improved.
- Companies are able to leverage a broader talent pool.
- The company better reflects the marketplace and creates a better reputation.
- Innovation is improved across the company.[xxxii]

Extra effort is needed on the part of leaders to build empathy, to kick the shit out of harmful biases and optimise for people's happiness. Mark Zuckerberg gets it in the neck for being removed from reality, a droid of sorts. But in 2017, in a quest to understand the make-up of society, Democrats to Republicans and the like, he went on a tour of all fifty US states meeting people on the ground. To understand. To build empathy.

A blatant PR exercise to distract from Facebook's (minute) role in the election of Donald Trump? Perhaps there was an element of that. But for him to dedicate that much time to such an expansive tour, confronted with angry voters, is a testament to his desire to build empathy to learn better leadership.

These companies look for it in hiring

Everyone is a leader, or expected to be in tech. The manager or director is leading for sure. But what's interesting in tech is individual contributors are encouraged, and trained, to display leadership characteristics. And grow more and more into the archetypal leader.

At Google they break down candidate evaluations into four different categories, and they keep these categories consistent across functions. From sales to finance to engineering, smart creatives tend to score well on all of these, regardless of what they do or at what level. The categories and their descriptions:

- *Leadership: We'll want to know how someone has flexed different muscles in various situations in order to mobilize a team. This can include asserting a leadership role at work or with an organization, or even helping a team succeed when they weren't officially appointed as the leader.*
- *Role-related knowledge: We look for people who have a variety of strengths and passions, not just isolated skill sets. We also want to make sure that candidates have the*

experience and the background that will set them up for success in the role. For engineering candidates in particular, we check out coding skills and technical areas of expertise.

- *General cognitive ability: We're less concerned about grades and transcripts and more interested in how a candidate thinks. We're likely to ask a candidate some role-related questions that provide insight into how they solve problems.*
- *Googleyness: We want to get a feel for what makes a candidate unique. We also want to make sure this is a place they'll thrive, so we look for signs around their comfort with ambiguity, bias to action, and collaborative nature.*[xxxiii]

PS: note the use of their own language

Communication – what great looks like

Let's go off-piste a moment, going from tech to the football pitch, to the sage words of arguably the game's greatest manager of all time, Sir Alex Ferguson:

There are some managers who will enter a dressing room at half-time with a pack of notes. When they talk to the players they will use their notes as prompts. I cannot imagine how that is an effective way to communicate. If you have command and control of your subject, you don't need notes. No player is going to believe that someone is in control of his material, or is an authority on a subject, if he has to keep resorting to notes. I relied on my memory and my own assessment and, that way, when I was talking to the players, I was able to maintain eye contact. I'm sure I got some stuff wrong. I'd miss a deflection or a foul but, in the grand scheme of things, those tiny details don't count. It's the message, the command of that message and its delivery that pack the punch. Everyone has their own style, but using notes when trying to motivate people is not mine.[xxxiv]

Command and control of your subject, and being authentic in your style. It's no wonder Ferguson is a sought-after inspirational lecturer for leaders in business and tech nowadays.

Let's look at what a great leader's communication looks like, in good times and bad. Let's start with the bad time. Covid-19.

At the beginning of Covid, it was clear the travel sector was getting shut down for an unknown time period. Airbnb was in the firing line of it all; it became clear they had to downsize to survive. In fact, they had to let go of 1,900 of their 7,500 employees. Devastating. How Airbnb's CEO Brian Chesky communicated this decision in a letter to those affected is a fucking masterclass in empathetic leadership, humanity even:

This is my seventh time talking to you from my house. Each time we've talked, I've shared good news and bad news, but today I have to share some very sad news.

When you've asked me about layoffs, I've said that nothing is off the table. Today, I must confirm that we are reducing the size of the Airbnb workforce. For a company like us whose mission is centered around belonging, this is incredibly difficult to confront, and it will be even harder for those who have to leave Airbnb. I am going to share as many details as I can on how I arrived at this decision, what we are doing for those leaving, and what will happen next.

Let me start with how we arrived at this decision. We are collectively living through the most harrowing crisis of our lifetime, and as it began to unfold, global travel came to a standstill. Airbnb's business has been hit hard, with revenue this year forecasted to be less than half of what we earned in 2019. In response, we raised $2 billion in capital and dramatically cut costs that touched nearly every corner of Airbnb.

While these actions were necessary, it became clear that we would have to go further when we faced two hard truths:

1. *We don't know exactly when travel will return.*
2. *When travel does return, it will look different.*

While we know Airbnb's business will fully recover, the changes it will undergo are not temporary or short-lived. Because of this, we need to make more fundamental changes to Airbnb by reducing the size of our workforce around a more focused business strategy.

Out of our 7,500 Airbnb employees, nearly 1,900 teammates will have to leave Airbnb, comprising around 25% of our company. Since we cannot afford to do everything that we used to, these cuts had to be mapped to a more focused business.

A more focused business

Travel in this new world will look different, and we need to evolve Airbnb accordingly. People will want options that are closer to home, safer, and more affordable. But people will also yearn for something that feels like it's been taken away from them – human connection. When we started Airbnb, it was about belonging and connection. This crisis has sharpened our focus to get back to our roots, back to the basics, back to what is truly special about Airbnb – everyday people who host their homes and offer experiences.

This means that we will need to reduce our investment in activities that do not directly support the core of our host community. We are pausing our efforts in Transportation and Airbnb Studios, and we have to scale back our investments in Hotels and Lux.

These decisions are not a reflection of the work from people on these teams, and it does not mean everyone on these teams will be leaving us. Additionally, teams across all of Airbnb will be impacted. Many teams will be reduced in size based on how well they map to where Airbnb is headed.

How we approached reductions

It was important that we had a clear set of principles, guided by our core values, for how we would approach reductions in our workforce. These were our guiding principles:

- *Map all reductions to our future business strategy and the capabilities we will need.*
- *Do as much as we can for those who are impacted.*
- *Be unwavering in our commitment to diversity.*
- *Optimize for 1:1 communication for those impacted.*
- *Wait to communicate any decisions until all details are landed – transparency of only partial information can make matters worse.*

I have done my best to stay true to these principles.

Process for making reductions

Our process started with creating a more focused business strategy built on a sustainable cost model. We assessed how each team mapped to our new strategy, and we determined the size and shape of each team going forward. We then did a comprehensive review of every team member and made decisions based on critical skills, and how well those skills matched our future business needs.

The result is that we will have to part with teammates that we love and value. We have great people leaving Airbnb, and other companies will be lucky to have them.

To take care of those that are leaving, we have looked across severance, equity, healthcare, and job support and done our best to treat everyone in a compassionate and thoughtful way.

Severance

Employees in the US will receive 14 weeks of base pay, plus one additional week for every year at Airbnb. Tenure will be rounded to the nearest year. For example, if someone has been at Airbnb for 3 years and 7 months, they will get an additional 4 weeks of salary, or 18 weeks of total pay. Outside the US, all employees will receive at least 14 weeks of pay, plus tenure increases consistent with their country-specific practices.

Equity

We are dropping the one-year cliff on equity for everyone we've hired in the past year so that everyone departing, regardless of how long they have been here, is a shareholder. Additionally, everyone leaving is eligible for the May 25 vesting date.

Healthcare

In the midst of a global health crisis of unknown duration, we want to limit the burden of healthcare costs. In the US, we will cover 12 months of health insurance through COBRA. In all other countries, we will cover health insurance costs through the end of 2020. This is because we're either legally unable to continue coverage, or our current plans will not allow for an extension. We will also provide four months of mental health support through KonTerra.

Job support

Our goal is to connect our teammates leaving Airbnb with new job opportunities. Here are five ways we can help:

- *Alumni Talent Directory* – We will be launching a public-facing website to help teammates leaving find new jobs. Departing employees can opt-in to have profiles, resumes, and work samples accessible to potential employers.
- *Alumni Placement Team* – For the remainder of 2020, a significant portion of Airbnb Recruiting will become an

Alumni Placement Team. Recruiters that are staying with Airbnb will provide support to departing employees to help them find their next job.
- *RiseSmart* – We are offering four months of career services through RiseSmart, a company that specializes in career transition and job placement services.
- *Employee Offered Alumni Support* – We are encouraging all remaining employees to opt-in to a program to assist departing teammates find their next role.
- *Laptops* – A computer is an important tool to find new work, so we are allowing everyone leaving to keep their Apple laptops.

Here is what will happen next

I want to provide clarity to all of you as soon as possible. We have employees in 24 countries, and the time it will take to provide clarity will vary based on local laws and practices. Some countries require notifications about employment to be received in a very specific way. While our process may differ by country, we have tried to be thoughtful in planning for every employee.

In the US and Canada, I can provide immediate clarity. Within the next few hours, those of you leaving Airbnb will receive a calendar invite to a departure meeting with a senior leader in your department. It was important to us that wherever we legally could, people were informed in a personal, 1:1 conversation. The final working day for departing employees based in the US and Canada will be Monday, May 11. We felt Monday would give people time to begin taking next steps and say goodbye – we understand and respect how important this is.

Some employees who are staying will have a new role, and will receive a meeting invite with the subject 'New Role' to learn more about it. For those of you in the US and Canada who are staying on the Airbnb team, you will not receive a calendar invite.

At 6pm pacific time, I will host a world@ meeting for our Asia-Pacific teams. At 12am pacific time, I will host a world@ meeting for our Europe and Middle East teams. Following each of these meetings, we'll proceed with next steps in each country based on local practices.

I've asked all Airbnb leaders to wait to bring their teams together until the end of this week out of respect to our teammates being impacted. I want to give everyone the next few days to process this, and I'll host a CEO Q&A again this Thursday at 4pm pacific time.

Some final words

As I have learned these past eight weeks, a crisis brings you clarity about what is truly important. Though we have been through a whirlwind, some things are more clear to me than ever before.

First, I am thankful for everyone here at Airbnb. Throughout this harrowing experience, I have been inspired by all of you. Even in the worst of circumstances, I've seen the very best of us. The world needs human connection now more than ever, and I know that Airbnb will rise to the occasion. I believe this because I believe in you.

Second, I have a deep feeling of love for all of you. Our mission is not merely about travel. When we started Airbnb, our original tagline was, 'Travel like a human.' The human part was always more important than the travel part.

What we are about is belonging, and at the center of belonging is love. To those of you staying,

One of the most important ways we can honor those who are leaving is for them to know that their contributions mattered, and that they will always be part of Airbnb's story. I am confident their work will live on, just like this mission will live on.

Dave Morrissey

To those leaving Airbnb,

I am truly sorry. Please know this is not your fault. The world will never stop seeking the qualities and talents that you brought to Airbnb ... that helped make Airbnb. I want to thank you, from the bottom of my heart, for sharing them with us.

Brian[xxxv]

Something else right? Now let's look at a more positive time. When Jeff Bezos decided to move from CEO of Amazon to chairman, marking a new era in the company, this was his final letter to shareholders as CEO. The *why*, ambition, tenacity, storytelling. All there, in spades:

In Amazon's 1997 letter to shareholders, our first, I talked about our hope to create an 'enduring franchise,' one that would reinvent what it means to serve customers by unlocking the internet's power. I noted that Amazon had grown from having 158 employees to 614, and that we had surpassed 1.5 million customer accounts. We had just gone public at a split-adjusted stock price of

$1.50 per share. I wrote that it was Day 1.

We've come a long way since then, and we are working harder than ever to serve and delight customers. Last year, we hired 500,000 employees and now directly employ 1.3 million people around the world. We have more than 200 million Prime members worldwide. More than 1.9 million small and medium- sized businesses sell in our store, and they make up close to 60% of our retail sales. Customers have connected more than 100 million smart home devices to Alexa. Amazon Web Services serves millions of customers and ended 2020 with a $50 billion annualized run rate. In 1997, we hadn't invented Prime, Marketplace, Alexa, or AWS. They weren't even ideas then, and none was preordained. We took great risk with each one and put sweat and ingenuity into each one.

Along the way, we've created $1.6 trillion of wealth for shareowners. Who are they? Your Chair is one, and my Amazon shares have made me wealthy. But more than 7/8ths of the shares, representing $1.4 trillion of wealth creation, are owned by others. Who are they? They're pension funds, universities, and 401(k)s, and they're Mary and Larry, who sent me this note out of the blue just as I was sitting down to write this shareholder letter:

March 5, 2021

Mr. Jeff Bezos
Executive Chairman
Amazon.com, Inc.
410 Terry Avenue North
Seattle, WA 98109

Dear Mr. Bezos,

Thanks for making Amazon a great company! We thought you would like to know how it has benefited our family.

Back in 1997 when you made Amazon public, our son, Ryan, was 12 years old and a voracious reader. For his birthday, , 1997, we bought two shares of your new book selling company, which was all we could afford at the time. Within a year or so, the shares split 2 for 1, then 3 for 1, then 2 for 1 again, giving him 24 shares. The shares were in our names because of his age. We meant to put it in custody for him but we never got around to it but he knew they were for him.

Several times over the years, Ryan would want to cash in the stock but we always said we would "buy" it from him and then eventually turn around and give it back to him as a "gift". It was kind of a running joke in the family.

Due to the exponential growth in value, we decided to split the stock between ourselves and both of our children, Ryan and Katy.

This year Ryan is buying a house and would like to sell some shares. After searching for the original certificates, we needed to convert the paper shares into digital before selling them. We noticed that the first share certificate was a very low number. issue # . I can't image how many more shares have been issued since that date!

Included is a copy of the th certificate of Amazon on , 1997 - 24 years ago. Those two shares have had a wonderful influence on our family. We all enjoyed watching Amazon value grow year after year and it's a story we love to tell others.

Congratulations on a great career as CEO of Amazon. We can't even imagine how hard you and your team have worked to make Amazon the most successful and inventive company on the planet. Now may you have time to relax and catch up on things you want to do, like space exploration!

We cannot wait to see where Amazon delivers next! Next Day to Mars!

Sincerely,

Mary and Larry

P.S. We wished we had bought 10 shares!

I am approached with similar stories all the time. I know people who've used their Amazon money for college, for emergencies, for houses, for vacations, to start their own business, for charity – and the list goes on. I'm proud of the wealth we've created for shareowners. It's significant, and it improves their lives. But I also know something else: it's not the largest part of the value we've created.

Create More Than You Consume

If you want to be successful in business (in life, actually), you have to create more than you consume. Your goal should be to create value for everyone you interact with. Any business that doesn't create value for those it touches, even if it appears successful on the surface, isn't long for this world. It's on the way out.

Remember that stock prices are not about the past. They are a prediction of future cash flows discounted back to the present. The stock market anticipates. I'm going to switch gears for a moment and talk about the past. How much value did we create for shareowners in 2020? This is a relatively easy question to answer because accounting systems are set up to answer it. Our net income in 2020 was $21.3 billion. If, instead of being a publicly traded company with thousands of owners, Amazon were a sole proprietorship with a single owner, that's how much the owner would have earned in 2020.

How about employees? This is also a reasonably easy value creation question to answer because we can look at compensation expense. What is an expense for a company is income for employees. In 2020, employees earned $80 billion, plus another $11 billion to include benefits and various payroll taxes, for a total of $91 billion.

How about third-party sellers? We have an internal team (the Selling Partner Services team) that works to answer that question. They estimate that, in 2020, third-party seller profits from selling on Amazon were between $25 billion and

$39 billion, and to be conservative here I'll go with $25 billion.

For customers, we have to break it down into consumer customers and AWS customers.

We'll do consumers first. We offer low prices, vast selection, and fast delivery, but imagine we ignore all of that for the purpose of this estimate and value only one thing: we save customers time.

Customers complete 28% of purchases on Amazon in three minutes or less, and half of all purchases are finished in less than 15 minutes. Compare that to the typical shopping trip to a physical store – driving, parking, searching store aisles, waiting in the checkout line, finding your car, and driving home.

Research suggests the typical physical store trip takes about an hour. If you assume that a typical Amazon purchase takes 15 minutes and that it saves you a couple of trips to a physical store a week, that's more than 75 hours a year saved. That's important. We're all busy in the early 21st century.

So that we can get a dollar figure, let's value the time savings at $10 per hour, which is conservative. Seventy-five hours multiplied by $10 an hour and subtracting the cost of Prime gives you value creation for each Prime member of about $630. We have 200 million Prime members, for a total in 2020 of $126 billion of value creation.

AWS is challenging to estimate because each customer's workload is so different, but we'll do it anyway, acknowledging up front that the error bars are high. Direct cost improvements from operating in the cloud versus on premises vary, but a reasonable estimate is 30%. Across AWS's entire 2020 revenue of $45 billion, that 30% would Imply customer value creation of $19 billion (what would have cost them $64 billion on their own cost $45 billion from AWS). The difficult part of this estimation exercise is that the direct cost reduction is the smallest portion of the customer benefit of moving to the cloud. The bigger benefit is the increased speed of software development – something that can significantly improve the customer's competitiveness and top line. We have no reasonable way of estimating that portion of customer *value except to say that it's almost certainly larger than the direct cost savings. To be conservative here (and remembering we're really only trying to get ballpark estimates), I'll say it's the same and call AWS customer value creation $38 billion in 2020.*

Adding AWS and consumer together gives us total customer value creation in 2020 of $164 billion.

Summarizing:
Shareholders - $21B
Employees - $91B
3P Sellers - $25B
Customers - $164B
Total - $301B

If each group had an income statement representing their interactions with Amazon, the numbers above would be the 'bottom lines' from those income statements. These numbers are part of the reason why people work for us, why sellers sell through us, and why customers buy from us. We create value for them. And this value creation is not a zero-sum game. It is not just moving money from one pocket to another. Draw the box big around all of society, and you'll find that invention is the root of all real value creation. And value created is best thought of as a metric for innovation.

Of course, our relationship with these constituencies and the value we create isn't exclusively dollars and cents. Money doesn't tell the whole story. Our relationship with shareholders, for example, is relatively simple. They invest and hold shares for a duration of their choosing. We provide direction to shareowners infrequently on matters such as annual meetings and the right process to vote their shares. And even then they can ignore those directions and just skip voting.

Our relationship with employees is a very different example. We have processes they follow and standards they meet. We require training and various certifications. Employees have to show up at appointed times.

Our interactions with employees are many, and they're fine-grained. It's not just about the pay and the benefits. It's about all the other detailed aspects of the relationship too.

Does your Chair take comfort in the outcome of the recent union vote in Bessemer? No, he doesn't. I think we need to do a better job for our employees. While the voting results were lopsided and our direct relationship with employees is strong, it's clear to me that we need a better vision for how we create value for employees – a vision for their success.

If you read some of the news reports, you might think we have no care for employees. In those reports, our employees are sometimes accused of being desperate souls and treated as robots. That's not accurate. They're sophisticated and thoughtful people who have options for where to work.

When we survey fulfillment center employees, 94% say they would recommend Amazon to a friend as a place to work.

Employees are able to take informal breaks throughout their shifts to stretch, get water, use the rest room, or talk to a manager, all without impacting their performance. These informal work breaks are in addition to the 30-minute lunch and 30-minute break built into their normal schedule.

We don't set unreasonable performance goals. We set achievable performance goals that take into account tenure and actual employee performance data.

Performance is evaluated over a long period of time as we know that a variety of things can impact performance in any given week, day, or hour. If employees are on track to miss a performance target over a period of time, their manager talks with them and provides coaching.

Coaching is also extended to employees who are excelling and in line for increased responsibilities. In fact, 82% of coaching is positive, provided to employees who are meeting or exceeding expectations. We terminate the employment of less than 2.6% of employees due to their inability to perform their jobs (and that number was even lower in 2020 because of operational impacts of COVID-19).

Earth's Best Employer and Earth's Safest Place to Work

The fact is, the large team of thousands of people who lead operations at Amazon have always cared deeply for our hourly employees, and we're proud of the work environment we've created. We're also proud of the fact that Amazon is a company that does more than just create jobs for computer scientists and people with advanced degrees. We create jobs for people who never got that advantage.

Despite what we've accomplished, it's clear to me that we need a better vision for our employees' success. We have always wanted to be Earth's Most Customer-Centric Company. We won't change that. It's what got us here. But I am committing us to an addition. We are going to be Earth's Best Employer and Earth's Safest Place to Work.

In my upcoming role as Executive Chair, I'm going to focus on new initiatives. I'm an inventor. It's what I enjoy the most and what I do best. It's where I create the most value. I'm excited to work alongside the large team of passionate people we have in Ops and help invent in this arena of Earth's Best Employer and Earth's Safest Place to Work. On the details, we at Amazon are always flexible, but on matters of vision we are stubborn and relentless. We have never failed when we set our minds to something, and we're not going to fail at this either.

We dive deep into safety issues. For example, about 40% of work-related injuries at Amazon are related to musculoskeletal disorders (MSDs), things like sprains or strains that can be caused by repetitive motions. MSDs are common in the type of work that we do and are more likely to occur during an employee's first six months. We need to invent solutions to reduce MSDs for new employees, many of whom might be working in a physical role for the first time.

One such program is WorkingWell – which we launched to 859,000 employees at 350 sites across North America and Europe in 2020 – where we coach small groups of employees on body mechanics, proactive wellness, and safety. In addition to reducing workplace injuries, these concepts have a positive impact on regular day-to-day activities outside work.

We're developing new automated staffing schedules that use sophisticated algorithms to rotate employees among jobs that use different muscle-tendon groups to decrease repetitive motion and help protect employees from MSD risks. This new technology is central to a job rotation program that we're rolling out throughout 2021.

Our increased attention to early MSD prevention is already achieving results. From 2019 to 2020, overall MSDs decreased by 32%, and MSDs resulting in time away from work decreased by more than half.

We employ 6,200 safety professionals at Amazon. They use the science of safety to solve complex problems and establish new industry best practices. In 2021, we'll invest more than $300 million into safety projects, including an initial $66 million to create technology that will help prevent collisions of forklifts and other types of industrial vehicles.

When we lead, others follow. Two and a half years ago, when we set a $15 minimum wage for our hourly employees, we did so because we wanted to lead on wages – not just run with the pack – and because we believed it was the right thing to do. A recent paper by economists at the University of California- Berkeley and Brandeis University analyzed the impact of our decision to raise our minimum starting pay to $15 per hour. Their assessment reflects what we've heard from employees, their families, and the communities they live in.

Our increase in starting wage boosted local economies across the country by benefiting not only our own employees but also other workers in the same community. The study showed that our pay raise resulted in a 4.7% increase in the average hourly wage among other employers in the same labor market.

And we're not done leading. If we want to be Earth's Best Employer, we shouldn't settle for 94% of employees saying they would recommend Amazon to a friend as a place to work. We have to aim for 100%. And we'll do that by continuing to lead on wages, on benefits, on upskilling opportunities, and in other ways that we will figure out over time.

If any shareowners are concerned that Earth's Best Employer and Earth's Safest Place to Work might dilute our focus on Earth's Most Customer-Centric Company, let me set your mind at ease. Think of it this way. If we can operate two businesses as different as consumer ecommerce and AWS, and do both at the highest level, we can certainly do the same with these two vision statements. In fact, I'm confident they will reinforce each other.

The Climate Pledge

In an earlier draft of this letter, I started this section with arguments and examples designed to demonstrate that human-induced climate change is real. But, bluntly, I think we can stop saying that now. You don't have to say that photosynthesis is real, or make the case that gravity is real, or that water boils at 100 degrees Celsius at sea level. These things are simply true, as is the reality of climate change.

Not long ago, most people believed that it would be good to address climate change, but they also thought it would cost a lot and would threaten jobs, competitiveness, and economic growth. We now know better. Smart action on climate change will not only stop bad things from happening, it will also make our economy more efficient, help drive technological change, and reduce risks. Combined, these can lead to more and better jobs, healthier and happier children, more productive workers, and a more prosperous future. This doesn't mean it will be easy. It won't be. The coming decade will be decisive. The economy in 2030 will need to be vastly different from what it is today, *and Amazon plans to be at the heart of the change. We launched The Climate Pledge together with Global Optimism in September 2019 because we wanted to help drive this positive revolution. We need to be part of a growing team of corporations that understand the imperatives and the opportunities of the 21st century.*

Now, less than two years later, 53 companies representing almost every sector of the economy have signed The Climate Pledge. Signatories such as Best Buy, IBM, Infosys, Mercedes-Benz, Microsoft, Siemens, and Verizon have committed to achieve net-zero carbon in their worldwide businesses by 2040, 10 years ahead of the Paris Agreement. The Pledge also requires them to measure and report greenhouse gas emissions on a regular basis; implement decarbonization strategies through real business changes and innovations; and neutralize any remaining emissions with additional, quantifiable, real, permanent, and socially beneficial offsets. Credible, quality offsets are precious, and we should reserve them to compensate for economic activities where low- carbon alternatives don't exist.

The Climate Pledge signatories are making meaningful, tangible, and ambitious commitments. Uber has a goal of operating as a zero-emission platform in Canada, Europe, and the U.S. by 2030, and Henkel plans to source 100% of the electricity it uses for production from renewable sources. Amazon is making progress toward our own goal of 100% renewable energy by 2025, five years ahead of our initial 2030 target. Amazon is the largest corporate buyer of renewable energy in the world. We have 62 utility-scale wind and solar projects and 125 solar rooftops on fulfillment and sort centers around the globe. These projects have the capacity to generate over 6.9 gigawatts and deliver more than 20 million megawatt-hours of energy annually.

Transportation is a major component of Amazon's business operations and the toughest part of our plan to meet net-zero carbon by 2040. To help rapidly accelerate the market for electric vehicle technology, and to help all companies transition to greener technologies, we invested more than $1 billion in Rivian – and ordered 100,000 electric delivery vans from the company. We've also partnered with Mahindra in India and Mercedes-Benz in Europe. These custom electric delivery vehicles from Rivian are already operational, and they first hit the road in Los Angeles this past February. Ten thousand new vehicles will be on the road as early as next year, and all 100,000 vehicles will be on the road by 2030 – saving millions of metric tons of carbon. A big reason we want companies to join The Climate Pledge is to signal to the marketplace that businesses should start inventing and developing new technologies that signatories need to make good on the Pledge. Our purchase of 100,000 Rivian electric vans is a perfect example.

To further accelerate investment in new technologies needed to build a zero- carbon economy, we introduced the Climate Pledge Fund last June. The investment program started with $2 billion to invest in visionary companies that aim to facilitate the transition to a low-carbon economy. Amazon has already announced investments in CarbonCure Technologies, Pachama, Redwood Materials, Rivian, Turntide Technologies, ZeroAvia, and Infinium – and these are just some of the innovative companies we hope will build the zero-carbon economy of the future.

I have also personally allocated $10 billion to provide grants to help catalyze the systemic change we will need in the coming decade. We'll be supporting leading scientists, activists, NGOs, environmental justice organizations, and others working to fight climate change and protect the natural world. Late last year, I made my first round of grants to 16 organizations working on innovative and needle-moving solutions. It's going to take collective action from big companies, small companies, nation states, global organizations, and individuals, and I'm excited to be part of this journey and optimistic that humanity can come together to solve this challenge.

Differentiation is Survival and the Universe Wants You to be Typical

This is my last annual shareholder letter as the CEO of Amazon, and I have one last thing of utmost importance I feel compelled to teach. I hope all Amazonians take it to heart.

Grow Like Tech

Here is a passage from Richard Dawkins' (extraordinary) book The Blind Watchmaker. It's about a basic fact of biology.

> 'Staving off death is a thing that you have to work at. Left to itself – and that is what it is when it dies – the body tends to revert to a state of equilibrium with its environment. If you measure some quantity such as the temperature, the acidity, the water content or the electrical potential in a living body, you will typically find that it is markedly different from the corresponding measure in the surroundings. Our bodies, for instance, are usually hotter than our surroundings, and in cold climates they have to work hard to maintain the differential. When we die the work stops, the temperature differential starts to disappear, and we end up the same temperature as our surroundings. Not all animals work so hard to avoid coming into equilibrium with their surrounding temperature, but all animals do some comparable work. For instance, in a dry country, animals and plants work to maintain the fluid content of their cells, work against a natural tendency for water to flow from them into the dry outside world. If they fail they die. More generally, if living things didn't work actively to prevent it, they would eventually merge into their surroundings, and cease to exist as autonomous beings. That is what happens when they die.'

While the passage is not intended as a metaphor, it's nevertheless a fantastic one, and very relevant to Amazon. I would argue that it's relevant to all companies and all institutions and to each of our individual lives too. In what ways does the world pull at you in an attempt to make you normal? How much work does it take to maintain your distinctiveness? To keep alive the thing or things that make you special?

I know a happily married couple who have a running joke in their relationship. Not infrequently, the husband looks at the wife with faux

Dave Morrissey

distress and says to her, 'Can't you just be normal?' They both smile and laugh, and of course the deep truth is that her distinctiveness is something he loves about her. But, at the same time, it's also true that things would often be easier – take less energy – if we were a little more normal.

This phenomenon happens at all scale levels. Democracies are not normal. Tyranny is the historical norm. If we stopped doing all of the continuous hard work that is needed to maintain our distinctiveness in that regard, we would quickly come into equilibrium with tyranny.

We all know that distinctiveness – originality – is valuable. We are all taught to 'be yourself.' What I'm really asking you to do is to embrace and be realistic about how much energy it takes to maintain that distinctiveness. The world wants you to be typical – in a thousand ways, it pulls at you. Don't let it happen.

You have to pay a price for your distinctiveness, and it's worth it. The fairy tale version of 'be yourself' is that all the pain stops as soon as you allow your distinctiveness to shine. That version is misleading. Being yourself is worth it, but don't expect it to be easy or free. You'll have to put energy into it continuously.

The world will always try to make Amazon more typical – to bring us into equilibrium with our environment. It will take continuous effort, but we can and must be better than that.

* * *

As always, I attach our 1997 shareholder letter. It concluded with this: 'We at Amazon.com are grateful to our customers for their business and trust, to each other for our hard work, and to our shareholders for their support and encouragement.' That hasn't changed a bit. I want to especially thank Andy Jassy for agreeing to take on the CEO role. It's a hard job with a lot of responsibility. Andy is brilliant and has the highest of high standards. I guarantee you that Andy won't let the universe make us typical. He will muster the energy needed to keep alive in us what makes us special. That won't be easy, but it is critical. I also predict it will be satisfying and oftentimes fun. Thank you, Andy.

To all of you: be kind, be original, create more than you consume, and never, never, never let the universe smooth you into your surroundings. It remains Day 1.

Sincerely,

Jeffrey P. Bezos
Founder and Chief Executive Officer
Amazon.com, Inc.

Chapter 9
MANAGING PEOPLE

TECHNOLOGY IS NOTHING. WHAT'S IMPORTANT IS THAT YOU HAVE A FAITH IN PEOPLE, THAT THEY'RE BASICALLY GOOD AND SMART, AND IF YOU GIVE THEM TOOLS, THEY'LL DO WONDERFUL THINGS WITH THEM.

— Steve Jobs

'People are our greatest asset' is espoused by many organisations in some shape or form, either explicitly like so, or implicitly through HR playbooks or gushings on the 'About Us' section of their website. Bullshit.

In fact, the HR/personnel department of every company suffers from a total identity crisis, a grand delusion. Ask yourself, when have you ever felt that the people in HR, recruiting, and so on are there to serve you? To understand who you are, how best to treat you, what path to take to you on, to look out for your success? Even worse, do they even act like 'humans'? Unfortunately the majority in these departments couldn't give a flying fuck about you, they merely toe the company line and try to hit whatever carelessly inhumane KPIs their manager gave them.

Across all facets of business, HR/recruiting/personnel management seems to be the area that has never evolved. We are in the exact same position as we were for decades. Employees on one side of the fence, HR the other side. Tech has been trying to change that, however. Unlike tech's exceptional effectiveness in areas like product development, capital management and so on, the caring of people has made progress, but only incrementally so.

On paper, tech's way of managing people is the best in class in the world of modern business. In this chapter I will outline the different ways tech has optimised the foundations and paths of people management. Tech's success sadly gets the better of it. These great practices to manage people get diluted with size. The bigger companies grow, the quicker bad actors creep in with their egos, often feigning incompetence or inability to learn, that throw all the good-natured policies out the window. And tech grows bigger, quicker, than anyone else, so the corporate perverts get their claws in quicker.

But let's not let the 'corporate perverts' disturb our look at how well tech has endeavoured to make their workplaces the best in class in modern society.

Let's first take a helicopter view, looking at organisational structures up high and wide.

Before proceeding, it's worth distinguishing between management and leadership. Management is coaching and leading people, on a one-to-one level, or one-to-a-few. Leadership is management, at scale. It's influencing and coaching widely.

Leadership is communicating through Netflix. Management is communicating through WhatsApp.

The world is flat, and fluid

Let's start with the organisational structure. The most striking difference between the look and feel of a tech organisational structure to that of the more traditional laggard companies is a conscious imperative to remove hierarchy where possible. In essence, to keep the structure as flat as possible. Steve Jobs famously said, 'You have to be run by ideas, not hierarchy.'[i]

Managers are there to serve their reports, or individual contributors as they are called, not to serve themselves or other managers. It's a different philosophy. Where it falls down is that humans are humans. Egos are still alive and well.

The old command-and-control, restricted-information and share-as-little-as- possible model doesn't work in the modern world of business, where trust and speed of decision-making are critical. Transparency is not just about sharing information, it's an assurance, as a company manager towards your team and your customers, that your company trusts each employee, at a fundamental level, to do the right thing for the company and themselves. Especially when enforced by reliable follow-up behaviour and results that back up that promise.[ii]

There are pitfalls to being overtly transparent in today's world, pitfalls that tech almost prides itself on – its self-awareness coupled with bullishness that openness is the correct course. Patreon chooses transparency for instance, but throws caution, openly, to the potential downsides of this choice:

- *Key information could leak and damage the company.*
- *The team could feel information overload via over-sharing.*
- *Information could be misinterpreted without proper context.*
- *Folks might share problems before having solutions; too much of that could shake confidence in leadership.*

They surmise then that 'despite these costs, we operate with high transparency to give our team the context they need to make great decisions.'

Google's Laszlo Bock summarised the attitude to removing hierarchy, and actually trusting employees:

Fundamentally, if you're an organization that says 'Our people are our greatest asset' (as most do), and you mean it, you must default to open. Otherwise, you're lying to your people and to yourself. You're saying people matter but treating them like they don't. Openness demonstrates to your employees that you believe they are trustworthy and have good judgment. And giving them more context about what is happening (and how and why) will enable them to do their jobs more effectively and contribute in ways a top-down manager couldn't anticipate.[iii]

There is a 'less is more' spirit when it comes to management practices in tech. Twilio's Lawson gives a pragmatic view, that runs against the capitalist mindset to 'add more headcount to boost growth':

I believe the goal isn't better collaboration; it's actually less collaboration. Great companies don't say: 'I need better customer support.' They say: 'We should reduce the need for customers to contact customer support.' In the same way, great companies reduce the need for teams, and individuals, to collaborate by standardizing or productizing the interactions between the groups. This frees up teams to spend more time innovating, and less time in internal coordination meetings. The key is treating other parts of the company as customers rather than collaborators.[iv]

Every org structure in tech is designed towards the customer and market environment. Spotify co-president and chief product and technology officer, Söderström, mused about how Apple and Amazon stack up their orgs, and how Spotify orients themselves towards the end user in comparison:

I talk about two orgs extremes, Amazon on one side and Apple on the other. This isn't necessarily true, but if you stereotype a little bit, Amazon is known for parallel teams. You run in parallel. You divide and conquer. You have the <u>two- pizza teams</u> and you're unblocked from reaching the consumer. That also results in a consumer experience where you might see three search boxes from three different teams on the screen at the same time. But it works. It's a trillion-dollar company.

It's not like there's nothing wrong with it, but it doesn't optimize for simple user experience, it optimizes for speed.

I think Apple is the opposite. They ship much, much slower than Amazon, but no one gets to put their own search box there. It is centrally synchronized. They managed to build something very complex that still feels like it was built by very few people for a single user. We chose to adopt more of that. We needed to synchronize the company and eat that complexity of music, podcasts, and audiobooks – and potentially other things – for the user, instead of just shipping our org chart to the user, saying, 'You figure it out.'

We built this org where we have three horizontal layers. We have a platform layer, which is the Spotify technology platform. We have the Spotify experience layer, which is all the applications, surfaces, mobile apps, cars, and desktops owned by a single person. Then we have a personalization layer. How do you choose between recommending a song, a podcast, or an audiobook for the same user at a certain moment? What is best for the user and for the company? We have these three horizontals that everything has to go through. It's a synchronization function that actually slows things down, but then these people are forced to eat all that complexity that would otherwise end up with the end user.

So these vertical businesses – the podcast business, the music business, and the audiobook business – can't actually just go and ship stuff to the user. They have to go through these synchronization functions. That was the big org change we haven't spoken much about externally. It is all in service of being able to do this without drastically increasing the complexity for users, to keep it simple. So far, we think it's working. We have quantitative metrics that say consumption on Spotify is way higher than any competitor, even though they only do one thing, like music.

Management is coded

In tech, culture is coded, values are coded, and management is coded, obviously. These coded behaviours are intended to cascade down to manager reports, thereby scaling desired excellence, standards of performance.

Standards, then, are the code in which human collaboration and discovery is written. Great managers know that if they want to build a cooperative, creative organisation, they will have to ensure that their employees use the relevant codes.[v]

Here is a look at Meta's management behaviours:

1. *They care about their team members.*
2. *They provide opportunities for growth.*
3. *They set clear expectations and goals.*
4. *They give frequent, actionable feedback.*
5. *They provide helpful resources.*
6. *They hold their team accountable to success.*
7. *They recognize outstanding work.*

Here are the ten behaviours that make a great manager at Google:

1. Is a good coach

Great managers are not simply great performers. They invest the time and energy to coach others.

Great managers share best practices so that their teams can grow.

2. Empowers team and does not micromanage

It's all about empowerment.

What are you doing to empower others on your team and across the organization?

Micromanagement is one of the great blunders of poor managers. Give your team space. Be flexible. Sometimes, you just need to get out of their way. No one likes a micromanager.

3. Creates an inclusive team environment, showing concern for success and well-being

Be inclusive. Embrace your team and make them part of the mission. Create an environment where anyone can ask a question, experiment and propose a new idea.

4. Is productive and results-oriented

Results matter, but you need to create a culture in which everyone can thrive to produce the desired results.

Show your team how to produce the results that you want. Don't just set goals and then expect outcomes.

5. Is a good communicator – listens and shares information

Too many managers fail because they can't communicate. Communication is not top-down or unidirectional. It's essential to be a good listener. Invest the time to get in the arena and listen to your team.

6. Supports career development and discusses performance

Don't focus on what your team can do for you. Focus on what you can do for them – and how you can work with them to advance the goals and mission of the organization.

Career development is essential – give your team the tools they need to thrive. Feedback (positive and constructive) is so important – make sure to get it right.

7. Has a clear vision/strategy for the team

If the manager doesn't have a clear vision and strategy, how can the team thrive?

It starts with the manager to set the tone and lay the foundation and direction for the team.

8. Has key technical skills to help advise the team

Substance matters.

Managers don't 'check out' when they become managers. Rather, they get in the weeds.

Not only can you help achieve better outcomes, but also you can gain credibility with your team when you demonstrate your technical expertise.

9. Collaborates across Google

Your team is not an island.

You must collaborate across the organization. You have expertise that someone in another group can use. They too have skills that can benefit you.

The more everyone shares, the more the organization rises. Collaboration leads to wonderful synergies.

10. Is a strong decision maker

Analysis is helpful. Strategy is important. Scenario testing provides focus. However, there is no replacement for being a strong decision maker.

You can spend unlimited time analyzing, strategizing and scenario-testing. It's the action that matters.[vi]

Best practices

One the best learnings I had at my time at Meta was on two simple words in combination, 'best practices'. A combination I never heard in previous jobs and industries.

Best practices meant the best way to do something. The best way to present a solution to a client. The best way to collaborate with an XFN partner. The best way to share learnings.

Best practices were the learnings and successes, codified. Shared through conversation, and scaled through replication. (The best) managers were the ones who unearthed best practices between individuals and teams and then surfaced them to others, highlighting what great looks like, so all ships could rise. 'They recognize outstanding work.'

And management best practices are no different; tech tends to share which management attitudes and programs are working best. HubSpot for instance have redefined employee needs:

	THEN	NOW
Focus	Pension	Purpose
Need	Good Boss	Great Colleagues
Hours	9-5	Whenever
Workplace	Office	Wherever
Tenure	Whole Career	Whatever

Psychological safety

A major investigation by Google, which sought to identify why some teams perform better than others, found that psychological safety was the single most important factor driving success, a result that has been widely replicated. 'Psychological safety was far and away the most important of the dynamics we found,' their report stated. 'And it affects pretty much every important dimension we look at for employees. Individuals on teams with higher psychological safety are less likely to leave Google, they're more likely to harness the power of diverse ideas from their teammates, they bring in more revenue, and they're rated as effective twice as often by executives.'[vii]

That's coming from Google. A company I'd argue is the most thorough and meticulous in its approach to data. The inputs, processes and outputs are the best in the world. It's a slam dunk.

The environment for work is crucial. How failure is treated. How great work is elevated. But the key differentiator is: do your manager and peers have your back? Trust and safety are crucial.

Tech is leading on this, especially from an unconscious bias perspective. Tackling diversity and inclusion (D&I) head-on is one approach tech is leading on. Patreon not only promotes its lean into D&I in its culture slides, they also get explicitly more prescriptive than most.

We build an inclusive environment because we believe that will give us the best chance at funding the creative class. We fight hard against unfair practices and trends that we see affecting underrepresented minorities at other tech companies. We want to reverse those trends by creating opportunities for anyone to succeed at Patreon.

Through language, they look to enforce a more balanced workplace:

Diversity and Inclusion messaging is important to us. There is no such thing as a diverse 'candidate' or 'person.' Please do not use that language.
'Teams' can be diverse or lack diversity, not individuals.
Also, some teammates prefer gender neutral pronouns. You can find pronoun preference in each person's Slack bio.
If someone slips up and uses improper language, speak up and correct them with compassion. Remember, all feedback at Patreon is KIND and DIRECT.

Let's cover a sort of side point on psychological safety, in relation to having 'smart' people in the room. Let the Stanford marshmallow experiment soak in for a moment …

Walter Mischel, a professor of psychology, challenged two groups to build the tallest possible structure using the following items: twenty pieces of uncooked spaghetti one yard of transparent tape, one yard of string and one standard- size marshmallow. The contest had one rule: The marshmallow had to end up on top. The fascinating part of the experiment, however, had less to do with the task than with the participants. Some of the teams consisted of business school students. The others consisted of kindergartners.

The business school students appeared to be collaborating, but in fact they were engaged in a process psychologists call status management. They were figuring out where they fit into the larger picture: who is in charge? Is it okay to criticise someone's idea? What are the rules here? Their interactions appear smooth, but their underlying behaviour is riddled with inefficiency, hesitation and subtle competition.

There is a punchy case for heightened listening in tech, and society in general to be honest.

Back to Google. A group of engineers examined 180 of Google's employee teams. They scrutinised team members' personality traits, backgrounds, hobbies and daily habits and found no predictive patterns of a group's success or failure. How teams were structured, how they measured their progress, and how often they met were also all over the map. After three years of collecting data, the researchers finally reached some conclusions about what made for cohesive and effective teams. What they found was that the most productive teams were the ones where members spoke in roughly the same proportion, known as 'equality in distribution of conversational turn-taking.' The best teams also had higher 'average social sensitivity,' which means they were good at intuiting one another's feelings based on things like tone of voice, facial expressions, and other nonverbal cues. In other words, Google found out that successful teams listened to one another.[viii]

In today's economy, effective listening is likely a significant part of your job. Nearly all job growth since 1980 has been in occupations with higher levels of social interaction, whereas positions that require predominantly analytical and mathematical reasoning – that can be turned into an algorithm – have been disappearing.

Virginia Woolf said, 'Words are full of echoes, of memories, of associations. They have been out and about, on people's lips, in their houses, in the streets, in the fields, for so many centuries.'

Effective listening is crucial to psychological safety in the workplace because it fosters open communication, encourages collaboration, and helps team members feel heard and valued. When team members feel psychologically safe, they are more likely to take interpersonal risks, leading to increased innovation and productivity. Without it, tech can't innovate at speed.

Tool up

Giving employees the necessary tools to do a job is criminally underrated. I've worked in places where there was no Wi-Fi, and I was expected to run social media campaigns. How often have you been in an office space and needed a battery for something like your wireless mouse or laptop? Half an hour spent asking people if they have AA batteries, half an hour wasted, total struggle.

Tech optimises tooling up, giving the core tools to do the job, and supposedly 'fluffy tools', for the purpose of having people focus on their strengths and impact.

Ever wonder why engineers flock to companies like Google? Sure, the pay is good. But the support infrastructure is world-class. It's one thing to coddle developers with free lunch and tricycles, but Google really coddles developers with great infrastructure on which to build. When your tools direct nearly all of your energy towards the task at hand – serving customers and being creative – it's magical. The opposite is also true – when you're fighting your tools, it's a real morale hit.[ix]

When starting at a tech company, you are handed a laptop (predominantly MacBooks) and a phone. These are your primary tools for work. Used wherever, whenever. If something happens to them (lots of phones get lost over bank holiday weekends, funny that) an employee goes to the IT desk, where that team is goaled for speed and quality of service. Everything is tracked for time and quality.

Day 1 at any tech company worth its salt will have you equipped with everything you need to do your job. The laptop; the 'buddy' on your team to ask where to log your expenses, how to book time off. All with the purpose of empowering you to do your core job as quickly and effectively as possible.

Show care

Lori Goler, Meta's HR head, outlined that the very first priority manager behaviour to nail is to show care. That managers care about their team members.

It starts with finding managers who actually want to be managers rather than those who feel like they need to be managers in order to progress in their careers:

'It sounds basic, but it's harder than it sounds in an organization that's scaling quickly' to find these people, Goler said. Those who have that passion for leading a team are able to make personal connections with their employees and actually want to see them succeed.

Take the time to get to know and care about people. Note the little things – partner and kids' names, important family matters, what they care about outside of work essentially. Eric Schmidt believes in the three-week rule:

When you start a new position, for the first three weeks don't do anything. Listen to people, understand their issues and priorities, get to know and care about them, and earn their trust. So in fact, you are doing something: You are establishing a healthy relationship. And don't forget to make people smile.

Praise is underused and underappreciated as a management tool. When it is deserved, don't hold back.[x]

In a Gallup study, the total time spent discussing each employee's style and performance was roughly four hours per employee per year. And as one front-line supervisor said, 'If you can't spend four hours a year with each of your people, then you've either got too many people, or you shouldn't be a manager.'[xi]

Ed Catmull of Pixar believes the best managers acknowledge and make room for what they do not know – not just because humility is a virtue but because until one adopts that mindset, the most striking breakthroughs cannot occur. He says, and this should be framed for its simplicity:

Find, develop, and support good people, and they in turn will find, develop, and own good ideas.[xii]

Remove grey areas and assumptions

TRUST IS A SERIOUS PROBLEM, WE HAVE TO GET TO A NEW LEVEL OF TRANSPARENCY – ONLY THROUGH RADICAL TRANSPARENCY WILL WE GET TO RADICAL NEW LEVELS OF TRUST.

— Marc Benioff, CEO of Salesforce

With the speed of change, and avalanche upon avalanche of information in tech, keeping people aligned is key, with communication the driver.

Transparency and accountability are two key virtues of tech companies, where everyone knows their lane, or should do. Google has built one of the finest organisational machines in the history of business, creating not just a swimming pool of clear lanes for employees, but a sea of lanes. Primarily around these five areas:

1. Regular communication and updates: Google regularly communicates with its employees through company-wide meetings, newsletters, and other channels. This helps keep employees informed about company news, updates, and initiatives.
2. Open feedback channels: Google encourages its employees to provide feedback and share their opinions through various channels, such as surveys, town halls, and open forums. This helps ensure that employees feel heard and valued, and that their opinions are taken into account when making decisions.
3. Performance evaluations: Google uses a system of regular performance evaluations to provide feedback and set goals for its employees. This helps ensure that employees understand what is expected of them and have a clear path for career development.
4. Employee resource groups: Google has established employee resource groups (ERGs) for various communities within the company, such as LGBTQ+ employees, women, and ethnicity-based groups.
5. These groups provide a platform for employees to connect with each other, share their experiences, and advocate for change within the company.
6. Transparency in policies and practices: Google has publicly shared information about its policies and practices, such as its diversity and inclusion initiatives, its approach to data privacy, and its environmental sustainability goals. This helps ensure that employees and other stakeholders understand the company's values and commitments.

Remove barriers

What was most interesting about the role of managers at Facebook was their purpose in a strengths-based business. Not just interesting, it was downright refreshing.

Managers existed to get out of the way of their reports. They were there to remove barriers to their impact. Ensuring reports had the tools, training and belief to succeed. Removing crap from people's workdays isn't just a nice to have, it's a vital piece of burnout prevention and waste.

The time and effort required to complete many critical business tasks grew significantly between 2010 and 2015. Hiring a new employee took sixty-three days in 2015, up from forty-two days just five years earlier. Delivering an office IT project took more than ten months, up from less than nine months in 2010.

Entering into a B2B sales contract took 22 per cent longer than it did five years earlier. And in many cases, it's not just the amount of time that grew – the number of people required to complete these tasks increased as well. The implications for the economy are immense. Estimates by management scholars Gary Hamel and Michele Zanini suggest that corporate bureaucracy costs the US economy more than $3 trillion each year.[xiii]

Having previously 'siloed' teams working together is key. Bob Iger saw the magic of collaboration first-hand when he visited the Pixar offices, first sitting with John Lasseter and the animation team. Then he spent time with Ed Catmull and the engineering team where they described in detail the technological platform that served the whole creative enterprise. The animators and directors were constantly challenging the engineers to give them the tools with which they could fulfil their creative dreams – to make Paris feel like Paris, for instance. Ed and his team on the engineering side were always building tools on their own, which they then brought to the artists to inspire them to think in ways they hadn't before. 'Look at how we can make snow, or water, or mist!' Catmull showed Iger the most sophisticated animation tools ever invented, technological ingenuity that enabled creativity at its highest form. This yin and yang was the soul of Pixar. Everything flowed from it.

It's worth getting the 'nerds' at the front table to unlock growth, you hear.

Create leaders

Leadership is an elevated virtue in tech, as it leads in business, it makes a point to promote leaders within. Managers are expected to foster and highlight leadership behaviours in their reports. Zappos were ahead of the game here:

Our philosophy at Zappos is different. Rather than focusing on individuals as assets, we instead focus on building as our asset a pipeline of people in every single department with varying levels of skills and experience, ranging from entry level all the way up through senior management and leadership positions.

Our vision is for almost all of our hires to be entry level, but for the company to provide all the training and mentorship necessary so that any employee has the opportunity to become a senior leader within the company within five to seven years. For us, this is still a work in progress, but we're really excited about its future. Without continually growing and learning both personally and professionally, it's unlikely that any individual employee will still be with the company ten years from now.

Our goal at Zappos is for our employees to think of their work not as a job or career, but as a calling.[xiv]

Goal setting

'Plan the Work and Work the Plan' was the calling card for setting goals and establishing operational rigour at Facebook. Which I'd argue was more of a belief system than a prescriptive mental framework. It got buy-in to planning, which is half the battle.

By asking people questions about their plans and intentions, we increase the likelihood that they actually act on these plans and intentions. Research shows that if I ask you whether you're planning to buy a new computer in the next six months, you'll be 18 per cent more likely to go out and get one.[xv]

Instead, specifics are needed. Goals are most useful if they're framed in a positive, immediate, concrete, specific (PICS) format: positive refers to motivation – your goal should be something you move towards, not away from. Goals like 'I don't want to be fat anymore' are a recipe for threat lockdown – you're reinforcing the negative instead of using reinterpretation to change your mind's prediction to get excited about improving. For best results, eliminate conflicts first, then move towards what you want to achieve.

Immediate refers to time scale: your goals should be things that you decide to make progress on now, not 'someday' or 'eventually'. If you don't want to commit to working on a particular goal now, put it on your someday/maybe list and focus on something else. Concrete means you're able to see the results in the real world. Goals are achievements – you should know when you've accomplished what you set out to achieve. Setting goals like 'I want to be happy' won't work because they're not concrete – how would you know when you're done? When you reach the top of Mount Everest, you've achieved something tangible in the real world – that's concrete. Specific means you're able to define exactly what, when, and where you're going to achieve your goal. Climbing Mount Everest on a certain date in the near future is specific, which makes it easy for your mind to plan exactly how you'll go about accomplishing this.[xvi]

Google has taken the lead here with goaling. In late 1999, John Doerr gave a presentation at Google that changed the company, because it created a simple tool that let the founders institutionalise their 'think big' ethos. John sat on our board, and his firm, Kleiner Perkins, had recently invested in the company. The topic was a form of management by objectives called OKRs (to which we referred in the previous chapter), which John had learned from former Intel CEO Andy Grove. There are several characteristics that set OKRs apart from their typical underpromise-and-overdeliver corporate-objective brethren.[xvii]

OKRs are an individual's *objectives* (the strategic goals to accomplish) and *key results* (the way in which progress towards that goal is measured). Every employee updates and posts his/her OKRs company-wide every quarter, making it easy for anyone to quickly find anyone else's priorities. When you meet someone at Google and want to learn more about what they do, you go on Moma (Google's Intranet system) and read their OKRs. This isn't just a job title and description of the role, it's their first-person account of the stuff they are working on and care about. It's the fastest way to figure out what motivates them.

John Doerr introduced the OKR model to Google, which famously accelerated their scale to unprecedented levels. He fondly remembered one particular OKR, that brought the leading web browser to the world, and probably helped the OKR owner to become the CEO of that very company.

Larry Page and Sergey Brin turned to Sundar Pichai, who at the time was a Google product manager. They said to him they'd like to create the next- generation web browser and application development environment, which eventually became Google Chrome. Now, Sundar's genius was to translate that into both the correct objective, build the world's best browser, and the correct key results. So how will you measure – what will be the key results to tell you that you've built the best browser? Sundar could have chosen any number of measures, like click-throughs or revenues or how many times people came back to using Chrome. And by the way, any one of those nuanced and different key results would've taken his effort in a different direction.

What Sundar did brilliantly is say, 'We're simply going to measure success by the number of users.' So he boiled it down into a bold and beautiful OKR, where the main key result in the beginning was to reach twenty million weekly active users by the end of the year, starting from zero, by the way. This was a moonshot for sure. In fact, do you remember the internet back in 2008? It was very, very slow. We were using Internet Explorer, and the Chrome team missed their target. That comes with the territory when you set really audacious goals. So what matters is what Sundar then did. Did he give up? No, he kept the same timeless objective to build the world's best browser, but he set even more aggressive stretch goals. By 2010, he said his key result would be 111 million weekly active users. And they made that key result.[xviii]

Senior leaders who are new to Amazon are often surprised by how little time is spent discussing actual financial results or debating projected financial outputs. Bezos explains:

To be clear, we take these financial outputs seriously, but we believe that focusing our energy on the controllable inputs to our business is the most effective way to maximise financial outputs over time. Our annual goal setting process begins in the fall and concludes early in the new year after we've completed our peak holiday quarter. Our goal setting sessions are lengthy, spirited, and detail orientated. We have a high bar for the experience our customers deserve and a sense of urgency to improve that experience.

We've been using the same annual process for many years. For 2010, we have 452 detailed goals with owners, deliverables, and target completion dates.

These are not only the goals our teams set for themselves, but they are the ones we feel are most important to monitor. None of these goals are easy and many will not be achieved without invention. We review the status of each of these goals several times per year among our senior leadership team and add, remove and modify goals as we proceed.

A review of our current goals reveals more interesting statistics: 360 of 452 goals will have a direct impact on customer experience.

The word revenue is used eight times and free cash flow is used only four times. In the 452 goals, the terms net income, gross profit or margin, and operating profit are not used once.

Taken as a whole, the set of goals is indicative of our fundamental approach. Start with customers and work backwards. Listen to customers, but don't just listen to customers-also invent on their behalf. We can't assure you that we'll continue to obsess over customers. We have strong conviction that that approach – in the long term – is every bit as good for owners as it is for customers.

It's still Day 1.[xix]

Size matters

Small teams beat big teams. This is one of the tech movement's most cherished, universal beliefs. We believe in the power of small teams – whereas in traditional corporate structures, the size of the team equals the importance of the project.[xx]

And tech's rule of thumb when it comes to team size has to do with pizza. The two-pizza rule. Jeff Bezos wrote the 'two-pizza team' memo proposing that they divide the company into small teams in order to move faster. (The idea was that you could feed the whole team with two pizzas.) It plays to the rule of seven: every attendee over seven reduces the likelihood of making a good, quick, executable decision by 10 per cent.[xxi]

Size and then their purpose is key, according to Jeff Lawson:

Teams do their best work when each member of the team feels accountable to the customer, and a deep sense of purpose to serve the customer. Small teams enable that kind of connection and purpose, with a mission that comes from inside the team, driven by a primary interaction with the customer and their problems, not from executives.[xxii]

It's worth noting the essence of this thinking. Lawson is ex-Amazon and saw this two-pizza rule first-hand, so he has optimised it further at Twilio.

In recent years, however, the two-pizza rule has been scraped into the bin. The company's VP of operations, Chris Barbin, said that Amazon has moved from a two-pizza rule to a single-threaded leader model.

The original two-pizza rule meant that there was no one person who could take charge and make decisions on behalf of the team. This often led to problems when someone else had to step in and take control when things went wrong.

The new approach solves this problem by giving one person responsibility for leading the team, while still keeping the size of each team small enough so that they can work effectively together without having too much overhead or bureaucracy involved in their day-to-day operations.

As growth abounds, Reed Hastings has this guidance:

I've also found having a lean workforce has side advantages. Managing people well is hard and takes a lot of effort. Managing mediocre-performing employees is harder and more time consuming. By keeping our organization small and our teams lean, each manager has fewer people to manage and can therefore do a better job at it. When those lean teams are exclusively made up of exceptional-performing employees, the managers do better, the employees do better, and the entire team works better – and faster.[xxiii]

Focus on impact

Another piece of inspirational 'go get 'em' on the walls of Facebook was a poster reading 'Focus on Impact'.

What does that mean in practice? In Mark Zuckerberg's own words:

If we want to have the biggest impact, the best way to do this is to make sure we always focus on solving the most important problems. It sounds simple, but we think most companies do this poorly and waste a lot of time. We expect everyone at Facebook to be good at finding the biggest problems to work on.[xxiv]

Google has been famous for its 80/20 time. This tiers the priority and impact, while giving employees their beloved autonomy. It's a policy where it encourages Google employees to spend 80 per cent of their time on core projects, and roughly 20 per cent (or one day per week) on 'innovation' activities that speak to their personal interests and passions. Autonomy for employees and added innovation for Google are the outcomes.

Here is their view, straight from the horse's mouth:

The most valuable result of 20 percent time isn't the products and features that get created, it's the things that people learn when they try something new.

Most 20 percent projects require people to practice or develop skills outside of those they use on a day-to-day basis, often collaborating with colleagues they don't regularly work with. Even if these projects rarely yield some new, wow innovation, they always yield smarter smart creatives. As Urs Hölzle likes to point out, 20 percent time may be the best educational program a company can have.[xxv]

The innovations that have come from the 20 per cent time of Google employees are mind-blowing. There is the money maker AdSense. The sticky Google News. And G-fucking-mail. Not bad, not bad at all.

Onboarding

Starting a job at a tech company is a flurry of excitement and ambition. It isn't the here is your desk, here is your team and here is the employee handbook approach. It's immersive in culture. It's prescriptive in breadth of information. And it is aimed to have employees hit the ground running at ferocious speed.

It's all about giving employees the tools, access and context to hit the ground running. Asana are most certainly leaders in this space.

Although the process will look different from company to company, here are some onboarding best practices from Asana:

1. Provide clarity on what to expect before day one

Send an email a few days before your new hires start. Include the first day's schedule, logistics (how to enter the building, dress code, etc.), and if they should bring anything (a personal laptop, HR documents, etc.).

2. Create helpful resources to avoid repeat questions

For questions that come up with every new hire – like company terminology or how to use cross-functional software – create standardized documents to help. Iterate on them regularly, so you can incorporate new questions that come up. – Asana Tip –

Set up an onboarding project in Asana for each new employee. Break it up into sections and add tasks like 'Register for benefits' or 'Enroll in our 401k plan.'

3. Don't over-automate things

Relying on technology and automation (like custom templates in Asana) is a great way to streamline your workflow, but don't forget to tailor the experience to each person. It's easy to fall into the automation trap, so remember that onboarding is a personal experience – it's the first impression new hires will get when they join your company. Find small ways to make new hires feel welcome, not just like another number.

4. Make time for personal interactions

Make sure to schedule in time for new hires to meet other members of the team over lunch, coffee, or a casual one-on-one. Assigning an onboarding mentor to each new hire can also be helpful – their mentor acts as a facilitator and resource throughout their onboarding.

– Asana Tip –

Ask new hires to fill out their profile in Asana so teammates can easily match their face to their name and role.

5. Give context for every role

In addition to general and functional onboarding, provide a way for new hires to learn about other teams and functions across the company. This could take the form of monthly onboarding meetings where representatives from each team give new hires a brief overview, loose 1-1 meetings, or even a shadowing session.

Understanding cross-functional connections and goals encourages new hires to think holistically and will help them see where their work fits into the broader organization.

6. Onboarding should be a soft landing

A new hire's first week should be a balance of being excited, settling in, and some easy wins. It's important for the onboarding experience not to feel overwhelming and for new hires to accomplish things – even if they're small – in their first week.

Make a great first impression

Onboarding is one of the first steps you take towards setting your employees up for success, and it's an ever-evolving process. As more people join your company, new and different opportunities to improve *it will arise, so keep adapting. Get feedback often, find what works for your team, and continue iterating on it with each new hire.*

Onboarding is a huge group effort. So many people come together when someone is hired – HR, functional teams, coordinators, IT – that to have their efforts fall flat would be a huge disappointment. But by following these best practices, you can provide a great onboarding experience together.[xxvi]

Adding to this, tech institutes a buddy/mentor system, which is ideal in helping a new employee understand the culture quicker and know who best to engage with to get things done. The most successful onboarding programs help the new employees develop relationships within the company as soon as possible because relationships help build trust and trust is the core foundation of a great working environment.[xxvii]

Feedback is a gift, via management

We learned earlier how tech leans into failure and utilises feedback as a truth-seeking resilience builder in employees. How management drives the 'feedback is a gift' ethos in tech is interesting.

A culture of feedback giving and receiving fostered in tech is done via the soft touchpoints like 'Feedback is a Gift' coded in posters and in conversation. It's also scaled through the tech itself.

At Facebook, there was the Thanks tool. If you wanted to gush gratefulness to a colleague for their support on some project or other, you went to the dashboard in the internal company Wiki to post thanks to the employee(s).

This was visible to all other managers and colleagues. Transparency is key.

Google took this a step further, anyone getting a nod of praise from a colleague into a similar tool to Facebook's Thanks tool. The difference being recipients of praise got a $100 dollar spot bonus for each one. Talk about incentivising good efforts and deeds amongst colleagues.

Culture building or culture buying? Whatever way you cut it, it has worked.

And then there are employee surveys where employees can score the culture, mission, leadership, their direct manager and more. At Facebook they were called Pulse Surveys, run every quarter.

The most important question of the whole survey comes at the end: 'Do you feel action will be taken from the outcomes of the survey?' A testament to tech's quest for truth and accountability.

Paying people

Long story short, tech pays very well. That should not come as a surprise to anyone reading this book. Stories of tech companies going public, and creating thousands of millionaires is a common narrative in the media.

Tech doesn't have a straightforward salary either, it's a world of OTE. Which means 'on target earnings'. It's an expected total pay package including salary, commission and/or company bonus. Then there are the shares issued. Say you start at Amazon and you get offered ten shares; doesn't sound like much, but it's a nice 30,000 euros to you, and it will grow nicely. Shares then have different vesting periods – meaning you don't get access to them immediately – usually staggered over four years.

Tech companies including equity or stock options is a savvy practice, bringing a multitude of benefits, namely:

- Incentivizes employees: Equity can incentivize employees to work hard and contribute to the company's success because their financial rewards are tied to the performance of the company.
- Attracts and retains talent: Offering equity can help attract and retain top talent, as it provides employees with the opportunity to benefit financially from the company's growth and success.

- Aligns employee and company interests: Equity aligns the interests of employees and the company, as both benefit when the company performs well.
- Helps with cash flow: Equity can be a more attractive form of compensation for start-ups and early-stage companies, as it allows them to conserve cash while still offering employees a valuable form of compensation.
- Creates a sense of ownership: Equity can create a sense of ownership and loyalty among employees, as they feel they have a stake in the company's success.
- Can be tax-efficient: Depending on the type of equity or stock options offered, they can be more tax-efficient than other forms of compensation, providing additional financial benefits for employees.

Add in free food, phone bill paid, gym membership and other benefits, and life is rosy. Rent/mortgage, if you don't have kids, becomes your only real expense. If you balk at car ownership like I do, that is.

Reed Hasting's view of Netflix and pay gives a good insight into the mindset:

Pay Top of Market is Core to High Performance Culture. One outstanding employee gets more done and costs less than two adequate employees. We endeavour to have only outstanding employees.

And Netflix exudes total transparency when it comes to pay:

Good for each employee to understand their market value.

It's a healthy idea, not a traitorous one, to understand what other firms would pay you, by interviewing and talking to peers at other companies

- *Talk with your manager about what you find in terms of comp*
- *Stay mindful of company information*

eShares is a contrast to Netflix then who don't pay 'top of market' salaries, here is why:

1. We must earn our talent (we can't buy it).
2. The best people deeply value non-financial compensation (often more than financial).
3. Employees that optimise for top-of-market pay are often mercenaries and difficult to align.

Point three is the most crucial one there, as it filters out the 'rest and vest' people, that is those who jump between tech companies for salary increases and stock option rides.

Six years ago, Gravity Payments' CEO Dan Price, thirty-seven, discovered one of his employees was working a second job to make ends meet. His response? He gave her, and ultimately everyone in the company a raise to $70,000 per year. He paid for it by dropping his own $1.1 million salary to $70,000. He tweeted, 'Money buys happiness when you climb out of poverty. But going from well-off to very well-off doesn't make you happier. Doing what you believe is right, will.'

Six years after this decision that others said would destroy his business, Dan reports that revenue has tripled, the customer base has doubled, 70 per cent of his employees have paid down debt, many bought homes for the first time, 401(k) contributions grew by 155 per cent and turnover dropped in half. His business is now a Harvard Business School case study.

At the start of the pandemic, Dan says they lost 55 per cent of their revenue overnight. His loyal employees volunteered to take temporary pay cuts in order to prevent layoffs. They all weathered the storm. He paid everyone back and is now giving out raises.

His employees were so grateful they bought him a Tesla. And then he gave out more raises.

Dan Price made a choice to spiral up the happiness and abundance spiral, rather than down the fear and poverty spiral.[xxviii]

Dan Price, sound.

Meanwhile, Bezos said in an early shareholder letter: 'We know our success will be largely affected by our ability to attract and retain a motivated employee base, each of whom must think like, and therefore must actually be, an owner.'[xxix]

It pays to pay nicely

Coinbase recently set their stall on how they plan to optimise pay for employees, something I envisage others following their lead on:

Step 1: Increasing our compensation targets

In 2019, we made the decision to benchmark ourselves across a highly competitive set of peers and some of the largest tech companies in the world. This was an aggressive move for us at the time, as a small, private start-up. This year we've continued our commitment to top talent by further increasing our cash and equity compensation – from the 50th percentile amongst our peers to the 75th – across the entire company.

Step 2: Eliminating negotiations from the hiring process

Because our standard offers are world-class, we are officially eliminating negotiations on salary and equity from our recruiting process.

Anyone who wants to work in crypto belongs and is valued at Coinbase. It doesn't matter what your background is, where you went to school (or bootcamp), where you've worked before, or even what you've been paid before. If you pass our bar and are hired to do the same work, you get the same offer as the next candidate for a role.

Traditionally people expect they need to negotiate for the best package after being hired in a new job. Those that do this well tend to be rewarded, and those that don't lose out. These negotiations can disproportionately leave women and underrepresented minorities behind, and a disparity created early in someone's career can follow them for decades. We want to do everything we can to ensure that's not the experience at Coinbase. All employees in the same position, in the same location, receive the same salary and equity offer. No exceptions.

Eliminating negotiations doesn't mean all employees are paid the same after they begin working. In fact, we want *compensation differentiation, but it should be solely driven by demonstrated performance and outsized impact on our company and for our customers. We will continue to apply multipliers to our equity and cash rewards for high performers identified through our rigorous performance management process. This way, our high performers receive compensation commensurate with their impact, in addition to accelerated career development and a front row seat to building the cryptoeconomy.*

We are OK if we lose some candidates due to this decision – the best candidates for Coinbase are those who are looking for a highly competitive package and are ready to let their contributions speak for themselves.

Step 3: Adopting annual equity grants that drive predictable, real time compensation

Another goal of our new compensation program is to manage volatility and provide as much predictability for our employees as possible. Crypto has historically been volatile, and it's a reasonable assumption that our stock price may be, too. As we grow, we anticipate more candidates will value predictability in their annual compensation. Instead of a four-year new hire grant (standard at many tech companies), employees will receive annual grants, sized at one-year targets that vest in their entirety each year. An employee's multi-year equity compensation will no longer be dictated by our company valuation at a single point in time.

Some may say eliminating 4-year new hire grants could hurt retention; we disagree. We don't want employees to feel locked in at Coinbase based on grants awarded 3 or 4 years prior. We want to earn our employees' commitment every year and, likewise, expect them to earn their seat at Coinbase.

We are also eliminating the one-year cliff from our new hire grants. We expect new hires to add value on their first day, so it only makes sense for them to start vesting rewards for their contributions.

We also plan to make these annual grants for all employees together at one time, using one share price. This is designed to minimize disparate outcomes that can persist for years after one's start date. This is another way we are ensuring pay differences are due only to demonstrated performance. Everyone will have the same incentive to add value and grow our company together, which is important for our culture.[xxx]

Rating Performance

What determines pay and promotion when in tech? First off, it's key to understand what good performance looks like. As Prasad Setty explains, 'Traditional performance management systems make a big mistake. They combine two things that should be completely separate: performance evaluation and people development. Evaluation is necessary to distribute finite resources, like salary increases or bonus dollars. Development is just as necessary so people grow and improve. If you want people to grow, don't have those two conversations at the same time. Make development a constant back-and-forth between you and your team members, rather than a year-end surprise.'[xxxi]

Netflix outline their three necessary conditions for promotion:

1. Job has to be big enough

- *We might have an incredible manager of something, but we don't need a director of it because job isn't big enough. If an incredible manager left, we would replace with a manager, not a director.*

2. *Person has to be superstar in current role*

- *Could get the next level job here if applying from outside and we knew their talents well.*
- *Could get the next level job at peer firm that knew their talents well.*

3. *Person is an extraordinary role model for our culture and values.*[xxxii]

Optimising hiring

IT DOESN'T MAKE SENSE TO HIRE SMART PEOPLE AND TELL THEM WHAT TO DO. WE HIRE SMART PEOPLE SO THEY CAN TELL US WHAT TO DO.

— Steve Jobs

As I write this, six out of ten Londoners are applying for new jobs. There has never been a market so flush with people moving jobs. And guess who is going to clean up the best talent?

Hiring is not only a key focus in tech, it plays out as a mantra at many companies. Asana has the motto 'Always Be Recruiting', which is company-wide, across every level of employee.

Netflix in its culture deck stated that 'a great workplace is stunning colleagues. Great workplace is not espresso, lush benefits, sushi lunches, grand parties, or nice offices. We do some of these things, but only if they are efficient at attracting and retaining stunning colleagues.'

Uber (in the Travis Kalanick era) defined eight qualities it sought early on in employees:

1. *Vision*
2. *Quality Obsession*
3. *Innovation*
4. *Fierceness*
5. *Execution*
6. *Scale*
7. *Communication*
8. *Super Pumpedness**

*Those of us outside the US are allowed to balk a bit at that one.[xxxiii]

HubSpot know the value of culture as a hiring weapon. They say that culture is to recruiting as product is to marketing, in that customers are more easily attracted with a great product, whereas talented people are more easily attracted with a great culture.

Be open with the hires you want. Hootsuite does this brilliantly, by publicising who thrives at Hootsuite:

- *People who like to experiment and always try new things*
- *People who are self-directed and self-motivated*
- *People who never rest until the job is done*

Patreon goes even further, with their noticeboard of who should apply and why they stay, putting it all out there:

We hire people who are actually here to help creators get paid and that's what makes this place really unique.

In our most recent company-wide survey, 100% of our teammates answered 'Yes' when asked the question 'Is the work that your company does important?' 95% of the company responded that they understand how their individual work directly contributes to company mission.

We are also externally recognized for our team. The San Francisco Business Times named Patreon one of the top places to work in 2017, and we were named to similar lists in 2016.

People stay at Patreon because they love their teammates and our mission. Our employee attrition rate is ~1/3rd the national average.

Another weapon for hiring in tech is referrals. Good people follow good people, especially to good cultures. Some 60 per cent of hires tend to be referrals in tech companies. Tech has nice referral bonuses too, especially for engineers, upward of 1,500 euros.

There are three criteria Bezos instructs managers to consider when they are hiring: Will you admire this person? Will this person raise the average level of effectiveness of the group he or she is entering? Along what dimension might this person be a superstar?[xxxiv]

From very early on in Amazon's life, they knew they wanted to create a culture of builders – people who are curious, explorers. They like to invent. Even when they're experts, they are 'fresh' with a beginner's mind. They see the way the company does things as just the way they do things now. A builder's mentality helps us approach big, hard-to-solve opportunities with a humble conviction that success can come through iteration: invent, launch, reinvent, relaunch, start over, rinse, repeat, again and again. They know the path to success is anything but straight.[xxxv]

How do you hire great people and keep them from leaving? By giving them, first of all, a great mission – something that has real purpose, that has meaning. People want meaning in their lives.[xxxvi]

Amazon's hiring mantra is to hire well, rather than hire quickly. As such, they brought in the Bar Raiser programme to optimise their hiring, keeping the quality high and in tune with the culture, whilst scaling to a size unseen in history. We are talking going from 17,000 people in 2007 to almost 1.7 million in 2022:[xxxvii]

A Bar Raiser is an interviewer at Amazon who is brought into the hiring process to be an objective third party. By bringing in somebody who's not associated with the team, the best long-term hiring decisions are made and we can ensure that the company is always serving, surprising, and innovating for customers. The role of the Bar Raiser is to be a steward of Amazon's 16 Leadership Principles.[xxxviii]

Of course the Bar Raiser program is instrumental in reinforcing a key Amazon leadership principle: Hire and Develop the Best.

There are eight steps to the Bar Raiser hiring process, all pretty self-explanatory, but certainly more steps than a chat or three, as seen with candidates in other industries:

- Job description.
- Resume/CV review.
- Phone screen.
- In-house interview.
- Written feedback.
- Debrief/hiring meeting.
- Reference check.
- Offer through onboarding.

At other tech companies, the hiring process follows a similar path. In most cases after a phone screener (with the recruiting team), it follows a path like this:

- Hiring manager interview.
- Interview with three peers (checking for competence, experience and culture fit).
- Mock presentation to Hiring Manager and three peers.

This can all happen in the space of two to three weeks. To say interviewing for the tech companies is intense is an understatement.

Dave Morrissey

YOU CAN'T BUILD A GREAT COMPANY WITHOUT A GREAT TEAM, SO IT'S REALLY IMPORTANT TO PRIORITIZE HIRING AND BUILDING A STRONG CULTURE.

— Sam Altman

Letting people go

This is the horrible side of work life. Like relationships in life, when things aren't working out with either party, things have to come to an end. I'd love to say tech has optimised this part over other industries, but I haven't seen it. If anything, there can be more ruthlessness, as there is more at stake for HR and shitty leaders.

Netflix broke down the drain that poor performers bring, and their straightforward-ish solution:

If you have a team of five stunning employees and two adequate ones, the adequate ones will sap managers' energy, so they have less time for the top performers, reduce the quality of group discussions, lowering the team's overall IQ, force others to develop ways to work around them, reducing efficiency, drive staff who seek excellence to quit, and show the team you accept mediocrity, thus multiplying the problem.[xxxix]

Here is an approach that could seem utterly barmy in other industries. Tech invented the pay-to-quit phenomenon, first conjured up by Zappos and then adopted by Amazon. Once a year they offer to pay their associates (Amazon terminology) to leave. The first year the offer is made for $2,000. Then it goes up $1,000 a year until it reaches $5,000. The headline on the offer is 'Please Don't Take This Offer', which is the desired outcome. The goal of the initiative is to encourage people to take a moment and think about what they really want. In the long run, an employee staying somewhere they don't want to be isn't healthy for the employee or the company.[xl]

Training and constant learning

'We are a learning organism' is the latest mantra from tech companies, understanding that humility, curiosity and adaptability are the survive-to-thrive attitudes necessary for success in a rapidly changing environment.

As Jeff Lawson says, 'In most companies, "learning and development" is an HR function that means training – typically in a classroom, maybe online, where people learn skills. That's all valuable, but the kind of learning I'm talking about here is embedded in the very construction of the company and its culture, not just extracurricular activities that the most ambitious employees voluntarily undertake. It's on-the-job learning, taken to an extreme. The goal, always, is to find the truth. That must be our north star, the destination toward which we navigate.'[xli]

Some learning mechanisms that tech companies roll out are bootcamps, player coaches and mentorship programs. As well as constant on-the-job learning to seek and scale best practices. Bootcamps in particular are unique to tech, but could be applied elsewhere.

Bootcamps are short programs – from three months to a year – that train mid-career professionals to become developers. People join bootcamps often because they see a more promising career in coding, or merely because it piques their interest and they're interested in pursuing a more technical career. As opposed to four-year undergraduate degrees, bootcamp grads get a crash course in coding and quickly learn job-relevant skills needed to build a variety of websites and apps.[xlii]

Amazon have a programme called Career Choice, where they prepay 95 per cent of tuition for their employees to take courses for in-demand fields, such as aeroplane mechanics or nursing, regardless of whether the skills are relevant to a career at Amazon.

For creativity, with regard craftsmanship in particular, Meta had a nifty offering. There are Art Labs, a space that had everything from 3D printers to embroidery classes. There were even 'artists in residence', who were on hand to guide employees on their creative endeavours and run classes.

Time off

Imagine starting at a company and they tell you to take as much time off or holidays as you like; as long as you get your work done, do whatever you like. Utopia? Welcome to tech.

Not all tech companies have an unlimited vacation policy, but more and more are adopting the policy, especially post-Covid. Again, Netflix have led the charge. But they have a culture that supports it:

We'd found a way to give our high performers a little more control over their lives, and that control made everybody feel a little freer. Because of our high- talent density, our employees were already conscientious and responsible.

Because of our culture of candor, if anyone abused the system or took advantage of the freedom allotted, others would call them out directly and explain the undesirable impact of their actions.[xliii]

Reed himself has to be seen to enforce it. If he doesn't take time off, others won't. And then it needs to be encouraged through every meeting in the company:

Whenever I hear stories floating around about people not taking time off, it's time to put vacations on the agenda of a QBR meeting. This gives me an opportunity to talk about the type of environment we aspire to have and gives our leaders a chance to discuss, in small groups, techniques they use in order to achieve a healthy work-life balance for our workforce.[xliv]

Meta rolled out its fUel (yes that is a capital U amongst everything else in lower case) program, which stressed work-life balance accountability for, you guessed it, you. A key component of this was 'Recharge'. This entailed getting an extra month off, paid, whenever you did five years at the company. You could take this on top of annual leave. Cue a raft of employees rediscovering themselves on backpacking trips (in five-star hotels) across South America, South East Asia and the like.

The UK fintech Monzo followed Meta's lead. The online bank, which already offered a one-month unpaid sabbatical per year, boosted this to allow staff who have been in their roles for four years to take three months of paid leave either in one block or one month at a time.

Benefits

Tech changed the game when it comes to benefits. Free food. Gym memberships. Wellness benefits. 3D printing rooms for creativity. It's easy to just look at these things as gimmicks and a 'way to keep you working harder', but that misses the deeper purpose.

That being to foster autonomy, creativity and letting employees focus on impact.

'A Holistic Life' is what Hootsuite pride themselves on in regard to their approach to benefits and employee care:

Our quality of life is supported at work. There are things at the office like yoga, fresh juice, organic fruit, dogs, a gym and a nap room – not because it's a gimmick or because everyone is doing it, but because we are already people who pursue a healthy lifestyle and work-life balance.

Transportation, covered. Google, Meta and Apple in the Bay Area in particular cover the place with shuttle buses, taking their precious employees to and from work each day. This means employees don't have to worry about finding parking or paying for gas.

And then there is the food. Sweet merciful, Lord, the food.

Dave Morrissey

'We used to hire out our food service to a contractor,' said Ed Catmull, president and co-founder of Pixar. 'We didn't consider making food to be our core business. But when you hire it out, that food service company wants to make money, and the only way they can make money is to decrease the quality of the food or the service. They're not bad or greedy people; it's a structural problem. That's why we decided to take it over ourselves and give our people high-quality food at a reasonable price. Now we have really good food and people stay here instead of leaving, and they have the kind of conversations and encounters that help our business. It's pretty simple. We realized that food really is part of our core business.'[xlv]

A key reason for providing delicious, nutritious food is also time-saving, focus and culture building. Instead of going to a local deli or shop, worrying about bringing your wallet, standing in a long queue, rushing back to the office and not engaging with fellow employees, you have something much different. You have top-notch grub, and you break bread with your colleagues. It induces serendipitous conversations. I also believe it's behind the higher-than-normal coupling rate between employees. Tech seems to partner future married couples at a higher clip than seen elsewhere.

At Meta Dublin, the contractor Urban Picnic put on a show every day. Breakfast was famous. We are talking seven types of eggs here, people. Scrambled, normal and egg white. Boiled. Fried. Omelette. Poached. And a little bacon quiche thing. That's before all the bacon, sausages, army of freshly baked goods, juices and more and more.

On Thursdays, lunch featured cuisines from a different country. One week could be Japanese, the next week Jamaican, and Irish cuisine the week the weather distinctly changes from autumn to winter, lots of comforting mashed potato and gravy. Potatoes aside, my time spent eating at Meta expanded my taste palette, you'd swear I was Anthony Bourdain swanning around the office.

When you started at Meta, Facebook for most of its existence as a company of course, you were known to put on a bit of weight. The

'Facebook Fifteen'. Our competitors across the way waddled about with their 'Google Stone'.

Free transport and body shaming aside, there is a lot of compassion applied to benefits, which is admirable and should be emulated across other industries. At Google, when an employee dies, their spouse receives half pay from the company for ten years and their children get $1,000 per month until they turn nineteen. Yelp will pay for employees to travel for abortion access.

Whoop, the wearable tech company that provides sleep-tracking devices, is known for its innovative approach to employee wellness. They have hit two birds with one stone, by tying an employee wellness initiative to the product and customer value of the company. They practice what they preach: their employees receive a one-hundred-dollar bonus if they meet the Whoop recommended sleep goal of seven and a half hours per night.

Whoop has created a culture around optimising sleep and recovery, which is reflected in their sleep bonus policy. The company uses data from their sleep- tracking devices to determine if an employee has met the Whoop recommended goal and should be eligible for the bonus. Employees who meet this requirement will receive one hundred dollars on their next pay cheque.

Remote working

The war for talent was in the Cold War phase pre-pandemic, since, it's a full- blown world war, with those not leaned into tech finding themselves on the winning side. Companies that didn't provide their staff with tools like laptops in the first place scrambled. As for those with no semblance of doing business virtually over Zoom, Google Hangout, etc., they were in no man's land.

Tools are one thing, attitude to remote working is a whole other ball game. As I've written this book, the tech companies have been leading the charge with policies that show their attitude to remote work. It's a lesson in pragmatism, where they realise that work can be done remotely, and more importantly, many employees desire it. Post-pandemic, employees hold the cards.

Meta announced a ten-thousand-job boost in Europe at the beginning of 2022, fully remote roles would enable it to 'tap into talent' across the region. It said existing staff would be able to request to go fully remote and move countries if they wished, though remote staff would not be able to work from a local office. That's ten thousand people who will see Meta as a dandy place to work as they give choice and care. That's ten thousand people not going to any other company. It's no wonder the likes of Robinhood, Microsoft and Twitter are following suit with similar announcements.

Whatever policies tech or anyone else unlocks around remote working or a hybrid model or whatever, the winners will be those who lean into choice and comfort for their employees.

Team, not a family

Go on LinkedIn and check out the posts of people working in tech, I guarantee many will talk about how great it is to work in their 'Company X' family. The irony of it all. It's the biggest load of horseshit going in the land of tech. No one fires their family or 'manages up' to their parents. Or grandparents. 'I am skipping a level, managing up to my grandmother' … imagine.

Netflix, on the other hand, approaches it in a more palatable and realistic way. A professional sports team is a good metaphor for high talent density because athletes on professional teams:

- Demand excellence, counting on the manager to make sure every position is filled by the best person at any given time.
- Train to win, expecting to receive candid and continuous feedback about how to up their game from the coach and from one another.

- Know effort isn't enough, recognising that, if they put in a B performance despite an A for effort, they will be thanked and respectfully swapped out for another player.

eShares is managed like a professional sports team, not a start-up or a company:

No titles, just positions ...

We are all defined as eShares employees. We play positions like 'Sales', 'Product', 'Dev'. We are not defined with titles like 'Vice President' or 'Senior Analyst'.

'Org chart' is our current formation.

The 'org chart' changes depending on the goals of the organisation. We change the org chart frequently (sometimes every month). People move groups and change managers frequently. People are tied to positions, not titles.

Practice what you preach

A simple rule of thumb here as a manager: make sure you would work for yourself.

Google's Eric Schmidt bellows the same sentiment:

If you are so bad as a manager that you as a worker would hate working for you, then you have some work to do. The best tool we have found for this is the self-review: At least once per year, write a review of your own performance, then read it and see if you would work for you. And then, share it with the people who do in fact work for you. This will elicit greater insights than the standard 360-degree review process, because when you are initiating criticism of yourself it gives others the freedom to be more honest '[xlvi]

Dave Morrissey

A case for optimising happiness

As the robots start to take over the mundane tasks, the seemingly prehistoric managerial ways of command and control are futile.

Working in a tech company, every day you work with so many nationalities and cultures. You could have a meeting with your team in Dublin. Then have a call with a client in Germany. Then have another call with product managers in San Francisco and then a share-learnings call with a counterpart in Singapore.

Employees are demanding more of their work. With the breakdown of other sources of community, employees are looking more and more to their workplace to provide them with a sense of meaning and identity. They want to be recognised as individuals. They want a chance to express themselves and to gain meaningful prestige for that expression. Only you, the manager, can create the kind of environment where each person comes to know his or her strengths and expresses them productively.

At the same time, companies are searching for undiscovered reserves of value. Human nature is one of those last, vast reserves of value. If they are to increase their value, companies know they must tap these reserves. In the past they have tried to access the power of human nature by containing it and perfecting it, just as humankind has done with the other forces of nature. We now know why this cannot work: the power of human nature is that, unlike other forces of nature, it is not uniform. Instead its power lies in its idiosyncrasy, in the fact that each human's nature is different. If companies want to use this power, they must find a mechanism to unleash each human's nature, not contain it. You, the manager, are the best mechanism they have.

The *Harvard Business Review* focused its entire 2012 January–February issue on happiness. What they found was that the only route to employee happiness that also benefits shareholders is through a sense of fulfilment resulting from an important job done well. We should aspire not just to make employees 'happy,' but to do so by helping them achieve great things. In short, we should earn our employees' passionate advocacy for the company's mission and success by helping them earn the passionate advocacy of customers.[xlvii]

Improving emotional intelligence is the necessary ingredient for a bigger, ever- changing world. That is for managers to optimise happiness. The more human managers are today and tomorrow, the more valuable they become.

Improving EQ is a process, not a quick win. Why does improving emotional intelligence competence take months rather than days? Because the emotional centres of the brain, not just the neocortex, are involved. The neocortex, the thinking brain that learns technical skills and purely cognitive abilities, gains knowledge very quickly, but the emotional brain does not. To master a new behaviour, the emotional centres need repetition and practice. Improving your emotional intelligence, then, is akin to changing your habits. Brain circuits that carry leadership habits have to unlearn the old ones and replace them with the new ones.[xlviii]

Employee well-being is front and centre now in the era of the Great Resignation. Just look at the latest companies to offer staff a paid week off in the name of mental health:

- Nike
- Zalando
- Bumble
- LinkedIn
- Hootsuite
- Mozilla
- Fidelity Investments

All are companies changing the landscape of employee well-being by prioritising the mental health of their teams and offering extended time off. That's a policy for all.

Optimising happiness for each individual is the next blue ocean in tech.

Chapter 10
CUSTOMER-FIRST BUILDING

FIRST OF ALL, WE REALLY NEED TO CARE ABOUT THE PEOPLE WE ARE DESIGNING FOR, UNDERSTAND WHAT THEIR DREAMS AND DESIRES AND PRIORITIES ARE, AND THEN WE HAVE TO USE THAT UNDERSTANDING AS THE DRIVING FORCE OF THE WORK WE PUT FORWARD, BECAUSE THE SECOND WE KNOW WHAT QUESTIONS … ARE IMPORTANT, THEN ALL WE HAVE TO DO IS ANSWER THEM.[1]

— Bjarke Ingels, architect

When it comes to ideating and crafting products for customer use, tech does things a little differently. I should add a caveat that tech usually builds through software which is incredibly malleable and speedy when crafting products for general use. Software can be changed on the fly, so products and their features can change daily. The same can't be said for making desks or running a hotel. So it's important to remember when reading further that software is enabling a speed of product development never seen before.

This chapter looks to inform you as to how tech ideates and ships product; its lessons may not be entirely applicable to you and your business, but I hope you take away the mindset of tech building products for growth. A customer-focused, test-and-learn mindset is central to tech's product development, and that mindset will work wonders in other industries.

Tech makes products that are in the hands of billions of people. Never before has the world seen so many companies capable of serving billions of people. Sure we've had Coca-Cola, McDonald's, etc., but they took decades to get to a global scale.

And then there has been Toyota with its six sigma approach which was ideal for car manufacturing. It brought quality control to a new level. It reduced errors and enabled scalability that would have Henry Ford jumping out of his grave.

There is lots to learn from this new world of developing a product for a market. Tech 'ships' stuff, be it a fully-fledged product like an iPhone or a new way to edit a video in Snapchat. Never before have we seen product get to market in the speed and scale of the tech companies. Here is how.

Usage first, monetise second

THE BEST WAY TO CREATE A SUCCESSFUL PRODUCT OR COMPANY IS TO START BY IDENTIFYING A PROBLEM THAT MANY PEOPLE HAVE AND THEN BUILDING A SOLUTION THAT SOLVES THAT PROBLEM IN A WAY THAT IS EASY AND ENJOYABLE FOR USERS.

— Sam Altman

You are not here to make money. Worry about the money down the line. Profit? Chuckle.

It's a whole new world when it comes to business building and their economics. Business plans can get fucked. By the time a business plan has been concocted and stamped for approval it's too late, the market has moved forward.

Why? Because people's habits and expectations have accelerated. We expect transport to arrive at our feet after hitting a button on our phone in three minutes (Uber). We expect a book to arrive the next day after one click on an app (Amazon). We expect our life and entertainment to look and feel like we look and aspire to (Instagram and Netflix). Immediate fulfilment is where customers are. And tech meets them head-on.

Tech serves. Value is created. Money follows.

Done is better than perfect

IF YOU'RE NOT EMBARRASSED BY THE FIRST VERSION OF YOUR PRODUCT, YOU'VE LAUNCHED TOO LATE.[II]

— **Reid Hoffman, Founder of LinkedIn**

As Mark Zuckerberg says in his famous manifesto (in Facebook's S-1 filing): 'Try to build the best services over the long term by quickly releasing and learning from smaller iterations rather than [by] trying to get everything right all at once … We have the words "Done is better than perfect" painted on our walls to remind ourselves to always keep shipping.'

'Done is better than perfect.' Probably the most influential motto poster to adorn Meta's walls. A mantra to speed and conviction, those five words so succinctly flipped my thinking entirely. I'd spent the past few years thinking that Steve Jobs's perfectionist approach was the name of the game. In fact, the Masters of Scale podcast:

If you're Steve Jobs, you can wait for your product to be perfect. But there are almost no Steve Jobs in the world. The way for most entrepre-

neurs to create a great product is through a tight feedback loop with real customers using a real product. Don't fear imperfections. They won't make or break your company.

What will make or break you is speed – how quickly you'll build things that users actually love.

Characteristics of what psychologists view as healthy perfectionism include striving for excellence, holding others to similar standards, planning ahead and strong organisational skills. Healthy perfectionism is internally driven in the sense that it's motivated by strong personal values for things like quality and excellence. Conversely, unhealthy perfectionism is externally driven. External concerns show up over perceived parental pressures, needing approval, a tendency to ruminate over past performances or an intense worry about making mistakes. Healthy perfectionists exhibit a low concern for these outside factors.[iii]

Imagine a manager or leader saying to you that every idea you come up with is a bad idea? You would run a mile. In tech, that mindset breeds success, as ideas are nothing until put into existence. Netflix co-founder Marc Randolph reflected on this mindset in light of the early days of Netflix:

Every idea is a bad idea. No idea performs the way you expect once you collide it with reality. And the more I learn, the more I believe that it's true. And what that has forced me to do is say, 'I've got to stop thinking about things and I've got to just begin doing them, because that's the only way I'm going to figure out whether it's a good idea or a bad idea.' And that's hard for us. It's hard for people, because people don't like to fail.

They want their experiments to work, and so they do this terrible thing where you keep it in your head, where it's safe, and where it's warm, and where you can embellish it, and it's a great idea, as long as it's all imaginary and in the safety of your head. It can grow and you can add on divisions and you can pivot it into new areas, and you've built this huge castle in your mind. And then of course, if you ever decide to do it, of course, it's way too big and too complicated to do. So it's all about taking these bad ideas and colliding with the reality as quickly as possible.[iv]

Customer first, live in their shoes

IT'S VERY DIFFICULT TO DESIGN SOMETHING FOR SOMEONE IF YOU HAVE NO EMPATHY.

— Stewart Butterfield, co-founder of Flickr and Slack

The most customer-obsessed company in the world has a seemingly unorthodox method for product development, but it works wonders. It comes in the main form of two narratives. The first is known as the 'six-pager'. It is used to describe, review or propose just about any type of idea, process or business. The second narrative form is the PR/FAQ. This one is specifically linked to the 'working backwards' process for new product development.

SVP of Devices at Amazon, Dave Limp, says of the PR/FAQ doc that it's for 'any new product inside of Amazon, the first page of that product, that narrative is a press release, as if you were launching the product tomorrow. And then the next five pages are frequently asked questions; how is this going to be differentiated? How would it be priced? What invention do you have to solve to be able to do this, etc., etc.'[v]

The Amazon PR/FAQ uses the following template format for all documents:

- Headline, Subtitle, and Date
- Intro Paragraph
- Problem Paragraph
- Solution Paragraph
- Company Leader Quote

- How the Product/Service Works
- Customer Quote
- How to Get Started

The PR/FAQ document is an extremely effective way to manage product expectations and communication with all stakeholders. The FAQ section is an extremely effective way to capture the assumptions or perspectives of stakeholders in a consistent format, preserved for future reviews. It's problem- solving for customers before the heavy lifting of coding and development kicks off.

When the Federal Aviation Association approved the use of electronic devices during take-off and landing, Amazon loaded a test plane with 150 active Kindles just to be sure that their customers had full access.[vi]

From his Amazon days, Jeff Lawson admittedly brought a similar practice to Twilio.

At Twilio, the first step in defining a new product or feature is writing the press release. This may sound counterintuitive, as the press release is usually the last step before launching a product. But this practice is part of a process of 'working backward' from the customer need that has roots at Amazon.[vii]

He took things further, by fuelling this mindset with visual triggers, via a pair of Converse.

We decided that the prerequisite of customer focus was empathy, and the best way to build empathy for somebody is, as the saying goes, to walk a mile in their shoes. So we decided to articulate one of our core values as 'Wear the Customer's Shoes.' Then we took it one step further: we commissioned a run of Twilio-red Chuck Taylor Converse shoes, with the Twilio logo (which is round) opposite the Converse logo on the side of the shoes. We called them the TwilioCons, and we made a deal with customers. If they gave us a pair of their shoes, we'd give them a pair of ours.

Steve Jobs and Jony Ive didn't start with the idea for a product; they began by thinking about who it was for and what mattered to them. They got to the core of the needs, well in Apple's case, the desires of their customers.

Companies often create customer profiles – describing customers' stories, wants and needs – at the beginning of the product creation process but then drop them midway through the research and development process. This in turn leads to the unhelpful marketing cycle of working hard to make people want things, instead of making things that people want.[viii]

Humanisation is the process of using data to tell a story (narrative) about a real person's experience or behaviour. Quantifiable measures are helpful in the aggregate, but it's often necessary to reframe the measure into actual behaviour to really understand what's actually happening. Many businesses humanise by developing a series of personas: fictional profiles of people developed from data. When a team developed home cleaning products for P&G, market research data told them that two broad segments existed: people who valued regular deep cleaning ('Unless I'm on my hands and knees cleaning with bleach and elbow grease, I'm not satisfied.') and people who wanted cleaning to be quick and convenient ('I'm too busy to clean – as long as it looks good enough, I'm happy.') Using this information, they combined these characteristics with other data like household income, family statistics and hobbies to create a profile of a fictional person. Once the profile was developed, it became easier to use the data we had to make decisions – instead of relying on statistics to evaluate an idea, they could rely on their intuition by asking themselves if 'Wendy' would like it. Don't just present data – tell a story that helps people understand what's happening, and you'll find your analysis efforts more useful.[ix]

A problem with tech, of late particularly in the social media space, is that it goes too far without deep human psychology baked into the thought process. Jack Dorsey, co-founder of Twitter, says that if he could invent social media all over again, he would start by hiring social scientists alongside computer scientists.[x]

Build something people want

THE BEST - MAYBE THE ONLY? - REAL, DIRECT MEASURE OF 'INNOVATION' IS CHANGE IN HUMAN BEHAVIOUR.

— Stewart Butterfield, CEO, Slack

Slack's Butterfield is one of the best product CEOs out there. Like Jobs and Ive, he has an astute intuition for the needs of customers, and is damn good at articulating that to his staff:

Just as much as our job is to build something genuinely useful, something which really does make people's working lives simpler, more pleasant and more productive, our job is also to understand what people think they want and then translate the value of Slack into their terms.

A good part of that is 'just marketing,' but even the best slogans, ads, landing pages, PR campaigns, etc., will fall down if they are not supported by the experience people have when they hit our site, when they sign up for an account, when they first begin using the product and when they start using it day in, day out.

Therefore, 'understanding what people think they want and then translating the value of Slack into their terms' is something we all work on. It is the sum of the exercise of all our crafts. We do it with copy accompanying signup forms, with fast-loading pages, with good welcome emails, with comprehensive and accurate search, with purposeful loading screens, and with thoughtfully implemented and well-functioning features of all kinds.[xi]

Airbnb's mental framework to figure out what to build for their guests (not customers in their language) is something else, a model every service industry could replicate. Take it away, Brian Chesky:

If you want to build something that's truly viral you have to create a total mindfuck experience that you tell everyone about. We basically took one part of our product and we extrapolated what would a five star experience be. Then we went crazy. So a one, two, or three star experience is you get to your Airbnb and no one's there. You knock on the door. They don't open. That's a one star. Maybe it's a three star if they don't open, you have to wait 20 minutes. If they never show up and you're pissed and you need to get your money back, that's a one star experience. You're never using us again. So a five star experience is you knock on the door, they open the door, they let you in. Great. That's not a big deal. You're not going to tell every friend about it. You might say, 'I used Airbnb. It worked.' So we thought, 'What would a six star experience be?' A six star experience: You knock on the door, the host opens. 'Hey, I'm Reid.

Welcome to my house.' You're the host in this case. You would show them around. On the table would be a welcome gift. It would be a bottle of wine, maybe some candy. You'd open the fridge. There's water. You go to the bathroom, there's toiletries. The whole thing is great. That's a six star experience. You'd say, 'Wow I love this more than a hotel. I'm definitely going to use Airbnb again. It worked. Better than I expected.' What's a seven star experience? You knock on the door. Reid Hoffman opens. Get in. 'Welcome.

Here's my full kitchen. I know you like surfing. There's a surfboard waiting for you. I've booked lessons for you. It's going to be an amazing experience. By the way here's my car. You can use my car. And I also want to surprise you. There's this best restaurant in the city of San Francisco. I got you a table there.' And you're like, 'Whoa. This is way beyond.'

So what would a ten star check in be? A ten star check in would be The Beatles check in. In 1964. I'd get off the plane and there'd be 5,000 high school kids cheering my name with cars welcoming me to the country. I'd get to the front yard of your house and there'd be a press conference for me, and it would be just a mindfuck experience. So what would 11 star experience be? I would show up at the airport and you'd be there with Elon Musk and you're saying, 'You're going to space.' The point of the process is that maybe 9, 10, 11 are not feasible. But if you go through the crazy exercise of keep going, there's some sweet spot between they showed up and they opened the door and I went to space. That's the sweet spot. You have to almost design the extreme to come backwards. Suddenly, doesn't knowing my preferences and having a surfboard in the house seem not crazy and reasonable? It's actually kind of crazy logistically, but this is the kind of stuff that creates great experience.[xii]

Always add value

WE WANT TO BUILD TECHNOLOGY THAT EVERYBODY LOVES USING, AND THAT AFFECTS EVERYONE. WE WANT TO CREATE BEAUTIFUL, INTUITIVE SERVICES AND TECHNOLOGIES THAT ARE SO INCREDIBLY USEFUL THAT PEOPLE USE THEM TWICE A DAY. LIKE THEY USE A TOOTHBRUSH. THERE AREN'T THAT MANY THINGS PEOPLE USE TWICE A DAY.

— **Larry Page**

Flick on Netflix and take note of the little things. Like at the end of the episode, the service helps you more by skipping credits and playing the next episode.

Very simple, but removing a few seconds of somewhat trivial content if you are binge-watching something is of benefit to the viewer.

Our next company is not quite a tech company, but the way they optimise their customer experience screams tech. Everything is looked at for some level of marginal gain. The depth of psychological hacking is astounding. It's everyone's favourite walkabout on a weekend afternoon, of course – IKEA. Look at a handful of their hacks …

Maze-like design. IKEA as a maze is a popular meme … but also true. Even though there are exits and shortcuts, the store is designed for a shopper to see everything on offer in the showroom. And, again, the 'effort' of solving the maze increases the perception of value.

Writing down a list. IKEA makes pencil/paper available to write down the item number you want to pick up. While it's a memory aid, the act of writing also plays on a classic persuasion hack: consistency. Once you've written down an item, you'll want to 'follow through' on a purchase.

The power of smell. Finally, IKEA's famous cinnamon buns are often placed near the checkout. Smell is extremely powerful for memory recall. IKEA is linking what should be the most painful part of the experience (buying) with the soothing scent of home baking.

Indeed its first-ever psychological hack is the business model: sell furniture that requires the effort of self-assembly. A 2011 Harvard study found people assign higher value to self-assembled goods (willing to pay 63% more versus pre-assembled). And the phenomenon is aptly named 'The IKEA effect'.

Amazon is all about convenience … one-click buy, I mean come on. That makes for some trigger-happy buying. Their brown cardboard boxes landing at your gaff the next day (Prime baby, Prime).

With the Kindle, Amazon set out with an audacious goal of improving on the physical book:

We knew Kindle would have to get out of the way, just like a physical book, so readers would become engrossed in the words and forget they're reading on a device. We also knew we shouldn't try to copy every feature of a book – we could never out-book the book. We'd have to add new capabilities – ones that could never be possible with a traditional book.[xiii]

A landmark study of customer value was published by the *Harvard Business Review*, conceptually rooted in our old friend Abe Maslow's 'hierarchy of needs' pyramid. Thirty elements of customer value from 'reduces effort' to 'nostalgia' to 'anxiety reduction' to 'belonging' were studied against ten thousand customers for a cohort of fifty brands with Apple, Amazon and more in the mix.[xiv] Not surprisingly, the two most valued companies in the world, Apple and Amazon, operate in most of the categories of value add.

Then there is a slam dunk simplification that every entrepreneur, product manager or salesperson can abide by when thinking of what they are creating and offering to the market. From Aidan Corbett, CEO of Wayflyer:

'Are you offering a vitamin, or a painkiller?'

Lean product ideation

In the spirit of moving fast and pragmatically, tech goes greyhound lean. Although lean production techniques are powerful, they are only a manifestation of a high-functioning organisation that is committed to achieving maximum performance by employing the right measures of progress over the long term. Process is only the foundation on which a great company culture can develop. But without this foundation, efforts to encourage learning, creativity and innovation will fall flat.[xv]

Bootstrapping is one way tech gets its start. Either in a garage, or tucked away in a tech company for a moonshot. Bootstrappers take an idea and – using talent and professionalism – build a worthwhile business without the backing of investors and having little or no starting capital.

Building a strong business with a sound foundation and value takes time and many bootstrapped companies have achieved this by providing amazing products or services. Eventually, they reach the point, through solid strategies and sustainable profit, where the company grows to have a powerful position within their industry.

Many of the successful companies that we see today had their humble beginnings as bootstrapped enterprises. Examples of these include:

- Meta
- Apple
- Hewlett-Packard
- Microsoft
- Oracle
- eBay
- Cisco Systems
- SAP[xvi]

What does lean product ideation look like? If you ever saw *The Founder* with Michael Keaton that tells the story of McDonald's origins, you see it out in the open, on a tennis court. They drastically overhauled the way those items were prepared so that customers' orders could be fulfilled in a mere thirty seconds. Dragging their kitchen employees along to an empty tennis court, they used chalk to map out possible arrangements for the restaurant's various cooking appliances and prep stations, essentially user testing their way to the most efficient layout and an accompanying 'assembly line' approach to food preparation.[xvii]

Impact over effort right there.

Finding the shortest technical path in context is what engineers do for a living. It's what they're trained to do in computer science classes.

Dropbox got its start by taking a lean approach, through how they showed their prototype. The video was banal, a simple three-minute demonstration of the technology as it is meant to work, but it was targeted at a community of early adopters. CEO Drew Houston narrates the video personally, and as he's narrating, the viewer is watching his screen. As he describes the kinds of files he'd like to synchronise, the viewer can watch his mouse manipulate his computer. Of course, if you're paying attention, you start to notice that the files he's moving around are full of in-jokes and humorous references that were appreciated by this community of early adopters.

The effects were breathtaking. 'It drove hundreds of thousands of people to the website,' Houston has said. 'Our beta waiting list went from 5,000 people to 75,000 people literally overnight. It totally blew us away.' Houston had demonstrated that people wanted the product. It enabled him to raise more capital and continue product development with confidence. But it also enabled him to interact with the early adopters, develop practical knowledge and refine the product. That is the value of the lean start-up.[xviii]

The e-commerce revolution has changed the game for entrepreneurs.

It's never been easier to start a business and deliver products, thanks to all the tech companies driving the change. From the product, storage and distribution side, drop-shipping has been a welcome phenomenon.

This is a great option if you don't want to handle physical inventory or deal with shipping, but still want to offer a product. You can purchase wholesale goods and then sell them on your site, without ever touching them yourself! For example, if you sell make-up online, you can buy your products from China and ship them directly to customers on your website instead of storing them in a warehouse or shipping them out yourself. It's also great because it's beautifully scalable – if you get an order for ten bottles of shampoo, you only have to pay for those ten bottles until they've been sold. No need for bulk buying or storage space.

Setting up your 'store' has never been easier. Shopify is an e-commerce platform that allows you to create your own online store with no upfront cost. It's also incredibly easy to use, with templates that are designed to help you get started quickly. It also has many other features such as analytics and marketing tools that can help increase sales even further than they would be otherwise (especially if they were sold through another platform).

And then when it comes to quick and hassle-free funding, say needing $1 million for inventory and marketing expenses, you can go to Wayflyer and get that funding in about two hours.

We have gone from months and years to get a business going, to days. Hours, even.

Direct to consumer

THE MOST IMPORTANT THING IS TO BE USER-CENTRIC, WHICH MEANS YOU HAVE TO START WITH THE CUSTOMER EXPERIENCE AND WORK BACKWARDS TO THE TECHNOLOGY.

— Sam Altman

This leads us to the 'direct to consumer' model. Which, thanks to tech providing the tools and infrastructure, is a very attractive business model of recent times. It's all about going lean, vertical integrations and pragmatism.

Vertically integrated organisations do as much as possible in-house. The advantage of doing this is gaining total autonomy and control of their operational processes, including sourcing, manufacturing, logistics and customer orders. Vertically integrated supply chains are now popular with many DTC brands whose products are significantly different from industry standards. It also gives these companies total responsiveness and the ability to innovate rapidly. The other benefit is that every cost driver is known and controlled. Knowing exactly how much something costs to make is critical to getting your margins to work.

Advantages of launching a product with a DTC strategy? First, there are fewer barriers to entry; for example, no retail buyer is deciding you are not the next big thing and denying you a place on the shelf. Second, DTC allows you to test, iterate and innovate more quickly and cheaply. Third, DTC allows you to build a direct relationship with your customers and find out what you need to do to serve them better, and by looking after their interests, you build trust and loyalty.

The landscape has changed considerably over the past decade. Competition is more abundant, the cost of acquiring customers has increased and consumer expectations are higher. The DTC brands that came before and succeeded in changing consumers' buying habits and choices have set the bar high. Just turning up is no longer going to be a winning strategy. If you don't (or can't) spend lots of cash to promote your new product, your best bet is to find a significant unmet need (e.g. Snag Tights) or focus on a smaller niche, like repair putty Sugru. The challenge is that most brands are not trying to provide a completely revolutionary product or service (these are hard to find), but rather they are trying to invent a better mousetrap.

DTC brands are modern businesses. This modernity means they do things differently from what has come before. They are different because they know they need to be more nimble and innovative than their invariably better- resourced competition. They are unafraid to try new things.

Gathering and using your data is a prerequisite for all DTC brands and remains one of the key advantages over traditional retail lead businesses. Graze, allplants and Ugly use their review data to innovate and iterate their products. Bloom & Wild are obsessed with their net promoter score. Snag Tights use customer data to inform their marketing.

Ship fast

Product development has become a faster, more flexible process, where radically better products don't stand on the shoulders of giants, but on the shoulders of lots of iterations. The basis for success then, and for continual product excellence, is speed.[xix]

Meta's success with Instagram has a lot to do with its speed in adjusting to the market. Its ability to punch out new features is unrivalled. The birthing, and killing, of new products makes Meta the most innovative big company on earth.[xx]

Look at how Tesla moves at speed, it's unprecedented (sorry, that word again). In October 2013, a Tesla owner ran over a bit of debris on the freeway, which punctured the car's battery and started a fire. The Model S alerted the driver to the issue, and he safely pulled over and got out minutes before the car was engulfed in flames. But it was a PR disaster for Tesla. To make the car safer, Tesla decided to make it ride an inch higher at highway speeds. At most companies, this would have required a recall – costing the automaker tens or hundreds of millions of dollars, and creating a huge inconvenience to owners. But Tesla just issued an over-the-air update, modifying the suspension to increase the ride height at highway speeds by one inch – problem solved.

That's the tech mindset at work.[xxi]

It's worth noting that there is a misconception with tech shipping fast, as some believe it to be that tech moves so fast, that they are throwing shit at a wall and hoping it sticks. It's more considered than that. Sandboxes are the regulating framework to ensure shit is known to stick before it hits the wall.

A sandbox is a controlled environment where developers can experiment with new ideas and test them out before launching them to a wider audience. Here are some key elements of sandboxes for product development:

- Isolated environment: A sandbox is an isolated environment where developers can experiment with new ideas without affecting the existing product or user experience. This allows for rapid iteration and testing without the risk of disrupting existing customers or damaging the company's reputation.
- Clear goals: A sandbox should have clear goals and objectives that align with the company's overall product strategy. This ensures that developers are working towards a specific

outcome and that the experiments conducted in the sandbox are aligned with the company's vision and values.
- Data-driven: A sandbox should be data-driven, with developers using data to inform their decisions and track progress. This allows for objective evaluation of the success or failure of the experiment and helps developers make informed decisions about whether to continue or pivot.
- Collaborative: A sandbox should be a collaborative environment where developers, designers, and other stakeholders can work together to test and refine ideas. This encourages a culture of innovation and creativity and allows for cross-functional collaboration and learning.
- Iterative: A sandbox should be an iterative process, with developers testing and refining their ideas in a continuous cycle of experimentation and evaluation. This allows for rapid feedback and learning, leading to faster innovation and product development.

Mark Zuckerberg also had this to say:

Ship and iterate doesn't always work. After launching, some products will get better and gather momentum while others will wither. The problem is, by the time a product has gone to market there have been a significant amount of resources and emotion invested into it, which can get in the way of good decisions. Forgetting sunk costs is a tough lesson to heed, so in a ship-and- iterate model, leadership's job must be to feed the winners and starve the losers, regardless of prior investment. Products that get better and gather momentum should be rewarded with more resources; products that stagnate should not. To decide which efforts are winners and which are losers, use data. This has always been the case, but the difference in the Internet Century is how quickly data is available and how much of it there is. A key factor in picking the winners is to decide which data to use and to set up the systems so that it can be retrieved and analysed quickly. Using data will muffle the sunk-costs fallacy – that irrational tendency most humans have to count the amount of resources that have already been invested in a project as one of the reasons to continue to invest in the project ('We have already invested millions, we can't stop now').

Get to the front line

Get to the customers. Get to the truth. Get to the front line. Such is how tech masters value creation. Early on, the Airbnb founders learnt the value of getting to the front line.

While Blecharczyk stayed behind to code, Gebbia and Chesky flew to New York over a long weekend and started meeting hosts. One obvious problem was that hosts weren't presenting their properties online in an appealing way – the photos were grainy and usually taken with the primitive cell phones of the time. They reported this observation back in Mountain View, and Graham compared it to a challenge he had encountered at the online marketplace Viaweb, where he had to show naive retailers how to sell on the internet.

'What they needed to do was teach their hosts how to sell,' Graham says. 'That was the missing ingredient.' So in what has become a bit of oft-repeated Airbnb lore, Chesky and Gebbia returned to New York regularly over the weekends that winter after emailing hosts that the site was sending a professional photographer to their homes for free. Once in the city, they rented a high-quality camera and trudged around in the snow, knocking on doors and taking pictures of people's bedrooms and backyards. 'We were on a budget. I remember deliberating every little expense, like the quality of the tripod and whether we should go for the nice one or not,' Gebbia says.

In the parlance of the Valley, this kind of activity did not 'scale'. It was a wildly inefficient use of their time. But it helped the founders tune in to the needs of their earliest users and to recognise that large, rich, colourful photos of homes and good profile pictures of the hosts would make the experience on the site more compelling. 'Paul was the first person to give us permission to say, it's okay to think about things that may not scale, to break away from the mythology of Silicon Valley,' Gebbia says. 'We could actually think creatively around how to grow the business.'[xxii]

Feedback loops

Data has enabled quicker learning, as tech builds to learn, by means of what they call 'feedback loops'.

Before a product or feature reaches the public, it's put through its paces with employees, a process called 'dogfooding', meaning 'eating your own dog food', where employees get to play with the feature. Any bugs or mishaps are then flagged to engineers for fixing.

Then it's out to the public. Meta would launch a new product first in New Zealand, why? Because of the time zone and user base. It's hours ahead of other countries so any bugs can be quickly fixed, and the user base has strong connectivity and user behaviours, so good learnings are seen early.

Tech bears the lean methods of innovation through validated learning. Validated learning is the process of demonstrating empirically that a team has discovered valuable truths about a start-up's present and future business prospects. It is more concrete, more accurate and faster than market forecasting or classical business planning. It is the principal antidote to the lethal problem of achieving failure: successfully executing a plan that leads nowhere.[xxiii] Validated learning can come in a few forms.

A split-test experiment is one in which different versions of a product are offered to customers at the same time. By observing the changes in behaviour between the two groups, one can make inferences about the impact of the different variations. This technique was pioneered by direct mail advertisers.

And then there are cohort-based reports, which are the gold standard of learning metrics: they turn complex actions into people-based reports.

Each cohort analysis says, among the people who used our product in this period, here's how many of them exhibited each of the behaviours we care about.

Personalisation

HOW'S EVERYBODY DOING OUT THERE? ARE YOU GETTING ENOUGH SLEEP? DRINKING ENOUGH WATER? EATING SOME VEGETABLES HERE AND THERE? WE DON'T HAVE ANY BIG UPDATES THIS TIME AROUND, SO WE WANTED TO USE THIS SPACE TO REMIND YOU TO BE KIND TO YOURSELF AND THOSE AROUND YOU. THAT'S ALL. LOVE YA.

— Slack IOS app update

Whether you want to believe this or not, there is lot of humanity baked into the land of tech. From cute notifications like Slack's above, to personalising a service to your every whim.

Filtering stuff for you is one such personalisation marvel. Filtered recommendations. Amazon in one sense is the world's biggest product review site and has learnt a ton about what people like to buy.

The 'more like this' feature is responsible for a third of Amazon sales – a difference amounting to about $30 billion in 2014.

These filtered recommendation AIs are so valuable to Netflix that it has three hundred people working on its recommendation system, with a budget of $150 million.

Personalisation in tech has changed products almost entirely. It's the same general format, but every person's Netflix home screen to Facebook Newsfeed is completely different to anyone else's. As a result they are 'sticky' as hell.[xxiv]

It also means tech has become more personal. The tech bros have brought personality to the bytes. Gifs and emojis are now all over 'business tech' like LinkedIn and Slack.

Product development is a dance of lots of science-leading and sexy art, all for the benefit of you personally. Merging science and art like the Netflix home screen.

You can try this at home to see personalisation in action. Do a VPN test. Flick on Netflix and change the location of your browser from wherever you are to another country or region. See the algorithm working for you, but also the thumbnails, each telling a story in one image to give you context about the show, and hook you in. They are helping you navigate a mountain of choices to make.

Reducing friction

Tech's quest for simplification naturally cascades down to the life of the consumer, to make life easier for the consumer. Make it easier to understand and use a product, and consumption goes up.

And it's the simple small things that reduce friction. Netflix, in an effort to reduce friction and keep viewers watching, has introduced a new feature: 'Next episode'. Where one episode is finishing, a prompt for the next episode pops up and automatically brings you to that next episode in fifteen seconds. This saves you having to reach for the remote control to select the next episode, and keeps the binge-watching machine ticking along.

With reducing friction in tech, and all products and services, there is a bigger case for applying behavioural economics. Rory Sutherland is leading the charge on this, with fascinating takes on the shift to electric cars:

One of the things that's an obstacle to people in Britain buying electric cars is range anxiety. It's the fear that you will be stranded and unable to charge your car. So the way to sell electric cars is to disabuse people of this fear.

In the US, this is an irrelevant fear because there are several highways across the country where you can drive for two hours straight without seeing a single house. If you are on I-40, for example, you are heading east in a straight line and there's nothing on either side of that road for miles and miles.

But Britain is a tiny country. It's hard to drive 150 miles without driving into the sea. And if your charger isn't working, you will find another one some eight miles away.

The US has about 165,000 gas stations. The UK has a fifth of the US population and gets by with, let's say, eight and a half thousand gas stations. So the infrastructure problem in the UK is inordinately less than it is in the US.

So my point is that there are two ways to sell electric cars. One of the ways is to make them better and better and have longer and longer range and better and better performance. That's a perfectly noble endeavor. I'm not suggesting we should give up that game completely. But at some point, we will run up against the laws of physics because the cars can only go so fast.

The other way to sell electric cars is to stop making them so much better in terms of their range. People fear that a car without 350 miles of range is somehow inadequate, which might be true if you live in northern Utah. But I don't think that is true if you live in the Southeast of England. Any good systems thinker would ask: why are we improving this metric? And does the consumer notice or even care? And would we be far better off tweaking a psychological metric rather than an objective one?

Here's another example, Uber didn't reduce the wait time for cabs. But by having the Uber map, waiting for your cab becomes less painful.[xxv]

Market selection

MARKET MATTERS MOST; NEITHER A STELLAR TEAM NOR FANTASTIC PRODUCT WILL REDEEM A BAD MARKET. MARKETS THAT DON'T EXIST DON'T CARE HOW SMART YOU ARE.[xxvi]

— Marc Andreessen, venture capitalist and founder of Netscape and Ning.com

TAM, all about the TAM. Which is the 'total addressable market' for a product or company. That's where it starts, then it's getting the 'product-market fit'.

On Marc Andreessen's old blog, he calls getting to product-market fit the 'only thing that matters' for start-ups and offers a way of thinking about the life of the start-up that divides it into two distinct phases: before product-market fit and after. Once the product fits the market, a company is able to step on the gas, spending to promote a product that will actually sell.[xxvii]

Despite the fact that there are a handful of direct competitors and a muddled history of superficially similar tools, we are setting out to define a new market. And that means one can't limit oneself to tweaking the product; one needs to tweak the market too.[xxviii]

Josh Kaufman's "The Ten Ways to Evaluate a Market" provides a back-of-the- napkin method you can use to identify the attractiveness of any potential market:

Urgency – How badly do people want or need this right now? (Renting an old movie is typically low urgency; seeing the first showing of a new movie on opening night is high urgency, since it only happens once.)

Market Size – How many people are actively purchasing things like this? (The market for underwater basket weaving courses is very small; the market for cancer cures is massive.)

Pricing Potential – *What is the highest price a typical purchaser would be willing to spend for a solution? (Lollipops sell for $0.05; aircraft carriers sell for billions.)*

Cost of Customer Acquisition – *How easy is it to acquire a new customer? On average, how much will it cost to generate a sale, in both money and effort? (Restaurants built on high-traffic interstate highways spend little to bring in new customers. Government contractors can spend millions landing major procurement deals.)*

Cost of Value Delivery – *How much would it cost to create and deliver the value offered, both in money and effort? (Delivering files via the internet is almost free; inventing a product and building a factory costs millions.)*

Uniqueness of Offer – *How unique is your offer versus competing offerings in the market, and how easy is it for potential competitors to copy you? (There are many hair salons, but very few companies that offer private space travel.)*

Speed to Market – *How quickly can you create something to sell? (You can offer to mow a neighbor's lawn in minutes; opening a bank can take years.)*

Up-Front Investment – *How much will you have to invest before you're ready to sell? (To be a housekeeper, all you need is a set of inexpensive cleaning products. To mine for gold, you need millions to purchase land and excavating equipment.)*

Upsell Potential – *Are there related secondary offers that you could also present to purchasing customers? (Customers who purchase razors need shaving cream and extra blades as well; buy a Frisbee, and you won't need another unless you lose it.)*

Evergreen Potential – *Once the initial offer has been created, how much additional work will you have to put into it in order to continue selling? (Business consulting requires ongoing work to get paid; a book can be produced once, then sold over and over as-is.)*[xxix]

Tech companies have shown a brilliant way to get their products into the market: brazen brute force.

In the case of electric scooters from Lime and Bolt, they just showed up on sidewalks and started dropping them off. They didn't ask permission or even explain what they were doing. They just did it, and people loved them so much that cities had to start regulating them because they were getting in the way of other pedestrians and traffic.

Steal with pride

Tech companies often copy each other's products and services in order to remain competitive, or keep up with the Joneses. This practice is known as 'stealing with pride', or 'copying with pride'. Tech companies may copy different aspects of their competitors' products, such as the design, features or even the entire concept. They may also copy the business model, such as subscription plans, pricing or marketing strategies. In some cases, tech companies may even clone the entire product. This is a common practice in the tech industry, and it can be beneficial for companies if they are able to make improvements or add unique features to their own version of the product.

Look at ads systems. The interfaces where advertisers go to set up, traffic and analyse their ads on a platform.

Google set the best-in-class system back in the 2000s. Facebook took the best of it and built their own. Snapchat took replicated Facebook to an extent, making it more appealing to younger internet users. Each platform evolves for the platform before.

Look at ad products. The different formats an advertiser can use to advertise their wares, be it in video, image or AR form.

Snapchat created Stories. Instagram copied Stories. Even Linkedin copied Stories.

Such is the way of tech. They look externally and thieve what's good. Or 'steal with pride', rather.

Apple has always found inspiration from others (Latin for stealing ideas). The sector that has inspired Apple's modern-day strategy is the luxury industry. Apple decided to pursue scarcity to achieve outsized, irrational profits that are nearly impossible for new-money, gauche tech hardware brands to imitate.

The Cupertino firm controls 19.2 per cent of the smartphone market, but captures 87 per cent of global smartphone profits.[xxx]

Chinese tech companies stole with pride, building their own Google (Baidu), Amazon (Alibaba) and Facebook (Tencent). Mind you they will call themselves 'fast followers'. But now they have out-innovated their Western counterparts in areas like payments and creators, and the development of Super Apps (apps that do social media, financial services, entertainment, transport and more, all in one app).

Product managers

A certain type of person exists in tech companies tasked with overseeing product development and market deployment at tech companies. They are the 'product owner'. It's their baby. They work with engineers and sales in tandem (well that's the idea anyway). A product manager bridges customer needs and the product while keeping everything aligned with the company's vision. The responsibilities of a product manager range from leading the product team to maintaining communication among multiple stakeholders.[xxxi]

Great product managers are not a layer between customer needs and developers. In fact, they actually remove layers, eliminate preconceived solutions and erroneous presumptions, and streamline communications. Great product managers don't abstract the developer from the customer needs; instead, they facilitate understanding of customer problems. The more layers there are between people who use a product and people who create the product, the worse things get.

A product manager at Google would have the following roles:

Creating Product Road Maps and Developing Ideas

Of course, one of the most exciting aspects of being a product manager is coming up with new product ideas. This is a core responsibility of Google PMs. They look for new opportunities and develop ideas and pitch them internally to other stakeholders. Once approved, these ideas are then translated into concrete strategies by the PMs.

After they have shaped the strategies, product managers create a product road map to outline the entire process of product development to launch.

Staying on Top of the Market

Google PMs conduct extensive market research to stay on top of the market range. One way they do this is by talking to customers. They look for opportunities to enhance and optimise existing products and come up with completely transformative ideas.

A Google product manager needs to have a good understanding of the market, competition and its users. Knowing the user is an integral part of everything a PM in Google does, from creating product strategies to designing the product.

They also need to be aware of the market trends, to constantly keep their products relevant and be in a competitive position.

Acting as a Bridge Between Teams

A product manager role in a big tech company like Google requires efficient collaboration among multiple teams. Teamwork is an important part of any product manager role, but in a company like Google, it is integral.

A product manager at Google needs to link multiple teams together, including the design, engineering, marketing and finance teams. They need to keep everyone focused on a common goal.

Conducting Product Features Testing

Product managers at Google have the essential job of extensively testing new features to find any bugs or scope for improvement. This happens right before the launch of a product or a feature but is also an ongoing process.

With the help of volunteers around the world, PMs lead the process of gathering feedback. Once they gather enough information on the user experience and functionality, the product team gets back to work.

Google PMs need to be efficient in handling the debugging process. This process of finding bugs and improving features continues even after the launch – gathering feedback from both internal and external sources.

Experimental mindset and environment

Mindset, mindset, mindset. It's everything right? When it comes to building products and services, tech clearly thinks differently. How do you think differently in your industry? Get experimental and bake it into the culture, or policies.

At 3M, the company behind the Post-it, there is a company policy that 30 per cent of products must form a totally new strategy or product category.

Rather than betting the company on a major app redesign, tech starts by running smaller tests on navigation and onboarding flows. These won't necessarily immediately fix retention or engagement problems. But week over week, making small, incremental improvements of between 2 and 5 per cent, can translate into a massive increase to the bottom line. That's because small wins compound into big ones over time.

Mark Zuckerberg details the sheer extent of experimentation on the Facebook platform:

At any given point in time, there isn't just one version of Facebook running, there are probably 10,000. Any engineer at the company can basically decide that they want to test something. There are some rules on sensitive things, but in general, an engineer can test something, and they can launch a version of Facebook not to the whole community, but maybe to 10,000 people or 50,000 people – whatever is necessary to get a good test of an experience. And then, they get a readout of how that affected all of the different metrics and things that we care about. How were people connecting? How were people sharing? Do people have more friends in this version? Of course, business metrics, like how does this cost the efficiency of running the service, how much revenue are we making? It can even kick off qualitative studies and ask people how happy they are with this version. And then at the end of that, the engineer can come to their manager, and say, 'Hey, here's what I built, these are the results. Do we want to explore this further and do this?' And giving people the tools to be able to go get that data without having to argue whether their idea's good through layers of management before testing something, frees people up to move quicker. If the thing doesn't work, then we add that to our documentation of all the lessons that we've learned over time. If it does work, then we can incorporate those small changes into the base of what Facebook is – that now everyone else who is trying to build an improvement, that's the new baseline that they need to get against. [xxxii]

Guess what is in every meeting room at Meta, regardless of whether it is legal, HR, marketing, etc.? Bowls of random LEGO pieces. To foster thoughts of play and building.

Whatever is being built and sold, creating an environment of ideas and experiments is a competitive advantage. Look at Warby Parker, the brand that has disrupted the spectacles industry.

Much of Warby Parker's recent success is due to the way they involved peers in evaluating ideas. In 2014, they created a program called Warbles, inviting everyone in the company to submit suggestions and requests for new technology features at any time. Before Warbles was introduced, they had received ten to twenty idea submissions per quarter. With the new program, the number of submissions jumped to nearly four hundred as employees trusted that the idea selection process was meritocratic. One of the suggestions led to the company overhauling how they conducted retail sales; another led to a new booking system for appointments.

Instead of limiting access to the ideas and leaving it up to managers to decide which ones to pursue and implement, Warby Parker made the suggestions completely transparent in a Google document. Everyone in the company could read and comment on them online and discuss them in a biweekly meeting.

But there's one twist: to give employees some guidance on which suggestions represent strategic priorities for the company, managers vote the promising ones up and the bad ones down. To avoid false positives and false negatives, the votes aren't binding. Technology teams can overrule managers by selecting a request that didn't receive a lot of votes and work to prove its value. 'They don't wait for permission to start building something,' says applied psychology expert Reb Rebele, who has worked on a study at Warby Parker. 'But they gather feedback from peers before rolling things out to customers. They start fast and then slow down.'[xxxiii]

Such an environment unlocks more marginal gains, which can have profound impacts. Google found this with the colour scheme on their home screen.

Google executives realised that the success of the greenish-blue shade was not conclusive. After all, who's to say that this particular shade is better than all other possible shades? Marissa Mayer, of Yahoo!, then a vice president at Google, came up with a more systematic trial. She divided the relevant part of the colour spectrum into forty constituent shades and then ran another test.

Users of Google Mail were randomly grouped into forty populations of 2.5 per cent and, as they visited the site at different times, were presented with different shades, and tracked. Google were thus able to determine the optimal shade, not through blue-sky thinking or slick narratives, but through testing.

They determined the optimum shade through trial and error. This approach is now a key part of Google's operation. As of 2010, the company was carrying out twelve thousand randomised control tests (RCTs) every year. This is an astonishing amount of experimentation and means that Google clocks up thousands of little failures. Each RCT may seem like nitpicking, but the cumulative effect starts to look very different. According to Google UK's managing director, Dan Cobley, the colour switch generated $200 million in additional annual revenue.

Speaking of colours on a screen, Netflix are militant in their testing of the artwork for each film and show. The data team at Netflix found that users look at the artwork first before deciding whether to click for more details. So they decided to run a number of experiments:

- First, they experimented with a simple A/B test to see if they could increase engagement by changing up the artwork by measuring click-through rates, play duration and other metrics.
- Next, they wanted to see if changing the artwork would contribute to increasing the total streaming hours across the product. They tested to find the best artwork for each title over a period of days, then served that artwork to other, future, watchers to see if that would result in a higher number of hours streamed.
- Finally, they experimented with finding a more efficient way of running the test by narrowing the number of users and time required to optimally find the winning variant for each test.

SERVICE TO OTHERS IS THE RENT YOU PAY FOR YOUR ROOM HERE ON EARTH.

— Muhammed Ali

Chapter 11
MEETINGS, MEETINGS, MEETINGS

MEETINGS ARE A USUALLY A BUG. IF YOU PROPERLY ROOT CAUSE THEM, YOU WILL FIND A TRUST ISSUE, A CLARITY ISSUE, OR A MISSING API. MEETINGS CAN PAPER OVER THESE, BUT IT'S MUCH BETTER TO FIX ROOT CAUSE.

— Tobias Lütke

Across every aspect of business, across every industry, across every country, there is a universal component to working life. It's an inescapable phenomenon. Yawned at, and during, by many. Accepted as a necessary evil by, well, everyone. It exists as a constant default with an unadaptable nature in most organisations, outside of tech. And yet it has a grip on so much of a business's everyday running; it's shocking that it is not looked at as something that can be optimised.

I am talking about meetings. 'Bloody meetings,' I hear you groan. Especially in a corporate world where we let ourselves have a meeting about a meeting, about a meeting.

Overall, about 15 per cent of an organisation's collective time is spent in meetings – a percentage that has increased every year since 2008.[i] And in industries bloated by bureaucracy and slow-moving decision-making, that sense that meetings take over from actual work is more pronounced. And if meeting time is seen as a necessary evil, does the collective say, 'Is there any way we can make these meetings more valuable for all involved?'

Tech does. Tech looks at a way to extract as much value and actionable outcomes from meetings as possible. Yes, meetings are optimised.

Indeed, asking the question of 'Can meetings be made better?' seems totally alien in other industries.

Meetings are optimised: from content to environment

The depth of thought and willingness to flex those thoughts in the cause of making meetings great again in tech is impressive to say the least. As Ed Catmull of Pixar famously opined, 'A room's dynamics are critical to any good discussion'.[ii]

What he refers to here is everything from lighting to the web conference software in a room, and beyond. As mentioned, most meeting rooms in Meta have little bowls of LEGO on the tables. Why? Because this implies an environment of building, which is core to Facebook's 'hacker culture'. And a space for creative thinking, which should always be optimised for in any modern company.

Meeting rooms aren't just optimised for creativity, but better transfer of ideas and insights. At Google they are setting up for the presentation of ideas, as best told by data. Eric Schmidt explains:

This is why most conference rooms at Google have two projectors. One of them is for videoconferencing with other offices or for projecting meeting notes. The other is for data. When discussing options and opinions, we start the meetings with data. We don't seek to convince by saying 'I think.' We convince by saying 'Let me show you.'[iii]

Every tech company worth its salt will have data and ideas almost ubiquitously shown over PowerPoint or Keynote. 'Deck building' is a language in itself in tech. Show your wares over slides, always. And that infers one must be ready, willing and able to present to small and large audiences week on week.

Unless you are working at Amazon, where you'd better get used to being more of an essayist than presenter. The same is seen at Google, docs are the lifeblood of information flow. Everything is typed in.

Hierarchy reduction

Beyond the make-up of the room, meetings in tech are optimised to ensure the best ideas, and truths, prevail. Go into a meeting with any Japanese company in a traditional industry like CPG or telecommunications, and you will witness hierarchy in corporatism at its most explicit. Underling reports aren't even allowed to enter the meeting room until the boss enters, never mind getting any chance to speak without being prompted to in the meeting itself.

Tech thinks and acts differently, to reduce any bias to hierarchy (HiPPO) with regard meeting content and outcomes.

Warby Parker, the DTC disruptor eyewear brand that has baked tech thinking into its DNA came up with a novel way to get around the hierarchy conundrum, especially after concluding that in a live setting, many personality types won't speak up with managers in the room. Instead of limiting access to the ideas and leaving it up to managers to decide which ones to pursue and implement, Warby Parker made the suggestions completely transparent in a Google document. Everyone in the company could read and comment on them online, and discuss them in a biweekly meeting.[iv]

Cut the crap

'Waffle.'

'Nonsense.'

'Bullshit.'

'Waste of time.'

'Kill me now.'

Just a few of the things colleagues say to each other leaving that weekly team meeting that went over the one hour allotted by twenty minutes. After listening through people from other teams flogging their glory projects, that have nothing to do with the priorities of the team they presented to. But they included some cat meme slides.

Efficiency, ruthless efficiency, lies at the heart of tech. So it's no surprise that the above is a no-no in tech. Tech looks to cut the crap and get to the point in meetings. Eric Schmidt tells it like it is:

Most businesspeople go to staff meetings. You have probably lived through hundreds of them, so you already know what their agenda is: Receive status updates, conduct administrivia, nap with eyes open, check email surreptitiously under the table, wonder what mistakes in life were made to warrant this torture. The problem with the typical staff meeting is that it is organised around functional updates, rather than around the key issues facing the team, so you may end up spending too much time on things that don't matter (do you really need a weekly update on everything?) and not enough on things that do. This structure also reinforces the organisational boxes around people – Pam is in quality control, Jason is the sales guy – rather than creating a forum where everyone has a stake in the key issues of the day.'[v]

Hootsuite's Ryan Holmes has three hacks to remove the nonsense of unproductive meetings:

1. *Just say no: Invited to a meeting you have doubts about? Reach out to the organizer and ask, 'Do you really need me?'*
2. *VIPs only – keep the guest list tight: Steve Jobs was a stickler for this principle, populating meetings with essential contributors only.*
3. *No agenda, no attenda: A meeting without an agenda is pointless. Equally important: a post-meeting action plan.*

Optimised for truth and removal of bias

Stemming from an engineer's way of seeing the world, meetings in tech have enjoyed the fruits that grow from their pragmatic mindset. By and large, meetings in tech companies across departments are optimised for the truth and the removal of bias (ego). Nowhere is this seen better than in the Braintrust meetings held at Pixar.

When a film is being created, say *Toy Story 19* (thanks to that bloody *Fast and Furious* franchise for leading the creative world into regurgitated ideas each year) the director of the film has to submit the latest draft to a group of fellow directors and company leaders. Those fellow peers would be seeing the draft for the very first time, and proceed to give unfiltered feedback to the owning director, who of course is so close to the work that they can't objectively review it.

The core purpose of the meeting is to ensure the best ideas, or best versions of ideas, win. Ed Catmull explains:

You are not your idea, and if you identify too closely with your ideas, you will take offense when they are challenged. To set up a healthy feedback system, you must remove power dynamics from the equation – you must enable yourself, in other words, to focus on the problem, not the person.[vi]

Walking your idea, your baby, that you have mollycoddled for over a year, into a room for your peers to openly butcher it to sausage meat will frighten the living shit out of most people. But Catmull encourages business leaders to push through the pain:

It is natural for people to fear that such an inherently critical environment will feel threatening and unpleasant, like a trip to the dentist. The key is to look at the viewpoints being offered, in any successful feedback group, as additive, not competitive. A competitive approach measures other ideas against your own, turning the discussion into a debate to be won or lost. An additive approach, on the other hand, starts with the understanding that each participant contributes something (even if it's only an idea that fuels the discussion – and ultimately doesn't work). The Braintrust is valuable because it broadens your perspective, allowing you to peer – at least briefly – through others' eyes.[vii]

And the essential ingredients of a Braintrust? 'Frank talk, spirited debate, laughter, and love'.

Optimising for decision-making

'Who is quarterbacking this meeting?' I once heard coming from someone in a meeting. After swallowing my low-level disgust at this Ivy League-educated product manager innocuously forcing more American ideals on the world of business, it illustrated perfectly the desire tech has to streamline decision-making in meetings.

At Meta, the greatest compass was the simple question, 'What is your desired outcome?'. As in, what do you want the client or colleague to understand and/or action after the meeting? A simple question, but it forces the mind to really focus on what the purpose of the meeting is and what needs to happen afterwards.

Concluding the meeting on what the next steps are, explicitly, enables each participant to leave with a plan of action, which should ideally stem from their desired outcomes drawn up before the meeting.

Making the best use of everyone's time and priorities is paramount to tech's attitude to meetings. Google has mastered the mindset and playbook thanks to leaning into that engineer/scientist mindset:

Dave Morrissey

Computer scientists hate inefficiency, so over the years Eric's team developed a series of rules for meetings that we found to be quite effective: Meetings should have a single decision-maker/owner. There must be a clear decision- maker at every point in the process, someone whose butt is on the line. A meeting between two groups of equals often doesn't result in a good outcome, because you end up compromising rather than making the best tough decisions.

Include someone more senior as the decision-maker. The decision-maker should be hands on. He or she should call the meeting, ensure that the content is good, set the objectives, determine the participants, and share the agenda (if possible) at least twenty-four hours in advance. After the meeting, the decision-maker (and no one else) should summarize decisions taken and action items by email to at least every participant – as well as any others who need to know – within forty-eight hours.

Even if a meeting is not a decision-making meeting – for example it's designed to share information or brainstorm solutions – it should have a clear owner.

Again, that owner should ensure that the right people are invited to the meeting, that there's a clear agenda, that the necessary prep work has been done in advance, and that action items are circulated promptly.

Meetings are not like government agencies – they should be easy to kill. Any meeting should have a purpose, and if that purpose isn't well defined or if the meeting fails to achieve that purpose, maybe the meeting should go away. The decision-maker needs to ask the hard questions: Is the meeting still useful? Is it too frequent / not frequent enough? Do people get the information they need? Meetings should be manageable in size. No more than eight people, ten at a stretch (but we would seriously discourage this). Everyone in the room should be able to give their input. If more people need to know the result of the meeting, make sure you have a process for communicating it rather than bringing them in as observers, which lowers the quality of the meeting and people's ability to talk openly.

Attendance at meetings is not a badge of importance. If you aren't needed, leave, or better yet, excuse yourself ahead of time. This is especially true of meetings with customers or partners. Many times we have walked into an 'intimate' meeting with a senior executive from one of our customers or partners, only to find the room full of people. We can't help it if customers feel the need to bring their entire org chart to the meeting, but we try to control our side. Fewer people is almost always better. Timekeeping matters. Begin meetings on time. End them on time. Leave enough time at the end to summarize findings and action items. If the meeting has accomplished its goal before its allotted time runs out, then end it early.

Remember, we are human: Schedule time for lunch and bio breaks, and be respectful of employees working in different time zones. They like to spend time with their families in the evenings in particular.[viii]

Types of meetings

There is quite an array of types of meetings in the world of tech. Each coming with its own purpose and make-up. Many may be in existence in your company and industry. Some of the below may be totally alien to your business. Whatever the case, I'm sure there will be some in here that may be of use to you and your business, so go throw them on for size and see if things work better as a result:

All-hands/townhalls

Let's start with a meeting type that's been evangelised by tech, in thanks to Mark Zuckerberg trying to empathise with society by essentially staging large Q&A sessions with locals in some far-flung state in the Midwest of the USA.

The townhall or all-hands is a chance for underlings to hear the latest developments from the leadership team, and usually ask them anything they want in relation to well, anything. Questions can range from what a company's approach to privacy will be to why certain sweets aren't stocked in the micro- kitchens anymore. Yes, the whole spectrum, from astounding to absurd.

These large-scale meetings can happen quarterly, weekly or on an ad-hoc basis for big company announcements. A cadence of weekly all-hands, coupled with a bigger version at the beginning of each quarter, tends to be the norm in tech companies.

At Meta, they happened weekly, every Friday afternoon, Pacific Time. Questions were submitted by staff and upvoted by 'Likes'. The top questions got answered by Mark mostly, along with Sheryl Sandberg and other C-level execs. Democracy in action, in a sense.

The pioneers of tech culture as we know it today, Netflix, were 'first to market' with all-hands as a powerful tool for communication and a transparent culture. Reed Hastings harked back to the early days of this meeting approach:

We started holding 'all-hands' meetings every Friday. Patty McCord would stand on a chair like a town crier to get everyone's attention and we would head out into the parking lot, which was the only place we had enough space for everyone in the company. I would pass out copies of the P&L and we would go through the weekly metrics. How many shipments had we done? What was the average revenue? How well were we able to fill client requests for their first and second choice of movies? We also created a strategy document that was filled with information we wouldn't want our competitors to know, and posted it on the bulletin board next to the coffee machine.[ix]

And the purpose, read desired outcome, of the meetings was crystal clear from the outset:

The number one goal for these meetings is to make sure that all leaders across the company are highly aligned on what I call our North Star: the general direction we are running in. We don't need to be aligned on how each department is going to get where they are going – that we leave to the individual areas – but we do need to make sure we are all moving in the same direction.[x]

As for LinkedIn, their all-hands happen on a biweekly cadence, which 'sets the tone for open, honest and constructive communication – one of our core values.'

OPR

In order to keep many departments all singing to the same tune week on week, the OPR-style meeting has been lauded as a weapon of efficiency that's helped Amazon fire on all cylinders since its inception. And the format has been stolen with pride by others like Twilio.

An OPR meeting is a meeting of an organization's board of directors or other leadership group that is open to all senior leadership. Essentially it's a weekly business review, in rapid-fire mode.

Like most things in tech, aside from the technology itself being built, no wheel has been reinvented here. As Jeff Lawson from Twilio explains:

Those big meetings with Andy Jassy grilling us provided a great (and fast) education. His approach was similar to one that professors in graduate programs, especially in law school, have been using for more than a century – and which in fact dates back to the fifth century BC. It's the Socratic method, named after the Greek philosopher Socrates. In this mode of teaching, students arrive to class having read the material (hopefully) and then the professor singles people out.[xi]

Daily stand-ups

The humble team meeting to kickstart the day or week. Simmering away with banal business updates and ego grooming project call-outs that could have been sent over email or Slack, sucking the life out of people's spirit, when its purpose is to get people informed and pumped. Not so at tech, bring the focus and energy or go home.

Again, Jeff at Twilio laser focused on this everyday meeting and found ways to optimise it.

Daily stand-up meetings are another foundational element of Agile. Every day the team starts with a meeting where everyone lets everyone else know what they did yesterday and what they are going to do today. The problem is that many developers absolutely hate meetings – not because engineers are antisocial, but because meetings occupy valuable time that could be better spent writing code. And like any meeting, daily stand-ups can be well run and efficient, or a boundless and unfocused waste of time.[xii]

And in order to force behaviours to make these meetings the best use of time, he enforced that a daily stand-up meeting couldn't last more than fifteen minutes:

We wanted it to be crisp, direct, and to the point. If something required further discussion, we noted it and met further after the daily meeting. The idea was to get the most actionable and valuable information in the least amount of time.

QBR/HBR

Quarterly business review and half business reviews do exactly what they say on the tin. These meetings are usually utilised in tech for departments to show off their highlights and lowlights (learnings) from the past quarter or half of the business year. Also heavily leaned on for client and partner means of engagement.

Walking meetings

First popularised by Steve Jobs who had meetings with employees over a stroll, it's become a meeting in vogue with tech leaders. Most famously Mark Zuckerberg. The $19 billion acquisition of WhatsApp by Facebook occurred after Jan Koum, one of its co-founders, had several meetings with the Facebook CEO.[xiii]

If you Google Image 'Facebook Building 20' you will see a Frank Gehry- designed building complex at Facebook's Menlo Park HQ, and you will see a garden roof, right above Zuck's fishbowl meeting room. Perfect for his meeting walkies.

Sprints

Want to solve a larger than business-as-usual problem, or unlock an opportunity as fast as possible? Kick into *sprint mode*.

There is all this noise around 'lean', 'agile' and 'scrums' in the ways to think now in business practice, in industries outside of tech. Lots of theory, lots of courses and trainings. A sprint is merely this mindset in action.

Bootcamps

With its origins in the engineering world, I've seen bootcamps spill into the other functions that make up tech organisations. Sales people, who need to have a decent grasp of the technology they are selling, can go to a one-month engineering bootcamp.

Oh, and at the end of the bootcamp, given the practicality of learning, they have to ship code to the product, that is the platform. Yes, from zero, to hero. Learning a new language and then adding to the product.

Hackathons

Imagine a banking CEO saying to their staff, 'Down your tools for a day or two, and go build what you think would be interesting and valuable to you, the customers and company'. Staff would think the CEO went a step too far with trying to keep up with the tech guys and their microdosing.

Hackathons are just that, at Meta they were anyway. Hack anything, was the culture. One person was sick of the restaurant queues so they set up cameras in the restaurants, and connected them to the internal employee video library. Suddenly every employee in the company could see what the queue was like at a restaurant in their location. This lent itself ideally to the strengths-focused nature of Facebook; you shouldn't have to queue for food when you could be crushing it on the job you were employed to do.

Of course hackathons aren't all for shits and giggles. They are a powerful weapon of focus to crank out new features, products, playbooks, and so on. Or as other industries and 'agile warriors' call them, sprints.

Reviews

The effervescent employee review meeting. Cadence and content are key. How often can come down to speed. Meta have a review meeting every six months. Google every one year.

Retrospectives

Tech doesn't always look and move forward, there is time for reflection, in order to at least unearth, and at best codify, learnings. These meetings do what they say on the tin, they look back at a certain moment in the company or quarter(s).

These meetings are rare enough in most tech companies, there simply isn't the time to look back when there is so much to build for the future.

Office hours

These meetings can be useful to downright deplorable. An hour of the host creating a platform to groom their ego or be visible.

They are time put in people's calendars for another department expert or leader to share expertise about a certain product or workstream, and answer any questions the guests may have. This can be useful as the host can learn how the sales team understands the new product and refine the go-to-market strategy, for instance.

For XFN collaboration, utilised pragmatically, Office hours are a valuable meeting tool.

Lunch and learns

Much like the office hours, these meetings are for expertise sharing and Q&As. Usually information about something that has scaled (is working) or is a nice- to-know.

Casual light content with lots of room for Q&As. Over food. A great use of time really.

1:1s

These are the periodic, usually weekly, meetings between manager and report.

Bill Campbell, executive coach to top leadership at Google, has nailed the essence of an optimised one-to-one meeting:

The manager should write down the top five things she wants to cover in the meeting, and the employee should do the same. When the separate lists are revealed, chances are that at least some of the items overlap. The mutual objective of any 1:1 meeting should be to solve problems, and if a manager and employee can't independently identify the same top problems that they should solve together, there are even bigger problems afoot. Bill also suggests a nice format for 1:1s, which we have adopted with good results: Performance on job requirements a. Could be sales figures b. Could be product delivery or product milestones c. Could be customer feedback or product quality d. Could be budget numbers. Relationship with peer groups (critical for company integration and cohesiveness) a. Product and Engineering b. Marketing and Product c. Sales and Engineering Management/Leadership a. Are you guiding/coaching your people? b. Are you weeding out the bad ones? c. Are you working hard at hiring? d. Are you able to get your people to do heroic things? Innovation (Best Practices) a. Are you constantly moving ahead ... thinking about how to continually get better? b. Are you constantly evaluating new technologies, new products, new practices? c. Do you measure yourself vs. the best in the industry/world?[xiv]

Offsites/retreats

The hallowed offsite. In tech these get-togethers away from the daily workspace for half a day up to three days are cherished. Not so much for the impact they have on the business – they can be incredibly wasteful of time and resources when not planned with care and purpose – but rather what they bring to the culture.

Getting to spend a few days with colleagues doing a few team goal planning exercises, followed by team bonding games and nights out on the piss, are invaluable in the sense of bringing people together.

Get tangible, impactful work done. And have a ball of fun together. In some country house or other country even. The results aren't always transparent but bonding occurs and these work moments leave a lasting memory in the humans that attended. Speaking of humans and meetings ...

Be human

Time is precious. Meetings are taking away people's lives, treat them as precious. Plain and simple.

Credit has to be given to tech for approaching meetings to be as efficient and effective as possible. Not just in the meetings themselves, but in the ethos of getting shit done before and after the meeting, the speed of booking in meetings. Here is what tech proposes:

Meet tomorrow?

End of week?
Early next week?

Saying, 'In a month we will circle back with dates to meet again,' sucks the buzz out of the session, and nothing happens. Tech squashes that behaviour.

Also, you could just give people time off meeting. Like Investment Day at LinkedIn. InDay is a day at LinkedIn where employees take all or part of the day off, once a month, from their regular work to explore new ideas, hack with friends, volunteer for special causes, invest in themselves or whatever inspires them.

Treat people as people, not numbers on a bloody spreadsheet. Or else.

KARMA POLICE
ARREST THIS MAN,
HE TALKS IN MATHS,
HE BUZZES LIKE A FRIDGE,
HE'S LIKE A DETUNED RADIO.

— Radiohead

Chapter 12
STORYTELLING & MARKETING

Tech talks a great game. Tech talks probably the best game in business land. Hard not to when it all starts with those big, bold visions really. And thanks to tech's ruthlessly efficient means of execution, it walks the walk, making it much easier than any other industry to talk up its existence in the world. Well, apart from the likes of Theranos and WeWork. More on them later in the chapter.

Beyond the 'make the world a better place' mantra, tech is rather good at marketing its wares and spinning a good yarn to generate press. Tech's marketing Svengali, Steve Jobs, did the industry a favour way back in 2001, when he positioned the iPod, a product with many competitors long since forgotten, as something that 'has a million songs in your pocket'. The marketing of technology got itself a benchmark to aspire to. Tech got its head out of its ass. Nobody cares about the mechanics of an iPod, really, it's what it does or adds to that person's everyday life that matters.

Tech's narrative in the public sphere of late hasn't been a bed of vibrant roses. Indeed 'Big Tech' has echoes of 'Big Oil' from not long ago. Concerns about tech's encroachment on privacy and jobs have dominated the narrative. Valid concerns for sure, but blown out of proportion by the media and then your mate in the pub, like everything.

Your mate rattling on about how Zuckerberg and Bezos are going to tag team your brain into their desired sex position, or more commonly ranting about AI and robots overtaking the human race, distracts us from seeing that it is humans driving this change, and other humans going with the change.

Edison pioneered it all. The 'Magician of Menlo Park'. Thomas Edison the supposed inventor of the light bulb, understood the context and perception drive needed to sell his new invention to the masses. Edison was not so much an inventor as a great product marketer. His image as an inventor was part of his carefully cultivated and controlled public relations/media strategy. He was opportunistic and extremely media savvy. He had a special office set up at Menlo Park and carefully designed the entire operation from a media perspective such that he was able to brand himself as the world's greatest inventor. He did not invent the light bulb. He improved on existing technology after having bought out other patent rights, and where competing patent rights were not so easily obtained, stole technology by directly infringing on those claims. Edison used Menlo Park as a means to his marketing ends. We are seeing a similar godlike inventor narrative play out for Elon Musk today.

Edison's ingenious marketing strategy with the light bulb was in selecting the location of his first customers – the financial institutions in Lower Manhattan. Seeing the windows of the financial district aglow by night demonstrated electric lighting technology to the metro population living across the Hudson River in New Jersey.

Articulating progress is a challenge to master for tech. The future is a tricky concept to convey to most of society. Humans are averse to change. We are hardwired to resist change. Part of the brain – the amygdala – interprets change as a threat and releases the hormones for fear, fight, or flight. Your body is actually protecting you from change.

This aversion to change is at odds with what we see and hear about Moore's law or the latest hyped tech offering (looking at you, virtual reality). So why would that person at the bar who hasn't changed their style of shoes and orders the same drink every day, be sitting there flicking away on the newest iPhone, and talking about an idea he has for an app (likely a quicker way to order the same drink he does every day as the barperson has gradually become less receptive to his orders, as they are fed up with hearing about the same bloody app idea)? Why is this?

Stories of course. We humans navigate the world through narratives.

Storytelling brings runways

Storytelling in tech allows the new and abstract to be consumable to the everyday person. The complex software and never-before-seen hardware can quickly be slotted into needs and desires. It opens wallets. It also opens bank accounts, big bank accounts.

As mentioned earlier, Amazon has had more access to cheaper capital for a longer period than any firm in modern times. Most successful VC-backed tech companies in the '90s raised less than $50 million before showing a return to investors. By comparison, Amazon raised $2.1 billion in investors' money before the company (sort of) broke even. Amazon has exploded this tradition, replacing profits with vision and growth, via storytelling. The story is compelling and simple – the power couple of messaging. The story: Earth's Biggest Store. The strategy: Huge investments in consumer benefits that stand the test of time – lower cost, greater selection and faster delivery.[i]

In addition, Amazon has trained the (Wall) Street to hold them to a different standard – to expect higher growth but lower profits. That enables the company to take the (substantial) incremental gross margin dollars it earns each year and plough more capital back into the business – and avoid that whole tax thing. And that in turn funds the digging of deeper and deeper moats around the business.

Scott Galloway continues to explain the impact the level of devastation Amazon's storytelling, years of masterful expectation management, has not just on competitors, but entire bloody industries:

The day Amazon announced it would enter the dental-supply business, dental- supply companies' stocks fell four to five percent. When Amazon reported it would sell prescription drugs, pharmacy stocks fell three to five percent. The day Amazon released a statement it would carry a small inventory of Nike shoes, sporting goods companies' stocks fell four to five percent.[ii]

Amazon may be the anomaly here, but don't discount the power of telling your story of groundbreaking product development and service. Even a turn of language can get you noticed.

Innovation: It's the next big thing. Or at least the next big word. According to the *Wall Street Journal*, some form of that word appeared in the annual and quarterly reports of US companies over thirty-three thousand times in 2011 alone.[iii]

Customer-centric, again

Marketing exists as a 360-degree weapon of value creation for tech, when done right, acting as a flywheel of profound growth. It is used to inspire, engage and convert a variety of stakeholders. From customers and end users, to investors and its own staff. Marketing in tech is an internal, and external, exercise to master.

To start, it has to be optimised towards the customer/end user. There is a narrative out there of tech company founders in pitch mode (hard selling – marketing's older, more aggressive brother) to venture capitalists and angel investors before talking to customers, but that's an overly idealised narrative that's taken hold. Another tech fairy tale.

It's not a chicken-and-egg-like scenario. Start from the point that you need happy customers using your product and talking about it in order to get further investment. Customer first, again. Steve Jobs wasn't talking to anyone else but the end user when he posited the iPod with its one-million-songs-in-your- pocket spiel.

That customer-first mentality is core to the marketing of Apple, and the other company to recently become worth one trillion dollars, Amazon. As Jeff Bezos put it in Brad Stone's 2013 book, *The Everything Store*, which adeptly tells the origin story of the company: 'If you want to get to the truth about what makes us different, it's this: We are genuinely customer-centric, we are genuinely long-term oriented, and we genuinely like to invent.'[iv]

Zappos, who got acquired by Amazon in 2009 for $1.2 billion, were quick to bring a 360-degree marketing view of the customer into every touchpoint of the business.

We receive thousands and thousands of phone calls and e-mails every single day, and we really view each contact as an opportunity to build the Zappos brand into being about the very best customer service and customer experience. Seeing every interaction through a branding lens instead of an expense-minimization lens means we run our call center very differently from most call centers.[v]

This is a crucial learning. The front line is where the game is won or lost. The best companies out there are now 'listening brands', finding ways to hear and understand what their customers are saying and doing, so they can adapt their product development and marketing to their needs. Creating clear and scalable feedback loops with the people using your product is a foundation for success. Listen first, always and then act.

Yakov Kagan was formerly a growth lead at Uber. Yakov's job was finding out who a clearing customer (someone who can't complete transactions, in layman's terms) is and what they want. Who they are is not just a matter of demographics. It is also what Yakov calls 'psychographics'. Psychographics is more than just understanding age, gender, location, education and so on; it is also a study of consumers based on their activities, interests, values and opinions. Yakov used questionnaires, landing pages, surveys and thousands of interviews to determine who a clearing customer is and how they think. After all these tests, they now understand their psychographic customer is matched to a forty-five-to-sixty-four-year-old female who is proactive about her health.[vi]

Get others talking about you

The holy grail of marketing is when others talk about you, to the point of your brand becoming a verb. Marketers can only wet dream at the thought of what they are working on entering into the lexicon of colloquial shortcuts.

Whenever I get asked something I don't have the answer to, my first instinct is to respond with, 'Did you google it?'. Doing a video call lately? 'Let's get on a Zoom', even though we could use a range of different video conference platforms.

In Ireland, those salty-flavoured fried slices of potato the world calls crisps or chips carry their own everyday-ism term. 'Crisps' sounds alien and highfalutin to Irish people. In Ireland they are called 'Taytos', after the brand name for a leading crisp manufacturer. Naturally Tayto has the market share, and hearts of the nation.

The stickiness of becoming the norm, the verb, of a product or category brings glorious benefits. Your job as a marketer is to cement your brand in the minds of consumers and stakeholders. Thanks to superb product development to satisfy customer needs, one of those four Ps of marketing, tech has been able to fit into people's lives with gusto.

And ideally once customers talk about you, other segments of your business landscape do too, to help grow your top-of-mind dominance. The research firm CB Insights tracked the content of investor calls in 2018 and found that American executives brought up Amazon more often than they mentioned any other company, more than they mentioned President Trump – and almost as often as they talked about taxes.[vii]

Who may talk about you better than others? Early adopters: the customers who feel the need for the product most acutely. Those customers tend to be more forgiving of mistakes and are especially eager to give feedback. Find the people quickest to use your product, and cherish them.

Stay familiar in language

Getting into that heavenly space in marketing lore essentially boils down to familiarity. If you slot into people's lives in a useful and engaging way, they will talk about you. Before they adopt you, they need to get you. They need to understand what value you will bring, almost instantaneously nowadays.

Talking in bytes, processing power, machine learning and such, gets you nowhere most of the time.

Framing new products and services in the context of the familiar is inherently psychological. Tech marketers anchor new innovation to the familiar for relatability. When tech talks to investors, supposed techies themselves with decades of industry knowledge, familiarity connects the investor with a better grasp of the opportunity. 'Our company is the Uber of x, y or z' is a well-worn cliché in investor pitches.

Going back to 2001, when Steve Jobs announced the launch of the iPod, he began talking about how much he and people at Apple loved music. He commented that the current crop of MP3 players was disappointing and, in many cases, unusable. He then talked about what would make a great MP3 player; this included storing a lot of songs – say, one thousand – so you wouldn't have to keep synching it with your computer. And it would have to be small enough to fit in your pocket, he said. Plus, it should have a user interface that makes it quick and easy to find the song you want.

On stage, he paused and said, 'Well, I have this perfect product right here in my pocket.' He pulled the product out of his front jeans pocket and said, 'The iPod. One thousand songs in your pocket.' At the same moment, the screen behind him reinforced the message. Within an hour, the Apple homepage was emblazoned with the same message. 'The iPod. 1,000 songs in your pocket.' It was very clear.

No mention of the number of gigabytes of storage, processor speeds and so on. Nobody gives a shit about that stuff really. What is in it for me? in simple and familiar language. Jobs knew, better than anyone.

In his cracking book *Hit Makers: How Things Become Popular*, Derek Thompson dwells on the need for familiarity at length. Both psychologists and media makers understand that most people are reliably drawn to new ideas that remind them of old ideas. They prefer surreptitiously familiar songs, storylines, clothing styles and interior decorating. Familiar ideas are processed faster and the sensation of quick and easy thinking – also known as fluency – is strong yet sneaky, so that people attribute the pleasure of the thought to the quality of the idea.[viii]

It's worth noting the mindset of most consumers, and the tension that exists as pointed out by Thompson. Most consumers are simultaneously neophilic – curious to discover new things – and deeply neophobic – afraid of anything that's too new. The best hit makers are gifted at creating moments of meaning by marrying new and old, anxiety and understanding. They are architects of familiar surprises.[ix]

From a marketing standpoint, tech doesn't talk about reinventing the wheel. It only makes the wheel go much faster.

Articulate the *why*, consistently and rigorously

Simon (Sinek) says again and again, people don't buy WHAT you do, they buy WHY you do it. What's missing there is that you have to remind people why you do it, over and over and over. Repetition is key, especially when selling products and services that are abstract or futuristic, to everyday consumers who are used to the now.

If you listen anytime to Zuckerberg or Bezos talk on quarterly earnings calls, conference keynotes or interviews, they always bring it back to the company's purpose and benefit to society. They articulate the *why* over and over. Bezos always talks about being the most customer-centric company on the planet, making things quicker and cheaper for customers. Zuckerberg is all about connecting the world.

Slack's Stewart Butterfield epitomises this remind-and-reflect on the *why* ethos. The following was an internal communication to Slack employees, marketing starts at home after all. It was titled 'We Don't Sell Saddles Here'. Take it away, Stewart:

What we are selling is not *the software product – the set of all the features, in their specific implementation – because there are just not many buyers for this software product. (People buy 'software' to address a need they already know they have or perform some specific task they need to perform, whether that is tracking sales contacts or editing video.)*

However, if we are selling 'a reduction in the cost of communication' or 'zero effort knowledge management' or 'making better decisions, faster' or 'all your team communication, instantly searchable, available wherever you go' or '75% less email' or some other valuable result of adopting Slack, we will find many more buyers.

That's why what we're selling is organizational transformation. The software just happens to be the part we're able to build & ship (and the means for us to get our cut).

We're selling a reduction in information overload, relief from stress, and a new ability to extract the enormous value of hitherto useless corporate archives.

We're selling better organizations, better teams. That's a good thing for people to buy and it is a much better thing for us to sell in the long run. We will be successful to the extent that we create better teams.

To see why, consider the hypothetical Acme Saddle Company. They could just sell saddles, and if so, they'd probably be selling on the basis of things like the quality of the leather they use or the fancy adornments their saddles include; they could be selling on the range of styles and sizes available, or on durability, or on price.

Or, they could sell horseback riding. Being successful at selling horseback riding means they grow the market for their product while giving the perfect context for talking about their saddles. It lets them position themselves as the leader and affords them different kinds of marketing and promotion opportunities (e.g., sponsoring school programs to promote riding to kids, working on land conservation or trail maps). It lets them think big and potentially be big.[x]

Measuring marketing

'Half my advertising spend is wasted; the trouble is, I don't know which half.' opined retail giant John Wanamaker way back in the early 1900s. It's been somewhat expected in decades since. It's being upended in this era of big tech. Accountability for each input is key to tech's growth engine. Marketing is never viewed as a fifty-fifty game.

Enter Eric Ries, who in recent times has helped shine a light on the path to twenty-twenty transparency for marketing efforts, not just in tech but business at large. He refers to the methodical means of measuring marketing correctly as innovation accounting. This is a way of evaluating progress when all the metrics typically used in an established company (revenue, customers, ROI, market share) are effectively zero. It provides a framework of chained leading indicators, each of which predicts success. Each link in the chain is essential and, when broken, demands immediate attention. It's a focusing device for teams, keeping their attention on the most important leap-of-faith assumptions. It's a common, mathematical vocabulary for negotiating the use of resources among competing functions, divisions or regions.[xi]

Understanding who your customers are early on is critical. Software can mould to their consumption behaviour, but marketers can tap into their desires and needs in untold ways if they so wish to get close to them. You will know what value you can bring to them, and therefore your company.

Then it's coding up the metrics for growth through marketing. The rate of growth depends primarily on three things: the profitability of each customer, the cost of acquiring new customers, and the repeat purchase rate of existing customers. The higher these values are, the faster the company will grow and the more profitable it will be. These are the drivers of the company's growth model.[xii]

Then it's testing time. The business and marketing functions of a start-up or bigger business should be considered as important as engineering and product development and therefore deserve an equally rigorous methodology to guide them.[xiii] In tech, the rigour engineers put into their work seeps into the marketing department. Once you know which metrics matter most to business growth, it's time to go test. An engineer's mindset is beneficial.

Scalable marketing

Underlying the growth mindset and hypothesis is scalability. Scale in marketing in tech is always the desired outcome. Find something that works and scale it up fast. If it can't scale, adapt or drop it.

A former colleague at Meta, James Chadwick, put together the 'Disruptors CMO Playbook', a superb call-to-arms for modern marketers to adopt the tech ways of working and scaling. James pointed out that the best out there 'prioritize 70-20-10' in that great companies know how to preserve the core *and* stimulate progress. Disruptor CMOs often use the 70-20-10 framework to ensure teams prioritise both proven methods and tests for new growth opportunities.[xiv]

Seventy per cent of marketing spend and resources goes to proven strategies. The 20 per cent is for new, innovative and engaging new audiences. Ten per cent then is a very experimental use of time and money; high risk, high reward. Tech looks to get to the 70 per cent

ASAP. Then they go play with the 20 per cent and 10 per cent, ideally moving those activities into the 70 per cent bucket in time.

An example of a 10 per cent working out was seen at Airbnb. In late 2009, a few months after it had graduated from YC (its incubator), Airbnb appeared to create a mechanism that automatically sent an email to anyone who posted a property for rent on Craigslist, even if that person had specified that they did not want to receive unsolicited messages.[xv] It was a hack, that paid off massively.

Uber starting off was in the 20 per cent territory, finding its feet, almost literally, in new cities. They pioneered a model to launch the service in a city and recorded it all in an online Google document to serve as a manual for Uber's entrance into new cities. Drivers should be solicited by combing through limo-fleet listings on Yelp, the online directory, or by visiting airport limo waiting lots. A launch party should bring together local media and tech luminaries, while a local celebrity should be selected as the first rider in the city and promoted in a blog post. They also used strategies to attract both drivers and riders, like offering subsidies and credits, and took some basic but important steps, like opening an Uber Twitter account in each city. The Google Doc would become a company bible; employees took to calling it 'the playbook'. 'Seattle,' says Austin Geidt, Uber's fourth employee, 'became the first iteration of our playbook.' It found its 70 per cent, and scaled like a virus.

Brand is more than a logo, more so with tech

The times they are a-changing for the once mighty logo. When consumers don't know the true value of the products they're looking for, they rely on corporate iconography to guide them. But when they can figure out the absolute value of a product on their own, they ignore advertisements and brands. That's why Itamar Simonson and Emanuel Rosen have named their theory 'absolute value'. The internet, they say, will be a brand-assassinating technology, flooding the world with information and drowning out the signal of advertising for many products.[xvi]

Me: 'Alexa, buy AA batteries.'

Alexa: 'I've added AA batteries to your basket …'

Now think of that Duracell bunny, running like a lunatic in all those ads, over all those years. One doesn't ask Alexa for the batteries from that cute bunny company. For everyday things like batteries, you just want a battery that does the job. The same can be said for a lot of CPG products. Who really gives a fuck about the brand of a dishwasher detergent?

Tracking the number of online purchases across one hundred million devices from five hundred different e-commerce retailers and marketplaces, Jumpshot reports that Amazon took a 97 per cent market share of online battery purchases in Q1 of 2018, along with a 94 per cent share of kitchen and dining product purchases, a 93 per cent share of home improvement tool purchases, a 92 per cent share of golf-related product purchases and a 91 per cent share of skincare product purchases.[xvii]

Tech is decimating the glory days of brands as they once were. Brands of the Don Draper *Mad Men* era. Brand today means service and experience, logos and taglines don't cut it anymore.

The e-commerce DTC brands are coming around to this need to apply 'brand' across all the customer touchpoints. Lucas London, co-founder and CEO of Lick, had this to say:

Having a great looking brand might lead to the misconception of premium prices; however, their brand image has always been at the heart of everything they do. Right from the beginning, we realized to succeed we would need to build a really strong consumer brand with multiple touch-points. When you have some people who only decorate a room every 5 to 7 years, it's going to be exceptionally hard to build a strong enough brand that people will keep coming back. Our way around this, as well as selling multiple products, is to build a community and create content to make sure that people are consistently engaging with the brand, even if they are not purchasing the product. The other great thing we are finding is that the younger demographic decorates their home much more frequently. They are also looking to personalize more than ever before. We want to inspire our customers weekly so that when they are ready to make a change, we are their first thought. When a strong brand is combined with being able to get everything you need and an unbelievable customer experience, we think we can create something special.[xviii]

Product-led marketing is becoming a marketing industry standard thanks to tech. Product-led marketing is a strategy where a company's product becomes the primary driver of its marketing efforts. Instead of relying on traditional marketing tactics like ads, cold-calling, and events, the product is designed to market itself by providing an exceptional user experience and delivering value to its customers.

Product-led marketing is rooted in the idea that the best way to acquire new customers is to make your product so good that people can't help but talk about it. When users have a great experience with your product, they're more likely to share it with their friends and colleagues, which can lead to viral growth.

The success of product-led marketing depends on a few key factors. First, the product must be user-friendly, intuitive, and deliver value to the customer.

Second, the product must have a clear value proposition that resonates with its target audience. Finally, the product must be easy to adopt, with a low barrier to entry, so that users can start using it immediately without needing extensive training.

One of the advantages of product-led marketing is that it can be more cost- effective than traditional marketing methods. Instead of spending a lot of money on advertising and promotion, companies can focus on building a great product and letting it do the marketing for them. This can result in higher customer acquisition rates, lower customer acquisition costs, and increased customer retention.

Zoom's success can be attributed to its product-led marketing approach, which focused on building a product that was easy to use, reliable, and accessible.

Zoom's user-friendly interface, seamless integration with other tools, and focus on user experience helped it become the go-to platform for remote work and virtual meetings. Covid kicking up work from home helped accelerate growth too of course. Right product, right time.

SWAG

Speaking of logos. If you ever visit the Silicon 'Spaces', like Silicon Valley or Silicon Docks (Dublin), Silicon Alley (New York) or Silicon Roundabout (London), you are likely to see wide-eyed, AirPod-budded twenty-somethings scurrying about fuelled by purpose and ambition, wearing hoodies, T-shirts and backpacks with logos adorned. No Nike, no GAP, no Carhartt, no Patagonia (well, they share a logo with tech company logos quite a bit actually) logos to be seen here. It's the logos of the tech companies, their own mighty brands in this new era of tech.

What do they call this new category of brand wear? SWAG.

Tech companies have their own internal e-commerce stores for SWAG. Buy SWAG for your clients and partners. Even buy SWAG as gifts for loved ones. Yes, baby grows are big. Instagram baby grows. Marketing from within, from birth.

Openness or vanity?

YOU'RE SO VAIN. YOU'RE SO VAIN.

— Carly Simon

Tech's marketing chops are sizzling more openly of late. The culture of openness is moving from the engineering department into the marketing department.

Some companies are putting it all out there, and it's admirable, great content. WeAreNetflix is a podcast from Netflix. In my view, the best in class at a tech company marketing itself. It's brimming with interviews from leaders and teams across the company. Here are just a few episode titles:

- 'Working Parents at Netflix'
- 'Launching TikTok for Netflix'
- 'Building a Studio in the Cloud'
- 'Netflix Culture: Feedback'

Employees openly sharing their work and life at Netflix. It was started in 2018, so somewhat ahead of the pack with a new medium in podcasting. It makes for an amazing hiring tool also.

One cautionary tale in how tech markets itself, or individuals market themselves under the guise of their tech employer. Particularly in this age of LinkedIn influencers, you must have something valuable to say; there is far too much noise out there, little depth. Ellen West, a communications leader at Google, always tells her team, 'To be a thought leader, you have to have a thought.'[xix]

Oversell at your mercy

The visionary lexicon of tech culture comes with downsides. The hyper self- actualisation, 'making the world a better place' mentality is sadly a perilous path with those of the headbanger, the narcissists and sociopaths, leaning.

The perils are either hyper-tech bro culture or putting lives at direct risk.

WeWork is one instance where a bombastic vision coupled with a tech bro culture collided to create one of the biggest valuation catastrophes in tech, and business, history. Essentially a real estate company masquerading as a tech company, it went from a valuation of $47 billion to $2.9 billion.[xx] Investors started to realise the company was a house of cards with overly leveraged property loans, no discernible technology to detract competitors, and an unhinged egotistical CEO in Adam Neumann.

And then there was Elizabeth Holmes of Theranos, who took the biscuit when it comes to unhinged CEOs. First off, she started dressing like Steve Jobs with the black turtleneck jumpers, even going so far as to have surgery on her voice box to sound more commanding. Then she promised the world a revolutionary way of medical testing, a prick of blood put in her machine could give patients the positive or negative on some two hundred illnesses, simultaneously. We are talking everything from chlamydia to cancer here. The technology was a crock, it would never work. And she covered it up, whilst still selling it big to the public and government. Thousands of people got the wrong diagnoses, with untold eventual outcomes. People most likely died.

In both instances the vision got people hyped, and steamrolled through reason, logic and morality. Big thinking is amazing, in the right hands.

Chapter 13
COMMUNITY AT LARGE

Tech is a mindset that permeates not just the world of business, but also society at large. And I can see your mind wandering towards, 'Yeah, Facebook is the reason for the Trump presidency, Amazon is destroying jobs for everyone and I am being spied on by all of them' ... However, I'm not going down that rabbit hole.

Let me take our minds out of the, somewhat justified but mostly OTT, gutter, and show you where the tech way can make your immediate community and broader society actually a 'better place'. Tech's mindset and actions are worth applying to areas like education, health and the climate, especially, before it's too late. So, let's start with the largest man-made entities in society, countries...

Countries at large

In the 'Data Is the New Gold' chapter I highlighted Xi Jinping and China's bold ambitions with data. That's the Chinese way. America's most striking similarity to the tech world is around the collective mission and vision of the nation.

Missions and visions are a celebrated differentiator of success between tech and others. Where can they be seen doing the business for a country? Well, in the greatest story ever told, a marketing masterpiece: the American dream.

The greatest place to live in the world. Where all your dreams come true, if you work hard enough, supposedly. The leader and protector of democratic values. The belief in the American dream is the greatest patriotic force that has graced this planet.

Sure, the country as a whole is a basket case of hypocrisy, fetishised capitalism, racism and American exceptionalism. But you can't deny the power of their narrative.

Side point, I believe the one-dollar bill to be the silent driver of the American dream. The one-dollar bill, coupled with American's tipping culture, provides the daily dopamine hits needed to keep the dream alive in people's minds. A barperson serves you a drink. A hotel porter takes your bags. A dollar tip here, a dollar tip there. The recipient of the dollar bill has a crisp note of currency, and the sense they are on track to achieve wealth and the American dream. Alas, it's a fallacy, especially when you consider the US as a world leader in income inequality.

Beliefs are one thing, execution another. A country that is killing it on the execution of tech is Estonia, the country that is recognised as the world's most advanced digital society.[i] And it is in turn termed as Europe's most entrepreneurial country by the World Economic Forum. It is the home of tech giants Skype, Wise, Bolt and Pipedrive.

Estonia's e-Residency program was launched in 2014 and is the first of its kind in the world. It allows non-Estonians to access Estonian services such as company formation, banking, payment processing, and taxation. E-residents are issued a digital ID smart card which they can use to sign documents. The program is aimed towards location-independent entrepreneurs such as software developers and writers. The program offers numerous benefits such as the ability to register a company in Estonia and access EU markets, reduced tax liability, access to secure digital services, and the ability to securely exchange documents.

Get how easy it is. You start by handing over €100, a photograph, and allowing your fingerprints to be taken. After a few weeks of verification, I have been issued with an identity card, a cryptographic key and a PIN code to access its national systems. I am now an official e-resident of the Republic of Estonia, as is the Japanese prime minister, and you will want to be one, too. And what's more, by doing so, you'll be part of a system that could not only reinvent public services for the internet age, but fundamentally redefine what it means to be a country.

Despite only half of the country having a phone line in 1991, by 1997, 97 per cent of Estonian schools were online. In 2000, cabinet meetings went paperless. By 2002, the government had built a free Wi-Fi network that covered most of the populated areas. By 2007, it had introduced e-voting, and by 2012 huge amounts of fibre-optic cabling were being laid – promising ultra-high-speed data connections – and 94 per cent of the country's tax returns were being made online, taking users an average of five minutes to fill in the parts that hadn't been automatically completed by the link between the tax office and local banks. Now, every task that can be done with a digital service is.

After all, these are Estonian digital services we're talking about: it's across the web, secured with your ID card.

And that's the opportunity, because Estonia is working on linking its tax office with its counterparts in other regions of the world. The Estonians want to offer the option for, say, UK citizens to run their UK companies through the Estonian system, which would in turn, in the background, with no extra work for the user, make sure that the UK tax office receives all the money it is legally due. A UK-based entrepreneur, they hope, will decide to open her business in Estonia, use an Estonian bank and pay for some Estonian services, even if the company was only going to be trading in the UK, because she would find Estonia's national infrastructure far easier to deal with than the UK's. In other words, a nation is now competing with its neighbours on the basis of the quality of its user interface. Just as you might switch your bank to one with a better mobile app, the Estonians hope you'll switch your business to a country with an infrastructure that is easier to use.

And you can apply to become an Estonian at any Estonian embassy, just show your passport and they set you up.[ii]

Israel, or should we say Start-Up Nation, the name coined by authors Dan Senor and Saul Singer, is another such country operating like a tech company. Given Israel's interesting dynamic caused by geography and political tensions since their country's founding, Israelis have been keenly aware that the future – both near and distant – is always in question. Every moment has strategic importance. As Mark Gerson, an American entrepreneur who has invested in several Israeli start-ups, described it:

When an Israeli man wants to date a woman, he asks her out that night. When an Israeli entrepreneur has a business idea, he will start it that week. The notion that one should accumulate credentials before launching a venture simply does not exist. This is actually good in business. Too much time can only teach you what can go wrong, not what could be transformative.

Technology companies and global investors are beating a path to Israel and finding unique combinations of audacity, creativity and drive everywhere they look. This may explain why, in addition to boasting the highest density of start- ups in the world (a total of 3,850 start-ups, one for every 1,844 Israelis), more Israeli companies are listed on the NASDAQ exchange than all companies from the entire European continent.[iii]

A country leading the way of 'impact over effort' a la tech companies and their engineers? Iceland. Trials of a four-day week in Iceland were an 'overwhelming success' and led to many workers moving to shorter hours, researchers have said. The trials run by Reykjavík City Council and the national government eventually included more than 2,500 workers, which amounts to about 1 per cent of Iceland's working population.

A range of workplaces took part, including preschools, offices, social service providers and hospitals. Many of them moved from a forty-hour week to a thirty-five- or thirty-six-hour week, researchers from UK think tank Autonomy and the Association for Sustainable Democracy (Alda) in Iceland said. The trials led unions to renegotiate working patterns, and now 86 per cent of Iceland's workforce have either moved to shorter hours for the same pay, or will gain the right to, the researchers said.

Note the countries leading here (Estonia, Israel and Iceland) are small and cohesive Petri dishes for a start-up ethos. Small is mighty in the need for innovation.

Credit where credit is due

Tech companies themselves deserve a lot more credit for what they do in local communities and social causes than the picture media paints of them.

Yes, a cynic would say, they just layer in work on community development and social causes to manipulate the self-actualisation motivators in employees ...

They encourage employees to reach their personal potential with their assigned work, while contributing positively to something greater than themselves.

The most striking contribution tech companies are making to the world is their leadership in fighting climate change. Tech companies will be carbon neutral before other industries get their finger out of their laggard holes. Many espouse their aim to be carbon neutral by 2030, with some already tracking ahead of those targets.

Google's vision for the future is one that is carbon-free, and Google and Alphabet CEO Sundar Pichai announced in 2020 that Google had eliminated its carbon legacy through purchasing carbon offsets.

Its next sustainability goal is running Google's business on carbon-free energy everywhere, starting with their data centres and campuses. Outside its own business, Google is working towards achieving its carbon-free vision with a variety of initiatives:

- Helping enable five gigawatts of new carbon-free energy through investment by 2030
- Helping more than 500 cities reduce one gigaton of carbon emissions annually by 2030
- Helping partners and organisations reduce their carbon usage and remove carbon from the atmosphere
- Through tools and information, helping one billion people make more sustainable choices by 2022[iv]

In addition to continuing its commitment to net zero greenhouse gas emissions for global operators and running on 100 per cent renewable energy, Meta has committed to reaching net zero greenhouse gas emissions for its value chain in 2030.

To achieve its goal, Meta is taking actions including:

- Evaluating materials with lower carbon impacts
- Designing products to be repairable and recyclable
- Extending the lifespan of hardware
- Ensuring responsible handling of products at the end of their lifecycle
- Working with key suppliers to help them set and reach their own emissions targets

Microsoft is upping the ante with its environmental goals, aiming to be carbon negative by 2030 and, by 2050, have removed from the environment all the carbon the company has emitted since it was founded.

Microsoft's approach is guided by seven principles:

- Grounding in science and math
- Taking responsibility for their carbon footprint
- Investing in carbon reduction and removal technology
- Empowering customers
- Ensuring transparency
- Advocating for carbon-related public policy initiatives
- Enlisting their employees in advancing innovation

On the employee level, there are forever 'give back to the community' initiatives on the go. As tech employees tend to be quite open and conscientious, dare I say 'woke'. LinkedIn for Good, the social impact arm of LinkedIn, takes this a step further by focusing on the underserved individuals included in the global economy. LinkedIn for Good's mission is to connect those from underserved communities to economic opportunity by providing them with the networks, skills and opportunities they need to succeed. In 2016 alone, LinkedIn for Good reached a combined one million youth, veterans, refugees, employees and non-profits.

Lest we forget the technology itself built by the tech companies and the good it can do. For example, the 'Donate' button on Facebook, which generated $2 billion for charities by 2019. And then there is Facebook's 'Safety Check' feature to allow people to update their family and friends on their status in the midst of a natural disaster, terrorist attacks and so on. Peace of mind that's invaluable.

Developers at tech companies are the silent heroes with features like these. It was seen in the Covid-19 pandemic too. In the course of a few weeks during March and April 2020 alone, many industries saw faster digital transformation than in the entire previous decade. Zoom became our corporate conference rooms, as well as the pub where we gathered after work. Google Classroom took the place of actual classrooms. Slack and other communication software became even more vital. Kerbside pickup, meal delivery and telehealth became the lifelines of retail, restaurant and healthcare industries, respectively.[v]

Education

It's long been claimed, as if it's a given that we must all roll with, that education, particularly third-level education, doesn't keep pace with the 'real world'. Theories and concepts in business, computer science and the like are outdated. Students graduate and enter the workforce to realise what they were taught in lectures has little resemblance to the actual needs of the workplace. Educational institutions move slowly. What if tech steps in?

We are seeing it now, in my hometown of Limerick, in my alma mater, the University of Limerick (UL). Fellow Limerick fellows, the Collison brothers of Stripe, are partnering with UL to launch a new, immersive software engineering course.

During the four-year course, students will complete five paid residencies of three to six months. Students will be part of professional teams working to improve access to financial services around the world, fighting the climate crisis and building next-generation instrumentation for healthcare.[vi] The students will learn on the job at Stripe of course, but also the likes of Shopify, Analog Devices, Shutterstock, Zalando and more.

It's a radically new approach to education in this field. And it oozes all the virtues of tech. A bias for action. Testing and learning, hands on. A pragmatic approach to growth. The program is also scalable. UL and the Collisons are optimising education for the better.

Hands-on learning has long been touted as the way forward, yet educational institutions never truly leaned into it due to a 'what worked last week will work this week' mindset. James Dyson advocates that we provide children with the tools they need not just to answer questions, but to ask questions:

The problem with academia is that it is about being good at remembering things like chemical formulae and theories, because that is what you have to regurgitate. But children are not allowed to learn through experimenting and experience. This is a great pity. You need both.[vii]

Back in 2011, a grassroots organisation, CoderDojo, sprung up to enable and empower young people to start coding. Anyone aged seven to seventeen can visit a Dojo where they can learn to code, build a website, create an app or a game and explore technology in an informal, creative and social environment. The movement has seen significant growth since its founding. There are now more than 1,900 verified Dojos in ninety-three countries, with new Dojos starting almost every day.[viii]

Health

Going straight to the ugly of the good and bad here. The Irish Health Service. If ever there was an organisation that could do with a tech lens, and blitzkrieg, applied to it, it's this organisation.

The HSE (Irish Health Service) has long been scorned as a Third World health service operating in one of the wealthiest countries per capita in the world. Benign inefficiencies abound, with a management layer that couldn't organise a piss-up in a brewery. It's decrepit, and frankly inhumane.

Management, staff training, supplies. All in dire need of change. But there is one glaring aspect of the service that could get the tech treatment. How data moves and flows. How doctors report diagnoses. How patient histories are logged. And every other information touchpoint. The software used for this will shock you.

Irish doctors and nurses have long suffered from excruciating weeks ranging from sixty to eighty hours on the front line. Admin work, logging patient details and so on takes up a significant amount of time. Some twelve to fifteen hours a week. Why? Because they have to use

MS-DOS. Yes, the blank black screen with the flicking box where you enter commands. A software that is over thirty-five years old. An update of the operating system to even Microsoft's Windows '95 (yes from the year 1995), would shave hours off a hospital staff's week. Who wouldn't want a 20 per cent efficiency gain for a service that saves lives?

My hope is that tech goes for the jugular of the health sector, in Ireland and beyond.

There are positive signals that this transformation is taking place, particularly with Amazon. Amazon have clearly proven themselves to be ruthlessly efficient in solving problems for customers in areas like retail, logistics and web infrastructure … all of which they made cheaper and more efficient for the end customer. The United States spends more on healthcare per capita than any other country in the world. In 2020, the US spent approximately $11,000 per person on healthcare, which is more than twice the average spending of other developed countries. High healthcare costs are a result of several factors, including high drug prices, high administrative costs, and high prices for medical procedures. Why not let them have a crack at health? Here are the ways they are taking on the flawed, and inhumane, US health sector:

- Amazon Pharmacy: Amazon launched its online pharmacy service in November 2020, allowing customers to purchase prescription medication and refills online. This move has put Amazon in direct competition with established players like CVS and Walgreens.
- Amazon Care: Amazon has also launched a virtual healthcare service called Amazon Care that provides users with virtual consultations and home visits from medical professionals. The service is currently available to Amazon employees in select locations.
- Alexa Healthcare Skills: Amazon has developed healthcare-specific skills for its virtual assistant, Alexa, such as

medication reminders, fitness tracking, and symptom checking.
- Health-related devices: Amazon has also developed a number of health- related devices, such as the Halo wearable fitness tracker and the Amazon Basics blood pressure monitor.
- Partnership with healthcare providers: Amazon has partnered with healthcare providers like Cerner and Beth Israel Deaconess Medical Center to integrate its services into their systems and improve patient care.

Climate

As seen earlier in the chapter, tech is doing a damn fine job doing their bit to tackle the climate crisis, leading the world of industry in cutting carbon. That's at a company-by-company level, but where can tech apply its strengths to the problem at a macro level? Enter Jeff Bezos and his 'selfish quest'.

Bezos recently fulfilled a boyhood dream of flying into space, on a rocket ship developed by his side-project from Amazon, Blue Origin. People understandably called out the world's richest man for looking to create a space tourism category that they deemed frivolous in light of the climate crisis. 'Why spend money on flying people to space when our planet is burning? Spend the money on that problem,' is the general consensus. But most have missed the point.

These 'space tourism' flights are merely practice runs to sharpen the processes to make flying into space akin to flying from New York to London. Bezos and Blue Origin are optimising the flight path for a much larger vision, of enabling a future where millions of people are living and working in space for the benefit of Earth. In order to preserve Earth, Blue Origin believes that humanity will need to expand, explore, find new energy and material resources and move industries that stress Earth into space. Blue Origin is working on this today by developing partially and fully reusable launch vehicles that are safe, low-cost and serve the needs of all civil, commercial and defence customers.[ix]

In short, all the heavy, dirty work that happens on Planet Earth, big industry, will be stored and operated in space. Earth will be like your favourite parks and rainforests, removing factories firing up smog. The Earth will be for humanity and beauty, human energy needs will be developed in space, eliminating carbon and any related climate issues. Not so selfish is our Jeff now, is he?

Closer to home, or Planet Earth as we call it, Amazon is doing its bit. Amazon today is at 40 per cent renewable energy by building fifteen utility-scale solar and wind farms. And they've put rooftop installations on their fulfilment centres and sortation centres around the world. They are committed to reaching 80 per cent renewable energy by 2040, and to be 100 per cent renewable by 2025.

Not only that, they're committing $100 million to reforestation. And a further

$2 billion recently to its Climate Pledge Fund, supporting entrepreneurs and innovators building products and services to help companies reduce their carbon impact and operate more sustainably.

Governments

Politics is all to play for with some saucy tech optimisation, which requires a mindset shift. Conservative laggards in charge won't cut it. Politics and governance need a lobotomy to change, but there is the possibility, and green shoots out there.

Governments partnering with tech is a great first step. The City of Pittsburgh asked if Twilio could find a way to keep its local 311 service, which lets people report non-emergency problems, up and running. The system was overwhelmed with so many calls that its dozen operators and seven IT support people could not cope. Things got even more difficult because operators and IT staff had to work remotely. Twilio's engineers worked with their developers to build, test and deploy a brand-new cloud-based contact centre – in just four days.[x]

Start-up incubators are a more medium- to long-term solution by the government to foster tech optimisation in its communities. An incubator is an organisation that hosts start-ups, equipping them with office space, access to tools and talent, training and investment opportunities.

One such incubator is in Paris, named Station F. It's a sprawling campus fitted with three thousand desks. That's a lot of room for a hell of a lot of companies. Facebook is a launch partner too. Every six months, Meta will work with ten to fifteen start-ups and help them as much as they can. There will be Meta engineers and weekly workshops so that young start-ups can learn from Meta. And I'm sure Meta will spot potential acquisitions quite early with this program.[xi]

Tech in social issues

Can the tech way cure our societal ills? So many people nowadays would say that the tech approach is doing the opposite; tech is doing more harm than good. I would agree with that point of view from the perspective of social media use amongst teens. Likes and comments optimised towards 'the perfect life' is brutally harmful to teens, and adults. It's a mental health bomb that's just ticking away.

For now let's stick to the positive. How is the tech way (actually) making the world a better place? With its lifeblood, data and insights. The 2011 documentary *Miss Representation* gives an inside look at the media and its message underscoring that young women need and want positive role models, and that the media has thus far neglected its unique opportunity to provide them.

What was fascinating was to see their analysis of children's films to see who the main protagonist was. They trawled through decades of popular films, for kids and adults, and coded what they saw. From female protagonists' screen time to female clothing on screen. Here are some findings:

1. Only 16% of women are the protagonists in movies.
2. Between 1937 and 2005 (68 years), there were only 13 female protagonists in animated movies and all of them were looking for romance except one.
3. Women in their twenties and thirties are only 39% of the population, but they make up 71% of characters and people on TV.
4. The media objectifies women as sex toys and unfairly stereotypes them.
5. Portraying women in a negative and deviant light is common.
6. Reality TV portrays women as manipulative, vindictive and on display for male judgement and objectification.
7. The female characters in G-rated movies are just as likely to wear revealing clothing as in R-rated movies.[xii]

That emphasis on coding up films to extract data in order to draw insights into a hypothesis, that's the tech way. Codifying stuff to get truth and then act.

Amazon joined the New York City Covid-19 Rapid Response Coalition to develop a conversational agent to enable at-risk and elderly New Yorkers to receive accurate and timely information about medical and other important needs.

Working with the CDC, Amazon's Alexa health team scrambled to build an experience that let US customers check their risk level for Covid-19 at home. A customer can ask, 'Alexa, what do I do if I think I have coronavirus?' Alexa then asks a series of questions about the person's symptoms and possible exposure. Based on those responses, Alexa then provides CDC-sourced guidance.[xiii]

Upon news of the Russian advance on Ukraine in 2022, Airbnb stepped up, big time. Airbnb.org is funding short-term housing for up to one hundred thousand people fleeing Ukraine. They support refugee guests regardless of nationality, race, ethnicity or how they identify.

Chapter 14
TECH YOURSELF

I'D RATHER BE A HYPOCRITE THAN THE SAME PERSON FOREVER.

— Adam Horowitz (Ad- Roc)

Your value to the economy will change because of tech, well to be precise, automation. It is important to realise and accept this now, because if your job can be automated, it will be.

Throughout this book we have gone through the inner workings of companies and organisations in the world of tech. We can now see how companies can thrive thanks to their cultures and execution. The question we can now ask is, are there principles and lessons from the world of tech that you can apply to your everyday, to optimise (sorry, a very techy way to say it) towards personal goals and ambitions you may have?

From maximising your impact in your day job to making improvements with how you are in relationships, to health and fitness targets you want to smash, you can apply the best of tech to yourself, to live a happier, healthier and more prosperous life.

In the marketing side of tech, there is a new breed of marketer with a term I reckon you could apply to yourself should you take on the learnings in this chapter, the *growth hacker*. Growth hackers are individuals who use creative, low-cost strategies to help businesses acquire and retain customers. Growth hackers often come from a range of backgrounds and disciplines, such as marketing, engineering, design, and product management. Growth hackers utilize data-driven experimentation and analysis to identify opportunities to quickly grow a company. They are focused on creating strategies that will result in rapid business growth and are often obsessive, curious and analytical. They are nimble, pragmatic and passionate as hell.

Let's look at seven key takeaways from the success of tech, and how they can apply to you and your own growth.

Impact over effort

Perfection. Perfection in one's work, one's relationship with a loved one, one's home and so on … are myths. Dangerous myths in fact. One's happiness lies in whether expectations are met or not. Perfection cannot be attained, ever, so why expect it?

Too often people try to achieve perfection when it comes to tasks at work. And they overdo it. Plans are made, milestones laid out, fellow employees briefed. It's very rare for anyone to ask what needs to be done and what is the quickest and easiest way to do it? In the modern way of working, such a person might be deemed lazy or disengaged.

But ask that question again as you sit down to any task. What is the least amount of effort I need to put in, to have the most amount of impact? Do I really need to write up a two-page plan that will take a day to construct in order to pitch an idea to management, or will quickly talking to one of the more enthusiastic managers about the idea help get it in motion just the same?

Be lean

The Lean Startup is a piece of tech lore at this stage. Amazon famously used old doors as desks for their employees so as to reduce costs and pass on savings to customers. Meta would be averse to hiring more people to cope with demand in order to keep the scrappy start-up culture as well as allowing the constraints in place to accelerate innovation. What can you take from these for your own life?

Their mental frameworks for lean business can be helpful for lean living. Does that car upgrade bring more value to you and your family? Forgoing that cost could open up more opportunities that increase your family's well-being, like an extra annual holiday. *The Lean Startup* model is a great mental model to minimise waste in your life and fill it with more elements of happiness.

A lean mindset will be good for your waistline too. It will also be crucial for your part in the fight for the BIG C, the climate. We are merely years away from a state of being when things available today will have to be forgone in our daily decision-making. Those avocadoes that travelled eight thousand kilometres from Peru to give your eggs-fucking-Benedict a healthy kick, forget about it. Lean will be a key virtue in the future, no harm in starting to lead that path yourself as soon as possible.

Ruthless prioritisation

Society, from work to play, is bloated with choice nowadays. In the workplace, across industries, there are many approaches we can take to driving impact and value. Think of the myriad of things you may be able to do in your workday, and think of how actually beneficial those actions will be to your personal goals, team goals, company goals, and so on.

Being crystal clear on the one, or very few things, you can do to drive impact has many benefits. First off, you will more likely get the one or few things done more proficiently. Less distraction. Multitasking is a myth as we have proven earlier on. Secondly, it's simply good for the head. Clarity and purpose unlock peace of mind.

Focus on strengths

While you prioritise, ask yourself, what are you good at and enjoy doing? Not so much what you are passionate about. The average person spends more than ninety thousand hours at work in their lifetime – one-third of many lifetimes. So that means you should probably 'follow your passion,' right? Not quite. What comes easily to you, or what have you mastered, that gives value and delight to others? That gives you energy? The answers will be your strengths.

An overlooked point regarding optimising to strengths is when to deploy your strength. Say you are a strong creative thinker who crafts ideas and strategies for brands. When do you do your best work? First thing in the morning when there is less noise? Or are you a late-night warrior? Your energy levels are finite. Ignore the hustle culture BS out there, nobody can go at 100 per cent 24/7.

The same can be said about going into a new role or company. Are you ready in the sense that your strength is the right fit for the role, team and culture? Hubristic humans – I am looking at you early twenty-something adults who join a company expecting to be CEO in a year – have a tendency to overdo it. And those on the other side of the spectrum go for positions with the assumption that they are not ready. Take a breather, read the room and pick your moments.

Be open

STAY HUNGRY, STAY FOOLISH.

— Steve Jobs

As detailed earlier, the secretive means of corporate activity is antiquated in modern work. Information is everywhere, keeping it locked up is a competitive disadvantage nowadays and fosters a negative culture. Sharing is a behaviour in the workplace that has allowed tech to thrive.

The question for you is, how can you distil more openness into your workday, or even relationships at home? Sharing learnings, experiences and problems can be hard. But would the short-term pain lead to medium- to long-term gain?

Test and learn

Tech companies have an experimental, incremental testing muscle in their DNA. Quick, cheap testing of hypotheses is the name of the game, building the learning muscle, an action bias to test constantly. This approach can directly be applied to your life.

Waking up half an hour earlier to go for a walk before work or read another chapter of your book, what does that do to your day? Cutting or adding different foods to your diet, how does that make you feel? When it comes to personal health and well-being, it's clear we could all benefit from a test-and- learn approach.

Data can help you, look at the benefits of leaning into data for your health thanks to the wearable fitness tracker Whoop:

- Sleep tracking: Whoop provides detailed information about your sleep patterns, including the amount of time you spend in each stage of sleep, the quality of your sleep, and how long it takes you to fall asleep. By tracking your sleep patterns, you can make adjustments to your lifestyle to improve the quality and duration of your sleep.
- Strain tracking: Whoop measures your body's physiological response to physical activity, known as strain. By tracking

your strain throughout the day, you can optimize your workouts and ensure that you're not overexerting yourself.
- Recovery tracking: Whoop measures your body's ability to recover from physical activity, providing insights into your body's readiness to take on physical challenges. This can help you avoid overtraining and reduce the risk of injury.
- Personalized recommendations: Based on the data collected from your Whoop device, the app provides personalized recommendations for optimizing your health and fitness, including guidance on sleep, hydration, and recovery.
- Community support: Whoop has a community of users who share insights and tips for optimizing health and fitness. By connecting with other Whoop users, you can learn from their experiences and get support and encouragement on your health and fitness journey.

This level of insight and data around your health, in real time, is unprecedented. Testing new levers like waking up earlier, working out ten minutes more than yesterday, drinking two fewer beers than the night before, will show you the impact there and then. What a time to be alive, and much, much healthier.

Attitude is everything

**I'M TRANSFORMING, I'M VIBRATING …
LOOK AT ME NOW, I'M GLOWING.**

— Nick Cave

Ultimately attitude is everything. Attitude is what sets people apart. An excited, idea-generating, problem-solving, caring colleague stands out from someone who sees cul-de-sacs, negative reactions and what's in it from them in the workplace. The best managers hire for attitude. The best teams have a shared progressive attitude.

From ten or so years working in tech I have seen three pillars of attitude work best. Those I have seen in others I worked with, and myself. These three pillars are key:

1. Curiosity
2. Persistence
3. Giving

Curiosity

WITHOUT EXPERIMENTATION, A WILLINGNESS TO ASK QUESTIONS AND TRY NEW THINGS, WE SHALL SURELY BECOME STATIC, REPETITIVE AND MORIBUND.

— Anthony Bourdain

Information is everywhere, you have to want to find it and then take action to find it. Desire to learn. Desire to experience. Openness to new ideas, different people, different perspectives. Act like a sponge.

Sidenote time. I'd argue the current means of testing intelligence at secondary level education is redundant at best, to very damaging at worst. In Ireland we have an exam at the end of your five or six years of secondary school with the results determining what level of points you can achieve to get a course in a further education institution. The Leaving Certificate (GCSE, SAT equivalent) is totally redundant, at least in the format I did it in, learning off by heart essays and data points on say the Norwegian fjord system.

It's measuring the intelligence levels of a small percentage of society. Intelligence comes in many different forms. At a high level, the Leaving Cert is designed for linear, computational intelligence (what computers can, but better than us humans).

I HAVE NO SPECIAL TALENT, I AM ONLY PASSIONATELY CURIOUS.

— Einstein

Persistence

FUCK YOU, I WON'T DO WHAT YOU TELL ME.

— Rage Against the Machine

I'm a bit of an ideas person. I fucking love ideas, be they from others and the environment around me, or even from myself, as you can see by my ramblings in this book, which 99 per cent are from others really. I was once a dreamer, but I needed to be a builder.

The idealist in me when I was younger thought that ideas were the hard part to crack in business and in life. How wrong I was. Ideas are easy. Executing those ideas, now that's a different story.

Having the balls to get an idea going, pushing it forward through craft and communication, having the resilience to overcome failure and setback, all to realise that idea. That's where it is at. That drive to do.

Ideas are plentiful. Ideas are 10 per cent of any initiative, project and so on. Ninety per cent is the tenacity and hard work to bring that idea to life.

Proactivity is key. Showing up (as early as possible) and doing. Doing. Doing. Doing. It's crucial.

Having a bias for action is a mental muscle to build. And it pays off in spades. Not just for impact, but for mental well-being. Action cures fear.

Giving

Good guys finish last. Fuck that. No more. We have to evolve.

Being nice to people in business and work life, there is a lot to be said for that. It pays to be sound. Adam Grant documented it in his seminal book *Give & Take*:

Successful collaboration requires a particular attitude. One has to be willing to offer one's insights to others; to share one's perspective; to impart one's wisdom. It is only by giving that we gain the opportunity, in turn, to receive. In fact, perhaps the most powerful evidence for the growing importance of diversity is that people with a giving attitude are becoming ever more successful.[i]

People with a giving attitude, a desire to serve others, will have a richer life. Being a prick can get you money and status, but you will be relationship poor. Play nice, and with sincerity. The results won't show themselves immediately, but life gets much better in time.

Jonathan Haidt at New York University's Stern School of Business shows that when leaders are not just fair but self-sacrificing, their employees are actually moved and inspired to become more loyal and committed themselves. As a consequence, they are more likely to go out of their way to be helpful and friendly to other employees, thus creating a self-reinforcing cycle. Daan Van Knippenberg of Rotterdam School of Management shows that employees of self-sacrificing leaders exhibit increased cooperation due to enhanced trust in their leaders. They also demonstrate higher productivity and see their leaders as more effective and charismatic.[ii]

One more, just to send this one home. Research by Harvard Business School professor Amy Edmondson shows that in the type of psychologically safe environment that Meyer helped create, people learn and innovate more. And it's givers who often create such an environment: in one study, engineers who shared ideas without expecting anything in return were more likely to play a major role in innovation, as they made it safe to exchange information.[iii]

Where your value will be

The story is told that the great Einstein was once asked how many feet are in a mile. Einstein's reply was, 'I don't know. Why would I fill my brain with facts I can find in two minutes in any standard reference book?'

A valuable lesson, emphasising the importance to use your mind to think, rather than use it as a warehouse for facts. Google stores the information, knowing when to google it is a much better use of our brain than the rote learning of yesteryear.

As automation looms, we have to accept that information is everywhere and the heavy lifting of finding info for the right context or moment will come to us. Be it via VR, Neuralink or other devices that haven't even been invented yet.

If you were to place your bet for which human work will be most valuable to you, and your children, it's best to look at areas humans do very well but machines cannot. Take a look at areas where human experiences are at the most vibrant.

The value of experience is rising. Luxury entertainment is increasing by 6.5 per cent annually. Spending at restaurants and bars increased 9 per cent in 2015 alone. The price of the average concert ticket has increased by nearly 400 per cent from 1981 to 2012 (Ticketmaster's 'fees' disgust me, for the record). Ditto for the price of healthcare in the United States, although their incredibly inhumane approach to healthcare bakes in exorbitant pricing.

The average US rate for babysitting is fifteen dollars per hour, twice the minimum wage. Personal coaches dispensing intensely personal attention for a very bodily experience are among the fastest-growing occupations. In hospice care, the cost of drugs and treatments is in decline, but the cost of home visits – experiential – is rising. The cost of weddings has no limit. These are not commodities, they are experiences, which humans excel at creating and consuming, not robots. Experiences are where money will be spent and made.[iv]

Be a curious, caring and courageous human. With stress on the human element in everything.

And be sure to practice what you preach. Nick Cave and Bad Seeds released the seminal song "Jubilee Street" in 2013, coincidentally a year into my Tech adventure, and the year I joined Facebook. These particular lyrics seared into my psyche, and a principle I've tried living and looking for in those around me:

"All those good people down on Jubilee Street
They ought to practice what they preach
Here they are to practice just what they preach
Those good people on Jubilee Street"

Power of the people

Throughout this book I have been hammering on about tech's way of working being the best-in-class way of working. To such an extent that I may have given tech a superiority complex.

The thing is, putting tech's way of working on an insurmountable pedestal is missing the point. Working with people, great people with great attitudes, is the key to working in the best way possible.

The best four days of 'work' I have ever experienced were not in tech, they were back in my time in the music industry. When I had the honour of being part of producer and master selector Mr Scruff's Ireland tour across Limerick, Dublin, Galway and Cork. I was his driver, and minor logistics helper, for the tour. What I learned and experienced in those four days changed me.

To begin with, he turned up with his own sound engineer, very unique for a touring DJ. A DJ nowadays turns up solo, with a USB stick and plugs into the decks and plays. Andy, aka Mr Scruff, not only turned up with a sound engineer and two bags of vinyl, but also got to each venue to get started on an almost eight-hour sound check.

When he played my hometown, a venue I ran gigs in and loved, Dolans Warehouse, he transformed the venue. I don't mean to get into the nerdy side of audiophilia, but he moved the subwoofers to line the stage, and brought red lighting to just half of the dancefloor. For its decades in operation, the speaker set-up had never been changed around. Local promoters, used to putting on heavy-hitting techno DJs in particular, walked into the room and were blown away by the improvement in sound and feel in the room. All this was created by Andy and his sound engineer tinkering away all day.

The following day we set off to Dublin for the next venue. To Tripod, the incredible gig space that sadly made way for a Pret-a-Manger. Driving up the motorway, Andy took out a clipboard, which had A4 sheets formatted with text boxes. The text boxes had the following headings:

What records worked well
What records didn't work well
What worked well at the venue
What didn't work well at the venue

In the 'what worked well' text box, Andy sketched out the speaker set-up redesign they did. I asked what he does with the sheets when he has written up his reflections, he said he sends them back to the promoter as helpful feedback, humbly citing, 'I hope it may be helpful to them to make that lovely space shine even more'. What care. What a wonderful giver.

The next day, we headed from Dublin to Galway. On that drive he was playing tunes on the car stereo. One record had me particularly hooked,

I asked where he came across it. He told this story of being on an island in the Caribbean, and he heard it on the speakers in the bar. He asked the barman what record it was and where it came from. The barman said a producer on the island created it, and there were only a hundred copies made. Andy got the address of the producer, and set off on a three-hour trek through a jungle to get the producer and get one of the hundred copies.

Such care taken to the craft.

Curiosity, persistence and giving. A four-day immersion in those virtuous attributes.

You don't necessarily need to work in tech in order to learn how to optimise your work and life to add value and 'make the world a better place', I'd recommend you seek and find groups of people that care, learn and give.

Everyone is creative

I'd like to end this chapter on something so inherently human, that the robots can't really take over. It is our greatest value add to society. That is, creativity. Having worked with some of the world's most successful and skilled people, one thing shocked me about many of their mindsets. It was this commonly uttered phrase:

'I am not creative.'

Bullshit. Everyone is creative. Some more so than others, yes, and they are the ones whose brand depends on it.

But there is a fallacy against creativity. Being creative doesn't mean painting the *Mona Lisa* or conceptualising an award-winning Superbowl ad. Being creative is putting one component together with another, to create something new. That is all.

Steve Jobs was hyper-creative because he was able to put a ton of 1s and 2s together to create game-changing 3s. Look at the iPhone. The phone was always in mass consumption. The camera was in mass consumption. The internet was in mass consumption. He merely had the vision. To bring them all together. 1 + 2 + 3 = iPhone = most successful product of all fucking time.

Creativity is combination. The more sources of knowledge and context you have, the better you are at combining them.

In his excellent book *The Creative Act: A Way of Being*, the iconic music producer Rick Rubin states:

Creativity is not a rare ability. It is not difficult to access. Creativity is a fundamental aspect of being human. It's our birthright. And it's for all of us.

To create is to bring something into existence that wasn't there before. It could be a conversation, the solution to a problem, a note to a friend, the rearrangement of furniture in a room, a new route home to avoid a traffic jam.

An accountant is creative. A banker is creative. How you do the dishes can be creative. You are creative. And you have to be more creative as automation looms. Don't worry, you are just getting more and more opportunities to be more human than ever, run with it.

The doers are the winners, as creation is easier than it's ever been. It is ten times easier today to make a simple video than ten years ago. It is a hundred times easier to create a small mechanical part (and 3D printing has yet to go properly mainstream) and make it real than a century ago. It is a thousand times easier today to write and publish a book than a thousand years ago.[v]

I hope this chapter is of some help. I don't mean it to be some self-help fluff. There are codes and learnings in the tech world, where I have seen good people becoming great, in every aspect of their lives. Take the learnings and run with them.

It's all possible; crawl, walk, run … just do it.

Grow Like Tech

Or, just google it.

CONCLUSION

Ask yourself the following questions ...

How would a very smart, well-funded competitor attack your company's core business or supposed 'USP'?

How could the competition take advantage of digital technologies to exploit weaknesses or skim off your most profitable customer segments?

What is the company doing to disrupt its own business in order to future-proof itself?

Is there an opportunity to build a platform that can offer increasing returns and value as usage grows for the sake of scale?

Do employees, and more importantly leaders, use the product regularly?

When you go through your pipeline of upcoming new major products and features, what percentage of them are built on unique technical insights or data?

Conclusion

How many product or technical specialists are on the senior leadership team?

Does the company aggressively reward and promote the people who have the biggest impact on creating excellent products and customer service?

Is hiring a top priority at the leadership level? And do leadership actually spend time on it?

Among your stronger employees, how many see themselves at the company in three years? And have you actually asked to find out?

How many would leave for a 10 per cent raise at another company? How much freedom do employees have?

Do leaders actually practice what they preach?

If there is someone who is truly innovative, does that person have the freedom to act on his ideas, regardless of their level?

Are decisions on new ideas based on product excellence, or profit? Who does better in the company, information hoarders or sharers?

Do silos between teams prevent the free flow of information and people?

If you have no good answer to all of these, then you need to consider a change of approach, be it at your company or within yourself. I hope this book serves as many people as possible. The world is experiencing increasing economic inequality. But I hope this book opens up a black box of how to do well, add value and create opportunity in whatever life you lead. To give you time back. To live a little bit better. To, actually, make the world a better place.

ACKNOWLEDGMENTS

This book has been 2 years in creation/tormented procrastination. But much, much longer than that in inspiration. It is the result of being fascinated by how people work together. People's purpose of work. The subtle cultural codes in each workplace. The "what good look like", and bad, and why. It's enthralled me, without me consciously knowing it for some time. From working in pubs as teenager, through to a multitude of coming of age jobs like door to door selling of lawn aeration. And then on to an invigorating stint in the music industry, and on to a decade plus in the world of tech. It's never been the company or brand or whatever that's been the fascination and learning, it's been the people. The people I have worked with, and worked around, have made me and this book.

So I would like to thank the people I have worked with, and inspired me both inside and outside the workplace. To that end, there are far too many to list here. But I will start with most thanks going to my family. Especially my mother Bernie, who always said "there is a book in you".

To everyone I've worked closely with, and that I can delightfully call a great friend to this day, and I hope you know who you are. To those who took a chance on hiring me a times when I seemed a bit of maverick or rogue decision, I am forever grateful. And also those who had the pain of managing me. Your decisions and guidance propelled me in ways you can't imagine. You are Conor Cronin, Dave O'Donovan, Joe Clarke, Catherine Flynn, Evin Gaffney, Daryl Hughes, Roy Cohen, Steve Carroll. Kris Boger and Paul Mears.

To all my great mates, in various Whatsapp groups and beyond. Thank you for the inspiration, especially in keeping things real and human, and hilarious.

And quite frankly to everyone I've had the joy of encountering, from the odd 30 min Zoom call, to a quick back and forth over Slack, it has had an impact. All our interactions with each other, in the world of work and most importantly outside work, matter.

Thank you.

Dave.

BIBLIOGRAPHY

Introduction

Statista. (2024). Number of daily active Facebook users worldwide as of 3rd quarter 2023, from https://www.statista.com/statistics/1092227/facebook-product-dau/

BBC. (n.d.). Amazon: The Truth Behind The Click [Television series episode]. In Panorama.Profgalloway.com. (n.d.). Apple, Thief. from https://www.profgalloway.com/apple-thief/Statista. (2024).

Number of daily active Facebook users worldwide as of 3rd quarter 2023.from https://www.statista.com/statistics/1092227/facebook-product-dau/

Fleximize. (n.d.). The Chinese Super-App Changing Tech, from https://fleximize.com/articles/006663/chinese-super-app-changing-tech

Huang, S. (2022, January 3). Apple Becomes First U.S. Company to Reach $3 Trillion Market Cap. NBC News. https://www.nbcnews.com/tech/apple/apple-becomes-first-us-company-reach-3-trillion-market-cap-rcna10767

Reiff, N. (2019, December 2). Decade in Review: Big Tech Gains Enormous Power. U.S. News & World Report. https://money.usnews.com/investing/stock-market-news/articles/2019-12-02/decade-in-review-big-tech-gains-enormous-power

Chapter 1: Change is Constant

Catmull, E., & Wallace, A. (2014). Creativity, Inc.: Overcoming the Unseen Forces That Stand in the Way of True Inspiration. Random House.

Chesky, B. (2021, November 30). Interview by N. Patel. Decoder [Audio podcast]. The Verge. https://www.theverge.com/22783422/airbnb-pandemic-ceo-brian-chesky-interview-travel-decoder-podcast

Duggan, W. (2013). Strategic Intuition: The Creative Spark in Human Achievement. Columbia University Press.

Galloway, S. (2017). The Four: The Hidden DNA of Amazon, Apple, Facebook and Google. Portfolio.

Judah, S. (2016). Meaningful: The Story of Ideas That Fly. Sceptre.

Lanier, J. (2013). Who Owns the Future? Simon & Schuster.

Mason, M. (2008). The Pirate's Dilemma: How Youth Culture Is Reinventing Capitalism. Free Press.

Mellon, J., & Chalabi, A. (2015). Think Like an Artist: and Lead a More Creative, Productive Life. Penguin.

Ries, E. (2017). The Startup Way: How Entrepreneurial Management Transforms Culture and Drives Growth. Currency.

Schmidt, E., Rosenberg, J., & Eagle, A. (2014). How Google Works. Grand Central Publishing.

Senor, D., & Singer, S. (2009). Start-up Nation: The Story of Israel's Economic Miracle. Twelve.

Swan, M. (2015). Blockchain: Blueprint for a New Economy. O'Reilly Media.

Chapter 2: The Why of Tech

Benioff, M., & Langley, K. (2019). Trailblazer: The Power of Business as the Greatest Platform for Change. Currency.

Bryant, A. (2011). The Corner Office: Indispensable and Unexpected Lessons from CEOs on How to Lead and Succeed. Times Books.

Cain, S. (2012). Quiet: The Power of Introverts in a World That Can't Stop Talking. Crown.

Catmull, E., & Wallace, A. (2014). Creativity, Inc.: Overcoming the Unseen Forces That Stand in the Way of True Inspiration. Random House.

Christensen, C. M. (1997). The Innovator's Dilemma: When New Technologies Cause Great Firms to Fail. Harvard Business Review Press.

Collins, J. (2001). Good to Great: Why Some Companies Make the Leap... and Others Don't. HarperBusiness.

Duhigg, C. (2012). The Power of Habit: Why We Do What We Do in Life and Business. Random House.

Economy, P. (2021, August 23). This Is the Way You Need to Write Down Your Goals for Faster Success. Inc., from https://www.inc.com/peter-economy/this-is-way-you-need-to-write-down-your-goals-for-faster-success.html

Galloway, S. (2017). The Four: The Hidden DNA of Amazon, Apple, Facebook and Google. Portfolio.

Hastings, R., & Meyer, E. (2020). No Rules Rules: Netflix and the Culture of Reinvention. Penguin Press.

Huang, S. (2022, January 3). Apple Becomes First U.S. Company to Reach $3 Trillion Market Cap. NBC News. from https://www.nbcnews.com/tech/apple/apple-becomes-first-us-company-reach-3-trillion-market-cap-rcna10767

Chapter 3: Culture Is Religion

Bezos, J. (2015). Amazon 2015 Shareholder Letter. Amazon.com, Inc.

Carmack, J. (Guest). (n.d.). Lex Friedman Podcast [Audio podcast].

Catmull, E., & Wallace, A. (2014). Creativity, Inc.: Overcoming the Unseen Forces That Stand in the Way of True Inspiration. Random House.

Clear, J. (2018). Atomic Habits: An Easy & Proven Way to Build Good Habits & Break Bad Ones. Penguin Random House.

Coyle, D. (2018). The Culture Code: The Secrets of Highly Successful Groups. Bantam.

Ferriss, T. (2016). Tools of Titans: The Tactics, Routines, and Habits of Billionaires, Icons, and World-Class Performers. Houghton Mifflin Harcourt.

Bibliography

Ferriss, T. (Host). (n.d.). Tim Ferriss Podcast [Audio podcast].

Galloway, S. (2017). The Four: The Hidden DNA of Amazon, Apple, Facebook and Google. Portfolio.

Grant, A. (2016). Originals: How Non-Conformists Move the World. Viking.

Hastings, R., & Meyer, E. (2020). No Rules Rules: Netflix and the Culture of Reinvention. Penguin Press.

Holmgren, L. (n.d.). Sample Project - OM300F06 Honors Report. University of Michigan-Dearborn. http://www-personal.umd.umich.edu/~yro/TenurePortfolio/

Horowitz, B. (2019). What You Do Is Who You Are: How to Create Your Business Culture. Harper Business.

Hsieh, T. (2010). Delivering Happiness: A Path to Profits, Passion, and Purpose. Grand Central Publishing.

Judah, S. (2016). Meaningful: The Story of Ideas That Fly. Sceptre.

Lawler, A. (2022). After Steve: How Apple Became a Trillion-Dollar Company and Lost Its Soul. William Morrow.

Mankins, M., & Garton, E. (2017). Time, Talent, Energy: Overcome Organizational Drag and Unleash Your Team's Productive Power. Harvard Business Review Press.

Mason, M. (2008). The Pirate's Dilemma: How Youth Culture Is Reinventing Capitalism. Free Press.Opensource.com. (n.d.). What is open source? Retrieved July 21, 2024, from https://opensource.com/resources/what-open-source

Ries, E. (2017). The Startup Way: How Entrepreneurial Management Transforms Culture and Drives Growth. Currency.

Robinson, K. (2011). Out of Our Minds: Learning to be Creative. Capstone.

Schiffer, Z. (2021, September 9). Apple's Slack Organizing: Interview with Zoe Schiffer. The Verge. https://www.theverge.com/22659497/apple-slack-organizing-zoe-schiffer-decoder-interview

Schmidt, E., & Rosenberg, J. (2014). How Google Works. Grand Central Publishing.

Sinek, S. (2009). Start with Why: How Great Leaders Inspire Everyone to Take Action. Portfolio.

Sull, C. K., & Sull, D. (2018, May). Why Great Employees Leave "Great Cultures". Harvard Business Review. https://hbr.org/2018/05/why-great-employees-leave-great-cultures

Sutherland, J., & Sutherland, J. J. (2014). Scrum: The Art of Doing Twice the Work in Half the Time. Crown Business.

Syed, M. (2019). Rebel Ideas: The Power of Diverse Thinking. John Murray.

Tines. (n.d.). About Us. Retrieved July 21, 2024, from https://www.tines.com/about

Vassallo, S. (2021). Ask Your Developer: How to Harness the Power of Software Developers and Win in the 21st Century. Harper Business.

Chapter 4: Growth Is God

Bezos, J. (2021). Invent and Wander: The Collected Writings of Jeff Bezos. Harvard Business Review Press.

Bibliography

Catmull, E., & Wallace, A. (2014). Creativity, Inc.: Overcoming the Unseen Forces That Stand in the Way of True Inspiration. Random House.

CB Insights. (n.d.). 15 Startup Pivot Success Stories, from https://www.cbinsights.com/research/startup-pivot-success-stories/

Clear, J. (2018). Atomic Habits: An Easy & Proven Way to Build Good Habits & Break Bad Ones. Penguin Random House.

Coinbase. (n.d.). Lighting up the map: How Coinbase plans to scale globally, 2024, from https://www.coinbase.com/blog/lighting-up-the-map-how-coinbase-plans-to-scale-globally-article

Davis, A., & Le Merle, M. C. (2017). Corporate Innovation in the Fifth Era: Lessons from Alphabet/Google, Amazon, Apple, Facebook, and Microsoft. Fifth Era Media.

Dumaine, B. (2020). Bezonomics: How Amazon Is Changing Our Lives, and What the World's Best Companies Are Learning from It.

Scribner.Frier, S. (2021). An Ugly Truth: Inside Facebook's Battle for Domination. The Bridge Street Press.

Galloway, S. (2017). The Four: The Hidden DNA of Amazon, Apple, Facebook and Google. Portfolio.

Hsieh, T. (2010). Delivering Happiness: A Path to Profits, Passion, and Purpose. Grand Central Publishing.

Investopedia. (n.d.). Companies That Succeeded With Bootstrapping, from https://www.investopedia.com/articles/investing/082814/companies-succeeded-bootstrapping.asp

Judah, S. (2016). Meaningful: The Story of Ideas That Fly. Sceptre.

Kaufman, J. (2012). The Personal MBA: A World-Class Business Education in a Single Volume. Portfolio.

Kelly, K. (2016). The Inevitable: Understanding the 12 Technological Forces That Will Shape Our Future. Viking.

Kerr, J. (2013). Legacy. Constable.

Kotter, J. P. (2014). Accelerate: Building Strategic Agility for a Faster-Moving World. Harvard Business Review Press.

Laszlo, B. (2015). Work Rules!: Insights from Inside Google That Will Transform How You Live and Lead. Twelve.Mellon,

J., & Chalabi, A. (2015). Think Like an Artist: and Lead a More Creative, Productive Life. Penguin.

Ries, E. (2011). The Lean Startup: How Today's Entrepreneurs Use Continuous Innovation to Create Radically Successful Businesses. Crown Business.

Schmidt, E., & Rosenberg, J. (2014). How Google Works. Grand Central Publishing.

Siu, E. (2021, October 27). AI Is No Longer Just a Trend. Here's How to Use It in Your Business Strategy. Fortune, from https://fortune.com/2021/10/27/ai-artificial-intelligence-business-strategy-data-accenture/

Sull, D., & Eisenhardt, K. M. (2015). Simple Rules: How to Thrive in a Complex World. Houghton Mifflin Harcourt.

Taplytics. (n.d.). How to Experiment Like Facebook and Netflix by Adopting the 10,000 Experiment Rule, from https://taplytics.com/blog/how-to-experiment-like-facebook-and-netflix-by-adopting-the-10000-experiment-rule/

Bibliography

Vassallo, S. (2021). Ask Your Developer: How to Harness the Power of Software Developers and Win in the 21st Century. Harper Business.

X, The Moonshot Factory. (n.d.). Homepage, from https://x.company/

Chapter 5: Data Is The New Gold

"All the Bells Say." Succession, season 3, episode 9, HBO, 2021.

Accenture. "AI Artificial Intelligence Business Strategy Data." Fortune, 27 Oct. 2021, fortune.com/2021/10/27/ai-artificial-intelligence-business-strategy-data-accenture/.

Marr, Bernard. "How Much Data Do We Create Every Day? The Mind-Blowing Stats Everyone Should Read." Forbes, 21 May 2018, www.forbes.com/sites/bernardmarr/2018/05/21/how-much-data-do-we-create-every-day-the-mind-blowing-stats-everyone-should-read/."

China Daily." 11 Dec. 2017, www.chinadaily.com.cn/a/201712/11/WS5a2dbce0a310eefe3e9a1453.html."

Generative AI Could Raise Global GDP by 7 Percent." Goldman Sachs, www.goldmansachs.com/insights/pages/generative-ai-could-raise-global-gdp-by-7-percent.html.

Galloway, Scott. The Four: The Hidden DNA of Amazon, Apple, Facebook and Google. Portfolio, 2017.

Stevens, Mike. The Direct to Consumer Playbook. Harriman House, 2021.

Schmidt, Eric, et al. How Google Works. Grand Central Publishing, 2014."Martech 2030." WPP, Aug. 2021, www.wpp.com/wpp-iq/2021/08/martech-2030.

Syed, Matthew. Black Box Thinking: The Surprising Truth About Success. John Murray, 2015.

Keating, Gina. Netflixed: The Epic Battle for America's Eyeballs. Portfolio, 2012.

Lawson, Jeff. Ask Your Developer: How to Harness the Power of Software Developers and Win in the 21st Century. Harper Business, 2021.

Kaufman, Josh. The Personal MBA: A World-Class Business Education in a Single Volume. Portfolio, 2010.

Tett, Gillian. Anthro Vision: A New Way to See in Business and Life. Simon & Schuster, 2021.

"Kevin De Bruyne Uses Data." Mirror, www.mirror.co.uk/sport/football/news/kevin-de-bruyne-uses-data-23870686.

"Why Is It So Hard to Become a Data-Driven Company." Harvard Business Review, Feb. 2021, hbr.org/2021/02/why-is-it-so-hard-to-become-a-data-driven-company.

"Gymshark Data Transformation." Think with Google, www.thinkwithgoogle.com/intl/en-gb/future-of-marketing/digital-transformation/gymshark-data-transformation/.

Galloway, Scott. "AI." Prof G, www.profgalloway.com/ai/."

Shein: The Mystery Behind the Largest Ecommerce Company in the World." Charged Retail, 11 June 2021, www.chargedretail.co.uk/2021/06/11/shein-the-mystery-behind-the-largest-ecommerce-company-in-the-world/.

Bibliography

Chapter 7: Fail Fast

Lawson, Jeff. Ask Your Developer: How to Harness the Power of Software Developers and Win in the 21st Century. Harper Business, 2021.

Bezos, Jeff. Invent and Wander: The Collected Writings of Jeff Bezos. Harvard Business Review Press, 2020.

Schmidt, Eric, and Jonathan Rosenberg. How Google Works. Grand Central Publishing, 2014.

Syed, Matthew. Black Box Thinking: The Surprising Truth About Success. Portfolio, 2015.

Hastings, Reed, and Erin Meyer. No Rules Rules: Netflix and the Culture of Reinvention. Penguin Press, 2020.

Ries, Eric. The Startup Way: How Entrepreneurial Management Transforms Culture and Drives Growth. Currency, 2017.

Kahneman, Daniel. Thinking, Fast and Slow. Farrar, Straus and Giroux, 2011.

Chapter 8: Leadership

Schmidt, Eric, and Jonathan Rosenberg. How Google Works. Grand Central Publishing, 2014.

Polsson, Ken. "Chronology of Apple Computer, Inc. 1984." Islandnet, 21 Aug. 2009, https://web.archive.org/web/20090821105822/http://www.islandnet.com/~kpolsson/applehis/appl1984.html.

"Leadership Principles." Amazon, https://www.amazon.jobs/en/principles.

Friedman, Zack. "The Best Managers at Google." Forbes, 30 Aug. 2018, https://www.forbes.com/sites/zackfriedman/2018/08/30/best-managers-google/?sh=66280a984f26.

Sinek, Simon. Start With Why: How Great Leaders Inspire Everyone to Take Action. Portfolio, 2009.

Lawson, Jeff. Ask Your Developer: How to Harness the Power of Software Developers and Win in the 21st Century. Harper Business, 2021.

Tuff, Chuck, and Paul Nunes. Corporate Innovation in the Fifth Era: Lessons from Alphabet/Google, Amazon, Apple, Facebook, and Microsoft. Fifth Era Media, 2016.

Catmull, Ed, and Amy Wallace. Creativity, Inc.: Overcoming the Unseen Forces That Stand in the Way of True Inspiration. Random House, 2014.

Santos, Rafael, et al. "A Comprehensive Review of Artificial Intelligence and Robotics." National Center for Biotechnology Information, 2018, https://www.ncbi.nlm.nih.gov/pmc/articles/PMC6050388/.

Butterfield, Stewart. "We Don't Sell Saddles Here." Medium, https://medium.com/@stewart/we-dont-sell-saddles-here-4c59524d650d.

Ernst, Porter. Alibaba's World: How One Remarkable Chinese Company Is Changing the Face of Global Business. St. Martin's Press, 2015.

Bryar, Bill, and Colin Bryar. Working Backwards: Insights, Stories, and Secrets from Inside Amazon. St. Martin's Press, 2021.

Bibliography

Stevens, Mike. The Direct to Consumer Playbook. Harriman House, 2021.

Hastings, Reed, and Erin Meyer. No Rules Rules: Netflix and the Culture of Reinvention. Penguin Press, 2020.

Coyle, Daniel. The Culture Code: The Secrets of Highly Successful Groups. Bantam, 2018.

Vance, Ashlee. Elon Musk: How the Billionaire CEO of SpaceX and Tesla is Shaping our Future. Ecco, 2015.

Ferguson, Alex, and Michael Moritz. Leading. Hachette Books, 2015.

Chesky, Brian. "A Message from Co-Founder and CEO Brian Chesky." Airbnb Newsroom, https://news.airbnb.com/a-message-from-co-founder-and-ceo-brian-chesky/.

Iger, Robert. The Ride of a Lifetime: Lessons Learned from 15 Years as CEO of the Walt Disney Company. Random House, 2019.

"How Jeff Bezos Makes Decisions." Fast Company, https://www.fastcompany.com/90578272/how-jeff-bezos-makes-decisions.

Holiday, Ryan. Ego is the Enemy. Portfolio, 2016.

"Harvard Business Review's 10 Must Reads on Leadership." Harvard Business Review Press, 2011.

Grant, Adam. Give and Take: Why Helping Others Drives Our Success. Viking, 2013.

Chapter 9: Managing People

Bock, L. (2015). Work Rules!: Insights from Inside Google That Will Transform How You Live and Lead. Twelve.

Buckingham, M., & Coffman, C. (1999). First Break All the Rules: What the World's Greatest Managers Do Differently. Simon & Schuster.

Catmull, E., & Wallace, A. (2014). Creativity, Inc.: Overcoming the Unseen Forces That Stand in the Way of True Inspiration. Random House.

Cohan, P. (2021). Ask Your Developer: How to Harness the Power of Software Developers and Win in the 21st Century. HarperBusiness.

Coyle, D. (2018). The Culture Code: The Secrets of Highly Successful Groups. Bantam.

Friedman, Z. (2018, August 30). Google Says The Best Managers Have These 10 Qualities. Forbes. https://www.forbes.com/sites/zackfriedman/2018/08/30/best-managers-google/?sh=f966c624f261

Hastings, R., & Meyer, E. (2020). No Rules Rules: Netflix and the Culture of Reinvention. Penguin Press.

Hsieh, T. (2010). Delivering Happiness: A Path to Profits, Passion, and Purpose. Grand Central Publishing.

Horowitz, B. (2014). The Hard Thing About Hard Things: Building a Business When There Are No Easy Answers. Harper Business.

Isaacson, W., & Bezos, J. (2021). Invent and Wander: The Collected Writings of Jeff Bezos. Harvard Business Review Press.

Kaufman, J. (2012). The Personal MBA: A World-Class Business Education in a Single Volume. Portfolio.

Bibliography

Mankins, M., & Garton, E. (2017). Time, Talent, Energy: Overcome Organizational Drag and Unleash Your Team's Productive Power. Harvard Business Review Press.

Page, S. E. (2019). The Diversity Bonus: How Great Teams Pay Off in the Knowledge Economy. Princeton University Press.

Ries, E. (2017). The Startup Way: How Entrepreneurial Management Transforms Culture and Drives Growth. Currency.

Schmidt, E., & Rosenberg, J. (2014). How Google Works. Grand Central Publishing.

Sinek, S. (2019). The Infinite Game. Portfolio.

Sutherland, J., & Sutherland, J. J. (2014). Scrum: The Art of Doing Twice the Work in Half the Time. Crown Business.

Vu, P. (2018). Culture Decks Decoded: Transform Your Culture Into a Visible, Conscious, and Tangible Asset. Phuong Vu.

Harvard Business Review. (2011). HBR's 10 Must Reads on Managing People. Harvard Business Review Press.

Chapter 10: Customer-First Building

Berger, J. (2013). Contagious: Why Things Catch On. Simon & Schuster.

Bezos, J., & Isaacson, W. (2021). Invent and Wander: The Collected Writings of Jeff Bezos. Harvard Business Review Press.

Butterfield, S. (2014, February 17). We Don't Sell Saddles Here. Medium. https://medium.com/@stewart/we-dont-sell-saddles-here-4c59524d650d

Cohan, P. (2021). Ask Your Developer: How to Harness the Power of Software Developers and Win in the 21st Century. Harper Business.

Ferriss, T. (2021, February 1). The Tim Ferriss Show Transcripts: Marc Randolph on Building Netflix, Battling Blockbuster, Negotiating with Amazon/Bezos, and Scraping the Barnacles Off the Hull (#496). Tim.blog. https://tim.blog/2021/02/01/marc-randolph-transcript/

Galloway, S. (2017). The Four: The Hidden DNA of Amazon, Apple, Facebook and Google. Portfolio.

Grant, A. (2016). Originals: How Non-conformists Change the World. WH Allen.

Hastings, R., & Meyer, E. (2020). No Rules Rules: Netflix and the Culture of Reinvention. Penguin Press.

Hoffman, R., & Yeh, J. (2018). Masters of Scale: Surprising Truths from the World's Most Successful Entrepreneurs. Currency.

Kaufman, J. (2012). The Personal MBA: A World-Class Business Education in a Single Volume. Portfolio.

Kelly, K. (2016). The Inevitable: Understanding the 12 Technological Forces That Will Shape Our Future. Viking.

Ries, E. (2011). The Lean Startup: How Constant Innovation Creates Radically Successful Businesses. Crown Business.

Schmidt, E., & Rosenberg, J. (2014). How Google Works. Grand Central Publishing.

Stone, B. (2017). The Upstarts: How Uber, Airbnb and the Killer Companies of the New Silicon Valley are Changing the World. Little, Brown and Company.

Bibliography

Syed, B. (2015). Meaningful: The Story of Ideas That Fly. Capstone.

Chapter 11: Meeting Meetings Meetings

Catmull, E., & Wallace, A. (2014). Creativity, Inc.: Overcoming the Unseen Forces That Stand in the Way of True Inspiration. Random House.

Cohan, P. (2021). Ask Your Developer: How to Harness the Power of Software Developers and Win in the 21st Century. HarperBusiness.

Grant, A. (2016). Originals: How Non-conformists Change the World.

WH Allen.Hastings, R., & Meyer, E. (2020). No Rules Rules: Netflix and the Culture of Reinvention. Penguin Press.Mankins, M., & Garton, E. (2017). Time, Talent, Energy: Overcome Organizational Drag and Unleash Your Team's Productive Power. Harvard Business Review Press.

Schmidt, E., & Rosenberg, J. (2014). How Google Works. Grand Central Publishing.

Stone, B. (2014, October 6). Zuckerberg's New Secret Weapon for Dealmaking: WhatsApp. Bloomberg. https://www.bloomberg.com/news/articles/2014-10-06/zuckerbergs-new-secret-weapon-for-deal-making-whatsapp

Chapter 12: Storytelling & Marketing

Berger, J. (2016). Contagious: Why Things Catch On. Simon & Schuster.

Butterfield, S. (2014, February 17). We Don't Sell Saddles Here. Medium. https://medium.com/@stewart/we-dont-sell-saddles-here-4c59524d650d

Dumaine, B. (2020). Bezonomics: How Amazon Is Changing Our Lives, and What the World's Best Companies Are Learning from It. Scribner.

Galloway, S. (2017). The Four: The Hidden DNA of Amazon, Apple, Facebook and Google. Portfolio.

Hsieh, T. (2010). Delivering Happiness: A Path to Profits, Passion, and Purpose. Grand Central Publishing.

Ries, E. (2011). The Lean Startup: How Constant Innovation Creates Radically Successful Businesses. Crown Business.

Ries, E. (2017). The Startup Way: How Entrepreneurial Management Transforms Culture and Drives Growth. Currency.

Schmidt, E., & Rosenberg, J. (2014). How Google Works. Grand Central Publishing.

Stevens, M. (2022). The Direct to Consumer Playbook: The Stories and Strategies of the Brands that Wrote the DTC Rules. Kogan Page.

Stone, B. (2017). The Upstarts: How Uber, Airbnb and the Killer Companies of the New Silicon Valley are Changing the World. Little, Brown and Company.

Thompson, D. (2017). Hit Makers: How to Succeed in an Age of Distraction. Penguin Press.

Chapter 13: Community at Large

Blue Origin. (n.d.). About Blue. Retrieved from https://www.blueorigin.com/about-blue

CoderDojo. (n.d.). About CoderDojo. Retrieved from https://coderdojo.com/movement/

Cohan, P. (2021). Ask Your Developer: How to Harness the Power of Software Developers and Win in the 21st Century. HarperBusiness.

Consumer Technology Association. (2021, May). 10 Tech Companies Setting Big Goals to Reduce Climate Impact. Retrieved from https://www.ces.tech/Articles/2021/May/10-Tech-Companies-Setting-Big-Goals-to-Reduce-Clim.aspx

Hammersley, B. (2015, February). Concerned about Brexit? Why not become an e-resident of Estonia. Wired UK. Retrieved from https://www.wired.co.uk/article/estonia-e-resident

Mandelbaum, R. (2017, January 17). Facebook to open Startup Garage at Station F in Paris. TechCrunch. Retrieved from https://techcrunch.com/2017/01/17/facebook-to-open-startup-garage-at-station-f-in-paris/

O'Brien, C. (2021, February 22). Tech companies team up with UL for radical computer science programme. The Irish Times. Retrieved from https://www.irishtimes.com/business/technology/tech-companies-team-up-with-ul-for-radical-computer-science-programme-1.4493307

Senor, D., & Singer, S. (2009). Start-Up Nation: The Story of Israel's Economic Miracle. Twelve.

Syed, M. (2015). Black Box Thinking: The Surprising Truth About Success. Portfolio. 1 https://korevoices.com/new-articles/2018/10/29/20-eye-opening-facts-from-missrepresentation

Chapter 14: Tech Yourself

1 Give & Take

1 https://hbr-org.cdn.ampproject.org/c/s/hbr.org/amp/2015/12/proof-that-positive-work-cultures-are-more-productive

1 Give and Take

1 The Inevitable

1 The Inevitable

ENDNOTES

Introduction

i. https://www.statista.com/statistics/1092227/facebook-product-dau/
ii. https://fleximize.com/articles/006663/chinese-super-app-changing-tech
iii. The Four: The Hidden DNA of Amazon, Apple, Facebook and Google
iv. BBC Panorama 'Amazon: The Truth Behind The Click'
v. https://www.nbcnews.com/tech/apple/apple-becomes-first-us-company-reach-3-trillion-market-cap-rcna10767
vi. https://money.usnews.com/investing/stock-market-news/articles/2019-12-02/decade-in-review-big-tech-gains-enormous-power
vii. https://www.profgalloway.com/apple-thief/

1. Change Is Constant

viii. Who owns the future?
ix. The Four: The Hidden DNA of Amazon, Apple, Facebook and Google.
x. Think Like an Artist.
xi. https://www.theverge.com/22783422/airbnb-pandemic-ceo-brian-chesky-interview-travel-decoder-podcast
xii. Strategic Intuition.
xiii. Start-Up Nation.
xiv. https://www.wpp.com/wpp-iq/2021/08/martech-2030
xv. https://newsroom.accenture.com/news/leading-companies-that-scaled-technology-innovation-during-covid-19-are-growing-revenue-five-times-faster-than-lagging-adopters.htm
xvi. Meaningful: The Story of Ideas That Fly.
xvii. Blockchain: Blueprint for a New Economy.
xviii. The Pirates Dilemma.
xix. How Google Works.
xx. How Google Works.
xxi. The Inevitable.
xxii. How Google Works.
xxiii. The Four: The Hidden DNA of Amazon, Apple, Facebook and Google.
xxiv. Ask Your Developer: How to Harness the Power of Software Developers and Win in the 21st Century.
xxv. The Four: The Hidden DNA of Amazon, Apple, Facebook and Google.
xxvi. Corporate Innovation in the Fifth Era: Lessons from Alphabet/Google, Amazon, Apple, Facebook, and Microsoft.
xxvii. Ask Your Developer: How to Harness the Power of Software Developers and Win in the 21st Century.

Endnotes

xxi. https://www.goldmansachs.com/insights/pages/generative-ai-could-raise-global-gdp-by-7-percent.html
xxii. The Four.
xxiii. Creativity.Inc
xxiv. Corporate Innovation in the Fifth Era: Lessons from Alphabet/Google, Amazon, Apple, Facebook, and Microsoft.
xxv. Corporate Innovation in the Fifth Era: Lessons from Alphabet/Google, Amazon, Apple, Facebook, and Microsoft.
xxvi. Ask Your Developer: How to Harness the Power of Software Developers and Win in the 21st Century.
xxvii. Bezonomics: How Amazon Is Changing Our Lives, and What the World's Best Companies Are Learning from It.
xxviii. Legacy.
xxix. Ask Your Developer: How to Harness the Power of Software Developers and Win in the 21st Century.

2. The Why of Tech

xxx. https://www.thoughtco.com/maslow-theory-self-actualization-4169662
xxxi. https://sacredstructures.org/mission/the-story-of-three-bricklayers-a-parable-about-the-power-of-purpose/
xxxii. The Startup Way: How Entrepreneurial Management Transforms Culture and Drives Growth.
xxxiii. Corporate Emotional Intelligence.
xxxiv. Ask Your Developer.
xxxv. Culture Decks Decoded.
xxxvi. Start With Why.
xxxvii. Originals: How Non-conformists Change the World.
xxxviii. Delivering Happiness.
xxxix. The Strategist: Be the Leader Your Business Needs.
xl. The Strategist: Be the Leader Your Business Needs.
xli. Meaningful: The Story of Ideas That Fly.
xlii. Corporate Innovation in the Fifth Era: Lessons from Alphabet/Google, Amazon, Apple, Facebook, and Microsoft.
xliii. Ask Your Developer: How to Harness the Power of Software Developers and Win in the 21st Century.
xliv. How Google Works.
xlv. How Google Works.
xlvi. How Google Works.
xlvii. Elon Musk: How the Billionaire CEO of SpaceX and Tesla is Shaping our Future.
xlviii. Alibaba's World: How One Remarkable Chinese Company Is Changing the Face of Global Business.
xlix. Brick by Brick – LEGO.
l. The Innovators Dilemma.
li. https://www.inc.com/peter-economy/this-is-way-you-need-to-write-down-your-goals-for-faster-success.html

Endnotes

xxiii. Start With Why.
xxiv. The Four.
xxv. Work Rules! Insight from Inside Google That Will Transform How You Live and Lead.
xxvi. No Rules Rules: Netflix and the Culture of Reinvention.
xxvii. Corporate Innovation in the Fifth Era: Lessons from Alphabet/Google, Amazon, Apple, Facebook, and Microsoft.
xxviii. How Google Works.
xxix. The Strategist: Be the Leader Your Business Needs.
xxx. The Startup Way: How Entrepreneurial Management Transforms Culture and Drives Growth.

3. Culture Is Religion

xxxi. https://hbr.org/2015/12/proof-that-positive-work-cultures-are-more-productive
xxxii. The Culture Code.
xxxiii. Creativity.Inc
xxxiv. Rebel Ideas: The Power of Diverse Thinking.
xxxv. The Pirates Dilemma.
xxxvi. Out of Our Minds: Learning to be Creative.
xxxvii. Time, Talent, Energy: Overcome Organizational Drag and Unleash Your Team's Productive Power.
xxxviii. Delivering Happiness.
xxxix. Corporate Innovation in the Fifth Era: Lessons from Alphabet/Google, Amazon, Apple, Facebook, and Microsoft.
xl. https://opensource.com/resources/what-open-source
xli. Lex Friedman Podcast: John Carmack.
xlii. The Pirates Dilemma.
xliii. After Steve.
xliv. The Startup Way: How Entrepreneurial Management Transforms Culture and Drives Growth.
xlv. Start With Why.
xlvi. What You Do Is Who You Are: How to Create Your Business Culture.
xlvii. Amazon 2015 Shareholder Letter.
xlviii. http://www-personal.umd.umich.edu/~yro/TenurePortfolio/sample
xlix. https://www.tines.com/about
l. The Culture Code.
li. What You Do Is Who You Are: How to create your business culture.
lii. No Rules Rules: Netflix and the Culture of Reinvention.
liii. Delivering Happiness.
liv. The Startup Way: How Entrepreneurial Management Transforms Culture and Drives Growth.
lv. Scrum: The Art of Doing Twice the Work in Half the Time.
lvi. Scrum: The Art of Doing Twice the Work in Half the Time.
lvii. https://www.theverge.com/22659497/apple-slack-organizing-zoe-schiffer-decoder-interview
lviii. Tools of Titans.

Endnotes

xxix. Work Rules!: Insight from Inside Google That Will Transform How You Live and Lead.
xxx. Tim Ferris Podcast.
xxxi. Originals: How Non-conformists Change the World.
xxxii. https://hbr-org.cdn.ampproject.org/c/s/hbr.org/amp/2015/12/proof-that-positive-work-cultures-are-more-productive
xxxiii. https://www.hrmagazine.co.uk/content/features/implementing-a-learn-it-all-culture
xxxiv. Time, Talent, Energy: Overcome Organizational Drag and Unleash Your Team's Productive Power.
xxxv. Ask Your Developer: How to Harness the Power of Software Developers and Win in the 21st Century.
xxxvi. Ask Your Developer: How to Harness the Power of Software Developers and Win in the 21st Century.
xxxvii. Corporate Innovation in the Fifth Era: Lessons from Alphabet/Google, Amazon, Apple, Facebook, and Microsoft.
xxxviii. Delivering Happiness.
xxxix. Little Bets.
xl. Ask Your Developer: How to Harness the Power of Software Developers and Win in the 21st Century.
xli. No Rules Rules: Netflix and the Culture of Reinvention.
xlii. Work Rules!: Insight from Inside Google That Will Transform How You Live and Lead.
xliii. Atomic Habits.
xliv. https://hbr.org/2018/05/why-great-employees-leave-great-cultures?
xlv. https://hbr-org.cdn.ampproject.org/c/s/hbr.org/amp/2015/12/proof-that-positive-work-cultures-are-more-productive
xlvi. No Rules Rules: Netflix and the Culture of Reinvention.
xlvii. The Four: The Hidden DNA of Amazon, Apple, Facebook and Google.
xlviii. https://hbr-org.cdn.ampproject.org/c/s/hbr.org/amp/2015/12/proof-that-positive-work-cultures-are-more-productive

4. Growth Is God

xlix. Corporate Innovation in the Fifth Era: Lessons from Alphabet/Google, Amazon, Apple, Facebook, and Microsoft.
l. Bezonomics: How Amazon Is Changing Our Lives, and What the World's Best Companies Are Learning from It.
li. https://www.coinbase.com/blog/lighting-up-the-map-how-coinbase-plans-to-scale-globally-article
lii. https://www.investopedia.com/articles/investing/082814/companies-succeeded-bootstrapping.asp
liii. Ask Your Developer.
liv. https://fortune.com/2021/10/27/ai-artificial-intelligence-business-strategy-data-accenture/
lv. The One Thing: The Surprisingly Simple Truth Behind Extraordinary Results.

Endnotes

viii. Work Rules!: Insight from Inside Google That Will Transform How You Live and Lead.
ix. The Lean Startup: How Constant Innovation Creates Radically Successful Businesses.
x. https://taplytics.com/blog/how-to-experiment-like-facebook-and-netflix-by-adopting-the-10000-experiment-rule/
xi. The Personal MBA: A World-Class Business Education in a Single Volume.
xii. Atomic Habits.
xiii. How Google Works.
xiv. Creativity.Inc
xv. The Four: The Hidden DNA of Amazon, Apple, Facebook and Google.
xvi. An Ugly Truth.
xvii. The Four: The Hidden DNA of Amazon, Apple, Facebook and Google.
xviii. Think Like an Artist.
xix. The Inevitable.
xx. Invent and Wander.
xxi. Little Bets: How breakthrough ideas emerge from small discoveries.
xxii. Delivering Happiness.
xxiii. How Google Works.
xxiv. The Four: The Hidden DNA of Amazon, Apple, Facebook and Google.
xxv. Invent and Wander.
xxvi. https://x.company/
xxvii. Legacy.
xxviii. The Lean Startup.
xxix. https://www.cbinsights.com/research/startup-pivot-success-stories/
xxx. Little Bets: How breakthrough ideas emerge from small discoveries.

5. Data Is the New Gold

xxxi. Succession, Season 3, Episode 9 'All the Bells Say'.
xxxii. https://fortune.com/2021/10/27/ai-artificial-intelligence-business-strategy-data-accenture/
xxxiii. https://www.forbes.com/sites/bernardmarr/2018/05/21/how-much-data-do-we-create-every-day-the-mind-blowing-stats-everyone-should-read/?sh=681c-c83260ba
xxxiv. The Four.
xxxv. https://www.chinadaily.com.cn/a/201712/11/WS5a2d bce0a310eefe3e9a1453.html
xxxvi. https://fortune.com/2021/10/27/ai-artificial-intelligence-business-strategy-data-accenture/
xxxvii. https://www.goldmansachs.com/insights/pages/generative-ai-could-raise-global-gdp-by-7-percent.html
xxxviii. The Four: The Hidden DNA of Amazon, Apple, Facebook and Google.
xxxix. The Direct to Consumer Playbook.
xl. How Google Works.
xli. https://www.wpp.com/wpp-iq/2021/08/martech-2030
xlii. Black Box Thinking: The Surprising Truth About Success.

Endnotes

xiii. The Four: The Hidden DNA of Amazon, Apple, Facebook and Google.
xiv. Netflixed.
xv. Ask Your Developer: How to Harness the Power of Software Developers and Win in the 21st Century.
xvi. The Personal MBA: A World-Class Business Education in a Single Volume.
xvii. Anthro Vision.
xviii. https://www.mirror.co.uk/sport/football/news/kevin-de-bruyne-uses-data-23870686
xix. https://hbr.org/2021/02/why-is-it-so-hard-to-become-a-data-driven-company
xx. https://www.thinkwithgoogle.com/intl/en-gb/future-of-marketing/digital-transformation/gymshark-data-transformation/
xxi. https://www.profgalloway.com/ai/
xxii. https://www.chargedretail.co.uk/2021/06/11/shein-the-mystery-behind-the-largest-ecommerce-company-in-the-world/

6. Be Open

xxiii. Alibaba's World: How One Remarkable Chinese Company Is Changing the Face of Global Business.
xxiv. Invent & Wander.
xxv. https://www-apipartnerships-com.cdn.ampproject.org/c/s/www.apipartnerships.com/types-of-technology-partnerships/amp/
xxvi. https://www.datacenterdynamics.com/en/news/report-apple-is-googles-largest-cloud-customer-for-storage/
xxvii. Ask Your Developer: How to Harness the Power of Software Developers and Win in the 21st Century.

7. Fail Fast

xxviii. Ask Your Developer: How to Harness the Power of Software Developers and Win in the 21st Century.
xxix. Invent and Wander.
xxx. How Google Works.
xxxi. Black Box Thinking: The Surprising Truth About Success.
xxxii. Invent and Wander.
xxxiii. No Rules Rules: Netflix and the Culture of Reinvention.
xxxiv. How Google Works.
xxxv. No Rules Rules: Netflix and the Culture of Reinvention.
xxxvi. Black Box Thinking: The Surprising Truth About Success.
xxxvii. The Startup Way: How Entrepreneurial Management Transforms Culture and Drives Growth.
xxxviii. Black Box Thinking: The Surprising Truth About Success.
xxxix. The Startup Way: How Entrepreneurial Management Transforms Culture and Drives Growth.
xl. Thinking Fast and Slow.

Endnotes

8. Leadership

i. How Google Works.
ii. https://web.archive.org/web/20090821105822/http://www.islandnet.com/~kpolsson/applehis/appl1984.html
iii. https://www.amazon.jobs/en/principles
iv. https://www.forbes.com/sites/zackfriedman/2018/08/30/best-managers-google/?sh=66280a984f26
v. Start With Why.
vi. Ask Your Developer: How to Harness the Power of Software Developers and Win in the 21st Century.
vii. Corporate Innovation in the Fifth Era: Lessons from Alphabet/Google, Amazon, Apple, Facebook, and Microsoft.
viii. Creativity.Inc
ix. https://www.ncbi.nlm.nih.gov/pmc/articles/PMC6050388/
x. https://medium.com/@stewart/we-dont-sell-saddles-here-4c59524d650d
xi. 'Alibaba's World: How One Remarkable Chinese Company Is Changing the Face of Global Business'.
xii. Working Backwards.
xiii. The Direct to Consumer Playbook.
xiv. No Rules Rules: Netflix and the Culture of Reinvention.
xv. No Rules Rules: Netflix and the Culture of Reinvention.
xvi. The Culture Code.
xvii. No Rules Rules: Netflix and the Culture of Reinvention.
xviii. Elon Musk: How the Billionaire CEO of SpaceX and Tesla is Shaping our Future.
xix. The Culture Code.
xx. Elon Musk: How the Billionaire CEO of SpaceX and Tesla is Shaping our Future.
xxi. Leading – Alex Ferguson.
xxii. Corporate Innovation in the Fifth Era: Lessons from Alphabet/Google, Amazon, Apple, Facebook, and Microsoft.
xxiii. Harvard Business School Press.
xxiv. The Ride of a Lifetime.
xxv. The Culture Code.
xxvi. https://www.theverge.com/22783422/airbnb-pandemic-ceo-brian-chesky-interview-travel-decoder-podcast
xxvii. https://www.theverge.com/22783422/airbnb-pandemic-ceo-brian-chesky-interview-travel-decoder-podcast
xxviii. TED Tech Podcast – Satya Nadella is building the future.
xxix. https://www.fastcompany.com/90578272/how-jeff-bezos-makes-decisions
xxx. Ego is the Enemy.
xxxi. HBR's 10 Must Reads on Leadership.
xxxii. Give and Take.
xxxiii. Give and Take.
xxxiv. Leading – Alex Ferguson.
xxxv. https://news.airbnb.com/a-message-from-co-founder-and-ceo-brian-chesky/

Endnotes

9. Managing People

i. How Google Works.
ii. Culture Decks Decoded.
iii. Work Rules!: Insight from Inside Google That Will Transform How You Live and Lead.
iv. Ask Your Developer: How to Harness the Power of Software Developers and Win in the 21st Century.
v. First Break All the Rules_ What the World's Greatest Managers Do Differently.
vi. https://www.forbes.com/sites/zackfriedman/2018/08/30/best-managers-google/?sh=f966c624f261
vii. Rebel Ideas: The Power of Diverse Thinking.
viii. The Culture Code.
ix. Ask Your Developer: How to Harness the Power of Software Developers and Win in the 21st Century.
x. How Google Works.
xi. Break all the rules.
xii. Creativity.Inc
xiii. Time, Talent, Energy: Overcome Organizational Drag and Unleash Your Team's Productive Power.
xiv. Delivering Happiness.
xv. Give and Take.
xvi. The Personal MBA: A World-Class Business Education in a Single Volume.
xvii. How Google Works.
xviii. https://tim.blog/2021/11/04/john-doerr-transcript/
xix. Invent and Wander.
xx. The Startup Way: How Entrepreneurial Management Transforms Culture and Drives Growth.
xxi. Time, Talent, Energy: Overcome Organizational Drag and Unleash Your Team's Productive Power.
xxii. Ask Your Developer: How to Harness the Power of Software Developers and Win in the 21st Century.
xxiii. No Rules Rules: Netflix and the Culture of Reinvention.
xxiv. https://www.cbsnews.com/news/ceo-zuckerberg-facebooks-5-core-values/
xxv. How Google Works.
xxvi. https://blog.asana.com/2017/06/onboarding-best-practices-new-employees/
xxvii. Culture Decks Decoded.
xxviii. https://www.opednews.com/articles/CEO-Ridiculed-for-Raising-by-Meryl-Ann-Butler-Minimum-Wage_Minimum-Wage-Living-Wage-210817-229.html
xxix. Invent and Wander.
xxx. https://blog.coinbase.com/how-coinbase-is-rethinking-its-approach-to-compensation-9aaf7d5d638e
xxxi. Work Rules!: Insight from Inside Google That Will Transform How You Live and Lead.
xxxii. No Rules Rules: Netflix and the Culture of Reinvention.
xxxiii. The Hard Thing About Hard Things.

Endnotes

xxxiv. Invent and Wander.
xxxv. Invent and Wander.
xxxvi. Invent and Wander.
xxxvii. https://www.statista.com/statistics/234488/number-of-amazon-employees/
xxxviii. https://www.aboutamazon.eu/news/working-at-amazon/what-is-a-bar-raiser-at-amazon\
xxxix. No Rules Rules: Netflix and the Culture of Reinvention.
xl. Invent and Wander.
xli. Ask Your Developer: How to Harness the Power of Software Developers and Win in the 21st Century.
xlii. Ask Your Developer: How to Harness the Power of Software Developers and Win in the 21st Century.
xliii. No Rules Rules: Netflix and the Culture of Reinvention.
xliv. No Rules Rules: Netflix and the Culture of Reinvention.
xlv. The Culture Code.
xlvi. How Google Works.
xlvii. Scrum: The Art of Doing Twice the Work in Half the Time.
xlviii. HBR's 10 Must Reads on Managing People.

10. Customer-First Building

xlix. Meaningful: The Story of Ideas That Fly.
l. The Personal MBA: A World-Class Business Education in a Single Volume.
li. Little Bets: How breakthrough ideas emerge from small discoveries.
lii. https://tim.blog/2021/02/01/marc-randolph-transcript/
liii. https://amazonchronicles.substack.com/p/working-backwards-dave-limp-on-amazons
liv. Invent and Wander.
lv. Ask Your Developer: How to Harness the Power of Software Developers and Win in the 21st Century.
lvi. Meaningful: The Story of Ideas That Fly.
lvii. The Personal MBA: A World-Class Business Education in a Single Volume.
lviii. Anthro Vision.
lix. https://medium.com/@stewart/we-dont-sell-saddles-here-4c59524d650d
lx. Masters of Scale.
lxi. Invent and Wander.
lxii. https://hbr.org/2016/09/the-elements-of-value
lxiii. No Rules Rules: Netflix and the Culture of Reinvention.
lxiv. https://www.investopedia.com/articles/investing/082814/companies-succeeded-bootstrapping.asp
lxv. https://www.subtraction.com/2018/01/23/design-lessons-from-mcdonalds/
lxvi. Ask Your Developer.
lxvii. How Google Works.
lxviii. The Four: The Hidden DNA of Amazon, Apple, Facebook and Google.
lxix. Ask Your Developer: How to Harness the Power of Software Developers and Win in the 21st Century.

Endnotes

- xxii. The Upstarts: How Uber, Airbnb and the Killer Companies of the New Silicon Valley are Changing the World.
- xxiii. The Lean Startup: How Constant Innovation Creates Radically Successful Businesses.
- xxiv. The Inevitable.
- xxv. https://www.yaagneshwaran.com/blog/rory-sutherland-behavioral-economics/
- xxvi. The Personal MBA: A World-Class Business Education in a Single Volume.
- xxvii. https://medium.com/@stewart/we-dont-sell-saddles-here-4c59524d650d
- xxviii. https://medium.com/@stewart/we-dont-sell-saddles-here-4c59524d650d
- xxix. The Personal MBA: A World-Class Business Education in a Single Volume.
- xxx. The Four: The Hidden DNA of Amazon, Apple, Facebook and Google.
- xxxi. https://markuphero.com/blog/being-a-product-manager-at-google-facebook-amazon/
- xxxii. https://taplytics.com/blog/how-to-experiment-like-facebook-and-netflix-by-adopting-the-10000-experiment-rule/
- xxxiii. Originals: How Non-conformists Change the World.

11. Meetings, Meetings, Meetings

- xxxiv. Time, Talent, Energy: Overcome Organizational Drag and Unleash Your Team's Productive Power.
- xxxv. Creativity.Inc
- xxxvi. How Google Works.
- xxxvii. Originals: How Non-conformists Change the World.
- xxxviii. How Google Works.
- xxxix. Creativity.Inc
- xl. Creativity.Inc
- xli. How Google Works.
- xlii. No Rules Rules: Netflix and the Culture of Reinvention.
- xliii. No Rules Rules: Netflix and the Culture of Reinvention.
- xliv. Ask Your Developer: How to Harness the Power of Software Developers and Win in the 21st Century.
- xlv. Ask Your Developer: How to Harness the Power of Software Developers and Win in the 21st Century.
- xlvi. https://www.bloomberg.com/news/articles/2014-10-06/zuckerberg-s-new-secret-weapon-for-deal-making-whatsapp
- xlvii. How Google Works.

12. Storytelling & Marketing

- xlviii. The Four: The Hidden DNA of Amazon, Apple, Facebook and Google.
- xlix. The Four.
- l. How Google Works.
- li. Bezonomics: How Amazon Is Changing Our Lives, and What the World's Best Companies Are Learning from It.
- lii. Delivering Happiness.
- liii. The Direct to Consumer Playbook.

Endnotes

vii. Bezonomics: How Amazon Is Changing Our Lives, and What the World's Best Companies Are Learning from It.
viii. Hit Makers: How Things Become Popular.
ix. Hit Makers: How Things Become Popular.
x. https://medium.com/@stewart/we-dont-sell-saddles-here-4c59524d650d
xi. The Startup Way: How Entrepreneurial Management Transforms Culture and Drives Growth.
xii. The Startup Way: How Entrepreneurial Management Transforms Culture and Drives Growth.
xiii. The Lean Startup: How Constant Innovation Creates Radically Successful Businesses.
xiv. https://bettermarketing.pub/19-habits-of-successful-marketers-the-disruptor-cmo-playbook-ef5b142171a1
xv. The Upstarts: How Uber, Airbnb and the Killer Companies of the New Silicon Valley are Changing the World.
xvi. Hit Makers: How Things Become Popular.
xvii. https://martech.org/amazon-owns-more-than-90-market-share-across-5-different-product-categories-report/
xviii. The Direct to Consumer Playbook.
xix. How Google Works.
xx. https://www.businessinsider.com/wework-valuation-falls-47-billion-to-less-than-3-billion-2020-5?r=US&IR=T

13. Community at Large

xxi. https://www.wired.co.uk/article/estonia-e-resident
xxii. https://www.wired.co.uk/article/estonia-e-resident
xxiii. Start-Up Nation.
xxiv. https://www.ces.tech/Articles/2021/May/10-Tech-Companies-Setting-Big-Goals-to-Reduce-Clim.aspx
xxv. Ask Your Developer: How to Harness the Power of Software Developers and Win in the 21st Century.
xxvi. https://www.irishtimes.com/business/technology/tech-companies-team-up-with-ul-for-radical-computer-science-programme-1.4493307
xxvii. Black Box Thinking: The Surprising Truth About Success.
xxviii. https://coderdojo.com/movement/
xxix. https://www.blueorigin.com/about-blue
xxx. Ask Your Developer: How to Harness the Power of Software Developers and Win in the 21st Century.
xxxi. https://techcrunch.com/2017/01/17/facebook-to-open-startup-garage-at-station-f-in-paris/
xxxii. https://korevoices.com/new-articles/2018/10/29/20-eye-opening-facts-from-miss-representation
xxxiii. Invent and Wander.

14. Tech Yourself

 i. Give & Take.
 ii. https://hbr-org.cdn.ampproject.org/c/s/hbr.org/amp/2015/12/proof-that-positive-work-cultures-are-more-productive
 iii. Give and Take.
 iv. The Inevitable.
 v. The Inevitable.

Printed in Great Britain
by Amazon